PUSHING BOULDERS

PUSHING BOULDERS

OPPRESSED TO INSPIRED

AN AUTOBIOGRAPHY

ATHOL WILLIAMS

THEART
Press

ALSO BY ATHOL WILLIAMS

Poetry	Children's books
Bumper Cars	*What is Happening to Oaky?*
Talking to a Tree*	*Oaky the Happy Tree*
Heap of Stones*	*Oaky and the Sun*
*as AE Ballakisten	

First published by Theart Press in 2016
www.theartpressbooks.com
© Athol Williams 2016
All rights reserved.
www.atholwilliams.com
ISBN 978-0-9946676-6-3
ISBN 978-0-9946823-4-5 (Hard cover)

Production, design and
print managed by Staging Post
10 Orange Street, Sunnyside
Auckland Park 2092
South Africa
+2711 628 3200
www.stagingpost.co.za

Cover design by Shawn Paikin
Set in Sabon 10.5/15.5pt
Printed and bound by ABC Press, Cape Town
Job no. 002832

Also available as an e-book:
d-PDF 978-0-9946676-9-4
ePUB 978-0-9946677-0-0
mobi file 978-0-9946677-1-7

Dedicated to my brother, Nicholas

Contents

Acknowledgements

◎

A special thank you to my family who supported me along all the paths I've travelled:

To my mother Mavis who set such a great example by pushing her boulders with resilience and grace, and for giving me the freedom to make sense of the world my way.

To my brothers Nicholas and Roscoe, and my nephew Aaron, who ceaselessly cheer me on as I push my boulders, and when it gets too heavy for me, lend a hand to push.

To my wife Taryn, who continues to be the leaves to my branches and the roots to my tree. I know I am twice as strong with you in my life.

Thank you to those who played vital roles in making the production of this book possible:

To Ulrike Hill who, with great energy and enthusiasm, gave shape to the book and helped me bring my story to life.

To Jonathan Amid who helped prepare the first versions of the manuscript.

To Klara Skinner and the Staging Post team for managing the process that magically produced a completed book.

Preface ◎

In Greek mythology, Sisyphus is a king condemned to pushing a large boulder up a hill. Each time he nears the summit, the boulder rolls back down. Sisyphus then descends the hill and starts pushing the boulder back up again. His curse is to repeat this fruitless task for eternity – never getting the boulder over the hill.

Every one of us is born into circumstances that play a major role in defining our life prospects. For some, these circumstances will ensure a life of comfort and prosperity, but for many the circumstances are dire. We are born with an enormous boulder that stands between us and a life of dignity and meaning, requiring us to push this boulder up an impossibly steep hill.

Whether people are oppressed on the basis of race, gender, religion, disability or any other social factor, the boulder which is the curse of their oppression can never be pushed over the hill: the oppressed are never free of their daily suffering and humiliation. Anyone who has lived under a repressive political regime such as apartheid in South Africa, or in a society that has institutionalised subjugation of citizens on some basis, often through invisible forces, or anyone who has faced more direct domination in a relationship or community, knows the weight of this boulder. They know, intimately, the near impossibility of pushing it up their hill.

While some may be *born* with boulders, others have boulders foisted upon them along their life's journey. A major career setback perhaps. Or a life-threatening disease. The heartbreak of a broken relationship or the death of a loved one. An act of violence perhaps. These are all boulders that suddenly fall onto our path and we find ourselves having to push these boulders in order to move forward.

Sometimes we make choices that lead us to a situation where we have to push a boulder. A political choice perhaps. A career or lifestyle choice. A choice to stand up against an injustice. Or a choice about wanting to escape from an oppressive environment or relationship. In these cases, there may be a choice between a path without a boulder and a path with a boulder, or perhaps a choice between a small boulder and a large one. Either way, our burden of boulder-pushing is our choice.

In different ways all of us end up in similar situations to Sisyphus, pushing a boulder, whether small or large, along a flat surface or up the steep incline of a hill. Most of us will push many boulders over the length of our life's journey. Sometimes we will have to push multiple boulders simultaneously.

This has been my experience. As I've travelled a path to fulfil my dreams I have had to overcome the inertia of boulders that I was born with (given that I was classified coloured* in apartheid South Africa the day I was born), boulders that suddenly appeared along my way, and boulders that I chose to push because they stood in the way of my dreams. The life prospects that I was born into were so dire that I needed to do something extraordinary to set myself free. This did not require the once-off pushing of a boulder, but rather a life-long struggle as I strived for a life of meaning.

For those born into forms of oppression or who find themselves in situations of constraint, it is our oppressors' hope that we do not even attempt to push back. And if we are determined enough to push, like Sisyphus, their hope is that we are never to get the boulder over the

---

* As repugnant as it is, discussing race is unavoidable given my context and its centrality to apartheid. I will identify interchangeably as either *coloured* or *black*; coloured when being specific about the actual classification inherited according to apartheid's rules, and black as a self-identity with all oppressed groups and our unified freedom struggle. On occasion I will use a more generic term, *non-white* to refer to all South African people who the apartheid regime set out as the subjects of their oppression, i.e. coloured, black and Indian. I hope these racial references cause neither confusion nor offence.

top of the hill before us. If by some miracle we do get it over the top we are certainly not to return to inspire and help others do the same.

Pushing Boulders is my story of *doing just this*. It is a story in which Sisyphus breaks the curse and succeeds, through great perseverance and toil, to push the boulder over the hill. It is my story of shattering my oppressors' hopes by reaching for the highest levels of education, and fulfilling my dream of freedom – political, socio-economic and spiritual freedom. As for all of us, there were many occasions when I could have chosen to live with the burdens that I inherited or acquired. But I chose to push the boulder. Every time. And every time the boulder came crashing down the hill I had to decide if I was going to accept defeat and fall in line with the plan my oppressors had for my life or put my shoulder to that boulder and start pushing. I chose to push.

This is my story of pushing multiple boulders of different shapes and sizes over hills of different contours and heights. It is the story of how my life changed so that it became my mission not just to push my own boulders, but to use my acquired boulder-pushing prowess to inspire and enable others to do the same.

While I hope this book will offer more than a leisurely read to pass time, perhaps some inspiration, it is not a self-help book, nor is it intended to be a presentation of a life worthy of emulation. It is my story, the good and the bad, the beautiful and the ugly. I present it here with the same spirit in which I presented my first book of poetry, *Heap of Stones* – the first lines of the first poem read:

> I lay my heart naked,
> my mind-door open wide;

Just as with poetry and diaries, an autobiography does lay the author's heart and life naked. I've kept a diary, of some form, for almost 30 years. *Pushing Boulders* serves as the ultimate diary entry; rather than a diary entry that reflects upon the events of a day, this book seeks to reflect the actions and thoughts of a lifetime, or at least the first 45 years of a life that I have sought to live with as much meaning as I could. As a diary entry it serves that wonderful purpose of preserving memory, giving a permanence to our days, for when written down, no matter how much our faculties fade, our actions and thoughts are never gone because we can always return to them on the page.

Autobiography, like a diary, serves to keep memory alive, to remind us of times and lives past. South Africa's colonial and apartheid past is one of erasing memory, of eliminating memories of lives past. Many of us have forgotten our origins, been robbed of our names, our languages, our native religions and customs. And so *Pushing Boulders* serves as a small stand in protest, a small act of resistance against this erasing of memory. During our fight for political freedom we sang 'we shall not, we shall not be moved'; this book serves as part of the choir that remembers our lives and that of our ancestors, and now sings, 'we shall not, we shall not be forgotten.'

As with all efforts to capture actual events, no matter how careful we are, invariably, we remember or interpret events differently to others. I have used original source material as far as I could but ultimately relied on my memory of events – what I present here is my version.

Breaking the mould ◉

They thought I was either an arms trader or diamond dealer. This was how my neighbours in the upmarket Johannesburg suburb of Morningside saw me. A neighbour explained to me that they had settled on diamond dealer because it was 'classier' than an arms trader. After all, I was always dressed in a suit and carried a briefcase.

We were standing alongside the newest addition to my car collection, a stunning brand new black BMW 650i, the third of four new BMWs that I drove over the years. Seeing me get out of the car compelled my neighbour to introduce himself and then to blurt out, 'I must ask, what *do* you do?'

'I run a strategy consulting firm,' I answered, 'Advising the CEOs of major corporations on their business strategies,' I continued, slightly taken aback by the directness of the question.

'Oh,' he laughed, and then proceeded to explain how he and his friends in the neighbourhood had been chattering about this coloured guy who arrived and left home at odd hours, driving a different exotic car each time. Seeing me arrive with BMW's latest creation, one of the first in the country, was just too much for him to bear, and thus the compulsion to approach me. Curious isn't it? Seeing a coloured man with exotic cars immediately led my neighbours to assume that I was involved in illegal activity. Good old South Africa!

I admit that having six exotic cars is rather unusual for anyone. In addition to the new BMW, I owned a Lamborghini, a classic Rolls Royce, a rare BMW 850i, a new Jaguar and a convertible Mustang Cobra. Except for the Rolls Royce, the cars were all black. I enjoyed cars. I enjoyed driving them and buying them – but had a real

1

problem selling them. Without intending to, within a short period I had assembled a mini-fleet, enough to rouse neighbourly curiosity.

It was 2006 and I was flying high. I was running my successful business founded three years earlier. The business had hit a vein of success that I could never have imagined, counting among our clients the CEOs of leading companies who we were advising on major strategic and financial initiatives. Even though we were a young company, we owned our own brand new office building in Woodmead that we fitted and furnished exactly as we wanted. Our boardroom overlooked the majestic Johannesburg and Sandton skylines. We were doing so well that we even owned a house in an estate overlooking the beach in Cape Town – it served as our local base for work, as well as a venue for holiday trips and parties.

This business success translated into financial success for me. I had a seven-digit bank balance. I owned a trendy townhouse in Morningside and would move into a mansion a few years later. I owned a house in upmarket Bryanston that stood on an acre of land and owned a further six acres of vacant riverside property north of Johannesburg. I enjoyed fine cigars and single-malt whiskys. I dined at the finest restaurants wherever I travelled, whether Cape Town, New York or London. I had visited over 40 countries and some of the world's most exotic locations including Monte Carlo, Paris, Miami, Puerto Rico and Bali where I stayed in five star hotels. I had taken 600 aeroplane flights, close to 200 of them internationally, the equivalent of flying around the earth 40 times or to the moon close to four times. My personal library contained 10,000 books. One wall sported degrees from the University of the Witwatersrand, Massachusetts Institute of Technology and the London Business School. As they say, *I was doing well for myself.*

But my life was not always this glamorous. And it would not continue to be this way for much longer. In fact, for most of my life it was the complete opposite.

For the first 24 years of my life, I lived under the oppressive apartheid regime in South Africa. This regime set out to relegate me, as a coloured person, to a life of subordination and deprivation. I was choked and constrained in every aspect of my life. Rising above my circumstances became my *modus operandi*. I would spend most of my years struggling to break free from the chains of this oppression, in a single-minded pursuit of my freedom that would take me from the depths of despair (including periods of living off charity hand-outs, suicidal thoughts and homelessness) to the heights of the top global universities and the global corporate world. I was filled with dreams, with drive to fulfil these dreams and with the no-holds-barred courage to do whatever it took to succeed.

The university degrees, which would later include those from Harvard, Oxford and London School of Economics, were not trophies to boast over, but channels through which I would attain my freedom and equip myself to work towards the socioeconomic freedom of others. The exotic lifestyle and material possessions, like cars and homes, were temporary means to an end. Soon I would shed these shackles, along with the shackles of apartheid.

The song, 'Something Inside', by British singer Labi Siffre had a powerful effect on me. It talked about growing taller in response to the building of barriers and running faster in response to our rights being taken further away. This song awoke something powerful within me. As the apartheid government built their barriers along racial lines, I grew taller so that I could overcome them. The more they sought to take away my rights to freedom and dignity, the faster I ran to retrieve these. Growing taller and running faster meant that I would strive to educate myself, despite their efforts to deprive me of an education.

Education would be my key to freedom. Books would set me free. And so I cast my sights as far as I could, to the best universities in the world, to gain the highest quality education and to give myself access to the highest paying jobs. I would grow so tall, and run so fast, that apartheid would never be able to contain me. I would gain the strength to push whatever boulder was set before me.

To run and to escape would become leitmotifs throughout my life. In my teens I would run away from home on more than one occasion.

3

I would leave my home city and home country in search of a better life. But none of my escapes were as daring and dramatic as my first one. I was only five years old.

I just had to get away.

The rebel is revealed ☺

It wasn't about right or wrong; it was about knowing that I did not belong there, a knowing that does not entertain questions or conscience but gives one a singular purpose. I was confined to the hell of nursery school. I hated being there. I hated the feeling of being trapped in one place. I resented the order the school imposed on my otherwise free and adventurous life. I had to get away.

My family lived in a rented house at 553 Lansdowne Road in the Cape Town suburb of Lansdowne. The 'house' happened to be an old converted police station where I was born five years earlier on 20 June 1970. An old police station was a rather inauspicious place in which to enter the world – I've often wondered what the symbolic meaning might be of being born there.

It was a simple dwelling on a busy street. Along the pavement in front was a low brick wall and a small wooden gate. Our tiny front garden was dominated by a hibiscus tree which mushroomed across half the width of our house. Inside was a simple layout – a lounge and two bedrooms led off to the right of the long narrow passage while to the left was the bathroom and kitchen. We had no toilet in the house – we had to go outside into the backyard to use the toilet. My younger brother, Nick, and I slept on a metal-framed double bunk bed and my older sister, Amanda, had a single bed. We three shared one bedroom, while our parents occupied the other.

Nick and I were inseparable. He was three years my junior but we were best friends, a close friendship that would continue through the years, and still continues today. We spent all of our time running around in our backyard or wandering the scrappy grounds at the back of our house. Two huge mounds of garbage stood like invitations to curious explorers such as we were. I don't know where these garbage heaps came from but they were taller than we were. They offered an endless array of 'treasures' – glass bottles of different colours and sizes, odd-shaped chunks of greasy metal car parts and a host of other unknown objects. I loved hurling the glass bottles against the wall at the back of our house, feeling great satisfaction in seeing and hearing the bottles shatter. We weren't the only treasure hunters there: occasionally we had to dodge families of rats. We loved climbing the loquat and fig trees and chasing the many chickens that my parents kept. Those were blissfully carefree days.

A path of orange gravel ran along the side of our house all the way to a cluster of factories situated a few hundred metres away. On the other side of the gravel path was the Salvation Army building. I had absolutely no idea what the Salvation Army was. All I knew was that a marching band of people from the Salvation Army, dressed in hats and decorated suits, would periodically march up and down Lansdowne Road. The band was impressive, with drums and trumpets and cymbals and other shiny instruments. We would hear them coming from miles away and we would join the throngs of people that lined the street as the band marched by.

To my young mind, this is what the Salvation Army did; they practised for weeks and then marched up and down our road. They were the town's entertainers. But I soon discovered that there was a dark side to them; they also ran the nursery school that would become my prison.

I could not believe that my parents had enrolled me in the nursery school. I was separated from Nick, my exploration partner, and our daily adventures. Now I had to sit with a bunch of strange kids finger-painting or making potato prints or listening to mindless stories. I hated it! There were endless rules. I could not understand why I had to stand in line before entering the classroom or sit in a row on the floor with my forefinger on my lips as some sort of commitment not to speak. I was sure I was a prisoner being punished for some crime that I had not (yet) committed. The only respite from all the torture was playtime. If not for these brief breaks, I am convinced that I would have used my teacher's face for my potato prints. These breaks made me feel alive again. *Why couldn't we just play all day?*

The resentment of being there was reinforced when I was made to sleep every afternoon. I had no choice in the matter as the teacher insisted that we had to take a nap. I refused. What did I have to sleep for? I wasn't tired. After all, we were finger-painting not building a skyscraper!

I could never sleep during the day; that's what night-time was for. My teacher insisted and so there I was, herded on a daily basis with the rest of the other inmates to the sleeping room. The sleeping room consisted of a long row of what looked like stretchers used by ambulance men to carry away car crash victims. Sprawled out upon these 'beds' was a bunch of placid, sleepy kids and me, wide-eyed and frowning. I would lie there picturing the fun Nick was having at home, wondering if he had found any more treasures in the rubble heaps or perhaps discovered that the chickens had laid eggs. It didn't seem fair that I should be confined to these pretend-sleep sessions on a stretcher when I could be home living a life of adventure with my brother. Initially, I tried to explain to my teacher that I was not tired. She refused to make an exception. I had to sleep even if I was not tired. I was convinced she had been a jail warden at our house when it was still a police station.

And so each day I walked with dread across the gravel path to school, to endure the day's activities and then pretend to sleep when that torturous time arrived. From the moment I arrived at school all I could think about was going home. And when waiting that long became intolerable, all I could think about was to escape. When half a day at a nursery school feels like a lifetime, escape feels like achieving a lifetime of freedom. It was 1975, the year that my future music hero, Bruce Springsteen, released his hit 'Born to Run'. Even though I hadn't heard the song yet, its restless sense of independence and raw passion to run free seemed to have already filled my heart.

One day a chance to escape presented itself. It was playtime. I found myself apart from the others, walking along the wire perimeter fence. Just there, across the gravel path, was home. It was unbearable – I could see home, I could see freedom, I could see fun! I didn't know why I so intensely hated being at the school, but such intense emotions overcame me that I just had to do something right there and then.

The plan came to me as if I had been contemplating it for months. I slowly meandered along the fence keeping a watchful eye out for the warden or any other person who might foil my plan. The school had a large gate – the frame was made from galvanised steel tubing and the rest of the gate was the same wire mesh that surrounded the school. While the entire area of our playground was covered in bricks and tar, the gate was situated just beyond the tar into the gravel path. The underside of the gate was a few inches off the gravel. I estimated that with just a few inches of gravel removed I could squeeze my chubby little body under the gate. Still with a keen eye looking out for the warden I bent down on one knee and began scooping away gravel from under the gate. I dug my fingers desperately into the caked surface and shovelled as fast as I could. Eventually I got down on both knees and was now scooping with both hands.

I had been so focused on the digging that I lost track of the activities behind me. In a panic I turned around. No one had noticed. The hole was ready; I lay down on my belly, stuck my head and arms through the gap and pulled myself through. I lay there for a second, on the other side, waiting for a large hand to grab me by the collar or for my legs to be pulled, but nothing. I sprang to my feet, quickly glanced back into the playground to check that I was safe and that no one had seen me. I then sprinted across the gravel path as fast as my little legs would carry me; not once looking back. I had escaped, I was free! Like a prisoner who had just been released from a long and unjust sentence, I breathed the outside air as if breathing for the first time.

My escape was perfect. I headed straight home with visions of digging for treasures and chasing chickens.

I knocked on the front door and was greeted by my mother's smiling face. Then she looked at her watch and realised that I was home early. 'What are you doing home so early, Athol?' I hadn't anticipated this line of enquiry. I was free, why wasn't she celebrating, why couldn't she just admire my great escape and show her little son some affection? How about inviting him in. So there I stood on the doormat, with my mother standing in the doorway staring down at me. Eventually, looking down at my scuffed shoes, I mumbled something like, 'I don't like school. I ran away.'

Needless to say my freedom was short-lived. I found myself being dragged by the arm back across the gravel path. That very path which just a few minutes earlier carried me to freedom was now like a walking plank on the edge of a pirate ship – I could see the sharks circling below. I kicked and shrieked and tried to yank my arm free, but back to school I would go.

By this time, the warden had noticed that I was missing and had come into the playground to investigate. Mum and the warden held conference at the gate, looking in absolute horror at the hole that I had dug. One would swear that I had buried the dismembered body of a schoolmate there judging from the outrage these two expressed. Before I knew it, I was back inside, my bum still burning from Mum's hearty send-off and covered in orange gravel dirt.

That Sunday the Salvation Army band again marched down Lansdowne Road and for the first time I hated the band. I hated their uniforms. I hated their shiny trumpets. It took me a few years to realise that the Salvation Army was not a sadistic cult but in fact a global church that does incredible work in communities.

A few weeks later my mother joyfully declared that I no longer had to attend nursery school. On the *strong recommendation* of the school principal, my parents had decided to withdraw me from the school.

Freedom!

Running in my veins ☺

The name Athol Eden Williams is unlikely to conjure up an image of a brown-skinned African. There is much history embedded in names as they track the journeys that our forebears have travelled and the name choices that our parents made.

My parents named me after the acclaimed South African playwright, Athol Fugard, for no other reason than that they liked the name. It turned out to be prophetic as I too would become a writer. My middle name was taken from the Garden of Eden in the Bible, again for no profound reason. However, my surname is loaded with South African history, and coupled with yet another arbitrary name choice, reflecting more of the bizarre nature of a country under racist colonial rule.

By the time I was born, the racist laws, policies and practices, collectively known as apartheid, had already been in force for 22 years, instituted by the Afrikaner-dominated National Party when they came into power in 1948. Africans had suffered under European colonial rule for more than 300 years so the concept of racial segregation was in fact not new. The difference between apartheid and racial segregation in other parts of the world was the extent to which the racism was written into law and institutionalised.

The essence of apartheid was a belief in white supremacy and the creation and maintenance of white privilege. The intent of apartheid was expressed with distasteful clarity in 1943 by the National Party's Enlightenment (*sic*) Secretary Otto du Plessis:* 'The National Party

---

* *The Forum,* 16 January 1943

10

takes its stand with those who strive for the maintenance of a pure White race on the Dark Continent.' What did this mean for non-whites or 'non-Europeans' as we were so eloquently labelled? 'The National Party visualises a great destiny for the non-European people … under the guardianship of our Western European civilisation. The party's policy is … segregation and trusteeship.' Apartheid's architects and their followers assumed the position of representing Western European civilisation and set out for me to live under their 'guardianship'.

The apartheid plan would be achieved by separating the races and subjugating those who were not white. Thus, the foundation of apartheid was racial classification, and one's racial classification determined absolutely every aspect of your life – what social status you held, whether you could vote, whether you could own property, where you could live, the quality of the education you'd receive, which beaches, parks, toilets, restaurants you could frequent, who you could marry, which public transport you could use, what jobs were reserved for you. Essentially your race dictated, by law, the quality of your life and your life prospects.

The government created four race classifications – 'white' for those of European descent, 'Indian', for those of South Asian descent who were mainly from the Indian subcontinent, 'black' for those of African descent and 'coloured', a catch-all classification of people who fell into neither of the first three groups. As a coloured person, my identity, into which every aspect of my life was wrapped, was essentially defined as being 'miscellaneous' – not belonging to any group, just a mixture of leftover people, the unwanted by-product of white men's enslaving of our fathers and rape of our mothers.

The coloured race group consisted of brown-skinned peoples with a variety of origins including descendants of slaves from Indonesia, Malaysia and southern Africa, those born of mixed-race parents and descendants of indigenous Khoisan peoples.

The hierarchy of races proceeded from white as the most privileged, then Indian, coloured and finally black. Furtherance of white interests, as the primary goal of government policy, was emphasised by Prime Minister Hendrik Verwoerd in 1963: 'Our major task is to ensure that a White nation will prevail ... it is our aim to survive and to prosper as a White nation.' Non-whites, according to Verwoerd were not citizens or peers but 'those entrusted to our care', like children or pets. This belief was palpable in my early interactions with white South Africans, particularly those in the corporate world; their belief that I was under their guardianship and in their benevolent care requiring my obedience and gratitude.

Job reservation ensured for whites the high-paying jobs at birth, and for everyone else, the grunge work regardless of abilities or enterprise. In the Cape, whites obtained the prime real estate near Table Mountain, while coloureds and blacks were banished to townships on the periphery of the city. Still today, such spatial separation exists.

Being classified coloured at birth ordained that I be burdened with the countless disadvantages associated with this race, and that I inherit the cumulative disadvantages of centuries of oppression suffered by my forebears. A white child inherited vast privilege while I inherited oppression and disadvantage. As a coloured person my disadvantage would not only be tangible deprivation but the many unseen ways in which I was reminded of my sub-human status such as the harsh or patronising tones with which I was addressed, the fact that I was looked upon with suspicion when entering places frequented by whites and the fact that I would never be given the benefit of the doubt – I would always be guilty until I could prove myself innocent.

It was this very fact, that as a coloured person the societal structures were laid to predetermine my life as a third-class citizen, which would later spur me on to break free from these constraints.

The objective of apartheid was different to most oppressive regimes around the world. This white society did not seek to exterminate non-whites (as the Nazis tried to do with Jews) or drive them out of the country (as the Israelis are doing to Palestinians) but rather subjugate us as cheap labour. Coloureds and blacks, in particular, were intended to be uneducated docile labourers upon whose backs the South African economy and white privilege would be built.

Both my parents were born in Cape Town and classified coloured, since both had mixed African, Asian and European ancestry. My mother, Mavis, was born in 1950, the third youngest of eleven children. Her parents were both descendants of slaves brought by the Dutch from Indonesia, Malaysia and St Helena. Slaves or farm labourers were labelled with the names of their masters, so more than likely my mother's parents' surnames, Marthinus and Marshall, came from slave owners or farmers by these names.

In 1998, while attending a business conference in Indonesia, I joined a colleague in browsing the local markets. What perplexed me was that the locals spoke English to my colleague who was white, but to me they spoke in their local language. This eventually made sense to me when I realised the local people saw me as one of them given our physical resemblance.

When slaves were freed in 1834, many settled in an area of inner-city Cape Town known as District Six. This was where my mother's family lived. In 1966, the apartheid government declared District Six a whites-only area and so forcibly removed 60,000 coloured and black residents from the area. My mother's family was among those forcibly removed. Their home was destroyed. Family members were scattered to different parts of the Cape Flats. My mother went with her grandparents to Crawford, while her parents were relocated to Kew Town in Athlone, a densely populated slum where they were confined to a tiny third-floor flat, accessible only by stairs which they could barely climb.

The destruction of District Six would become one of the enduring symbols of apartheid's social engineering plans, yet would also serve as a unifying memory for the coloured population in the Cape.

My father, Edwin, was born in 1944, the third eldest of four brothers. My grandmother had mixed lineage, including European which explained her fair skin. My grandfather was a descendant of Indian indentured labourers named Ballakisten, who had arrived in Natal on South Africa's east coast.

'Indentured labourer' was a euphemism for slave; a new form of forced labour developed after the abolition of slavery within the British Empire. Between 1860 and 1911, over 150,000 Indians were imported on 384 ships to Natal, primarily to work on the sugar plantations. Many Indians opted to travel to South Africa and enter fixed-term servitude in the belief that their lives would improve, however this would not turn out to be the case. Labourers were housed in conditions of squalor in barracks on the plantations and, owing to limited employment prospects, labourers and their descendants continued working on the plantations even when their contracts were terminated. Some did return to India, but the vast majority stayed partly because they could not afford the return trip to India.

It was into this context that Mahatma Gandhi arrived in 1893 as a young lawyer. During the 21 years that he spent in South Africa, he fought against the injustices suffered by Indian South Africans and inspired other race groups to do the same. While Gandhi is famed for his political activism and leadership in India, it was in South Africa that he first encountered personal racial attacks and saw the brutality of British colonialism. And it was here that he developed his philosophy of *Satyagraha*, a form of active yet peaceful resistance.

While a few Ballakistens remain in Natal, the majority moved to the Transvaal (current-day Gauteng), either to the factories established by the sugar industry or in search of opportunity in the gold industry. As a result, my family came to be concentrated in Laudium near Pretoria, the township created for Indians under apartheid.

So if my father's line has the surname Ballakisten, where does my surname Williams come from?

Around 1915, my grandfather Maxwell Ballakisten travelled from Laudium to the Cape drawn by adventure and economic prospects. This was a tricky venture at the time, since the Immigrants Regulation Act of 1913 restricted the movement of Indians between provinces; Indians could only migrate between provinces if they held a permit to do so. In the early 1900s, Indians in the Transvaal were burdened with severe economic restrictions including the restriction against owning property. However, coloureds in the Cape suffered no such legal restriction and so Maxwell hatched a plan to leave the Transvaal for the Cape and reclassify as coloured and now we know from whom I inherited my proclivity to 'escape'.

In his book *Memoirs*, anti-apartheid stalwart Ahmed Kathrada refers to 'another ridiculous consequence of the Immigrants Regulation Act was that a sizeable number of Natal and Transvaal Indians managed to change their classification to Coloured in order to settle in the Cape'. My grandfather was one of them. To give an air of legitimacy to his assumed coloured classification my grandfather decided to change his surname, opting for one of the most common coloured surnames of the day, Williams. Maxwell Ballakisten thus became Maxwell Williams. I owe the surname Williams to no one in Wales which is the origin of the surname, just the rebellious pragmatism of my grandfather.

Memories of long journeys seemed to pulse through my veins owing to my ancestors coming from Southeast Asia, South Asia and West Africa. Most of these journeys were torturous. I too travelled many long journeys and lived at close to 40 addresses in the US, UK and South Africa. Thankfully most were as a free man, taking voluntary trips.

My parents married in 1966, when my father was 22 years old and my mother just 16. They had four children: Amanda born in 1968, myself, and then Nicholas (Nick) in 1973 and finally Roscoe in 1980. A picture of myself and my siblings tells the story of a long mixed and diverse ancestry. Amanda is fair skinned with green eyes and straight light brown hair, easily classified as white. Nick has dark skin and straight black hair, often assumed to be Indian. Roscoe has rounded features but with light brown skin, green eyes and light brown hair. And I have rounded features, curly black hair with features that would either make me a light-skinned African, a South American or, as I discovered, Indonesian. We are a mixed bag for sure, true to the literal meaning of the word *coloured*. This showed the absurdity of the racial classification system: if it was strictly applied to our family, we'd all be classified different races.

Neither of my parents completed high school – both had to leave school to go work to augment their families' incomes. This was the sad reality in coloured communities: many parents could not afford to have their children at school or, knowing that career prospects were severely limited, parents placed little value in education. My father had great intelligence and read widely, but had to live with the intense frustration of being limited to being a factory-floor worker in the textile industry for all of his working life owing to his lack of formal education and the system of job reservation. This frustration corroded his spirit.

By the time I was a teenager, I understood that a life of limitation awaited me, unless I did something outside of the script that had been written for my life.

Promise in a tragic land ◎

'Why is Mum crying?' Nick asked me as we lay in bed. We could hear my mother crying in the kitchen. This was not the first time that we heard her cry while sitting on her own.

'I don't know,' I replied, 'I think it's because Daddy is sick.'

By the time my mother was 27 years old, she had three young children. Without any help, she raised us. Without any transport, she walked great distances with us children in tow or patiently used the unreliable bus service that operated in our area. Life was a struggle for her that became immeasurably worse when, in April 1977, my father fell into a coma.

For a few weeks before the coma it seemed as though my father had lost his mind. Many were the nights when we would be woken by his erratic screams. I recall him complaining about a piece of candy that he was sucking – he shouted that the candy tasted like cabbage and was stringy. It was deeply unnerving for a seven-year-old to see his invincible father in such a state.

My father had been home without work for four months when his illness struck, which we would later learn were the extreme symptoms of diabetes. It was around this time that we first started hearing my mother's heart-sore sobs in the kitchen. We were barely making ends meet when my father was employed but now, with no income, my young mother was scared. Years later she told me that she really thought my father was going to die, that she feared for us.

The coma would last for ten days. My father would spend 23 days in Groote Schuur Hospital, most of the time in intensive care. Each evening we relied on a family friend, who drove his employer's delivery van, to take us to the hospital to visit him. One horrible scene that I remember from these hospital visits was seeing my father's legs tied, just above the ankles, to his hospital bed as he screamed and shook violently. Rather than appropriate straps, the hospital used thick industrial rope to tie his ankles which cut deep into the flesh as he convulsed. He would retain deep black scars just above his ankles from these ropes.

A despairing heaviness hung in our house while my father was in hospital and in the months after. I didn't appreciate how dire our situation was even as we became reliant on a charity for food. It became a weekly routine – Nick and I would be playing in the house when we would hear a knock at the door just before sunset on a Friday evening. We would race down the long passage to open the door. And there he would stand ... a stranger, holding two cardboard boxes filled with the most unusual foods. My mother would place the boxes on the kitchen table and Nick and I would be standing on the chairs getting our arms and heads all tangled up in Mum's hands as she tried to unpack the groceries.

It was on the occasion of one of these visits that I saw baby potatoes for the first time. I just couldn't stop giggling at these cute, tiny potatoes. It is strange how sights or sounds can trigger memories. Whenever I see baby potatoes now, I am drawn back to that kitchen where the cloud of despair had blown away for just a short time as we rejoiced in receiving these groceries.

The weekly deliveries came from a charity, the Lions Club, and would continue for two months. Even though my parents had siblings, everyone was struggling financially. If we did not receive these parcels, then we would surely have starved. No wonder my mother was filled with dread.

I have come to appreciate the vulnerability of people living at or below the breadline as we were, and that they are often unable to cope with shocks such as illness or sudden job loss, because there is no buffer of savings or a community able to support them. That image of the man with the boxes of groceries standing in our doorway with the setting sun behind him, has never left me. It continues to inspire the work that I now do to support others.

One of my favourite photos of this time is of Nick and I, sitting on the concrete *stoep* in our backyard. The background to the photo shows damaged, dirty walls with the occasional writing in crayon, most likely my handy work. We are dressed in matching T-shirts, which was how my mother always dressed us. Even in my teenage years, to my chagrin, I was wearing matching outfits with Nick and even with Roscoe when he came along. Nick has a plaster on his left knee and is sporting the goofiest smile, while I look on rather nonchalantly. What is most striking about the photo is our shoes. Nick's shoes are scuffed and scratched but not as bad as mine. Mine are so badly scuffed that you can hardly see that they are black shoes, and neither of my shoes has laces. It is a picture of two scruffy little boys sitting with a backdrop of dilapidation which so aptly captures the circumstances of my upbringing. My mother insists that it's a cute picture of us – who am I to argue.

An encounter with the American billionaire Donald Trump many years later would remind me of this photo.

I started Grade 1 in 1976, attending St Ignatius Primary School in Claremont, which was attached to the Catholic Church by the same name. It fell under the Administration of Coloured Affairs even though the school had a mix of races among the students and teachers, reflecting the mixed communities of Claremont and surrounding areas.

The mandatory minimum age for school entry was seven years old, so at just five-and-a-half I was much younger than my classmates. My mother's original plan was for me to attend nursery school for another year but with my opposition to nursery school my parents decided to enrol me in 'big school'. My mother figured that even if I struggled in Grade 1 and repeated the grade, it would be better than the embarrassment of dragging me back to nursery school each day after I'd dug holes like a rebellious mole around the school perimeter.

I loved Grade 1 and excelled academically. Where I couldn't wait to escape from nursery school I was excited about going to primary school. My Grade 1 teacher was Ms Morris, who had also been my father's Grade 1 teacher 26 years earlier. She was a tall, dark-skinned woman who was strict but known to be a good teacher. In my report she wrote that I had 'done excellent work' and that I was 'interested in all his lessons'.

And I *was* interested in my lessons, enjoying reading and learning to count with an abacus. My aggregate grade for the year was 95%. I was off to a good start in my schooling career. And to think that my mother was planning for me to be at nursery school doing finger painting!

While I innocently entered this new phase of my life, seismic shifts were taking place in Johannesburg, shifts that catapulted South Africa into international news for all the wrong reasons, and that would have a lasting impact on our country. In its continued efforts to subdue the majority, as all oppressive regimes do, the apartheid government commenced a programme of cultural imperialism which included imposing the language of the Afrikaner on all South Africans, requiring the compulsory use of Afrikaans as a language of instruction in all schools.

Tensions over this policy erupted into violence on 16 June 1976, when students took to the streets in the Johannesburg township of Soweto to oppose the use of Afrikaans. Crowds of students and residents ignored the police's call for them to return to their classes and homes. The police responded by firing live bullets into the crowds. The massacre left 575 people dead, 134 of whom were under the age of eighteen. The uprising spread countrywide as students abandoned school in droves. 'Liberation before Education' became the battle cry.

Meanwhile, battles raged in Cape Town over the racial classification of Claremont, where my school was located. Forced removals of black and coloured residents had already been going on for 16 years by this time, but still there were 'controversial areas' according to the authorities. Claremont was popular because of its location and proximity to shops, schools and public amenities, with a good network of buses and trains serving the area. Despite the cultural diversity of its inhabitants, the government declared Claremont a whites-only area, ordering the eviction of all non-whites. Just like that it became illegal for me to continue attending my primary school.

Professor Colin Bundy describes the destruction of District Six and forced removals from Claremont and other areas as 'ethnic cleansing', thus leaving Cape Town the most segregated city by 1980.* Alongside forced removals, the government planned huge construction projects of townships to accommodate those that had been forcibly removed. Coloured people, the largest group of people affected by forced removals in Cape Town, were accommodated in these newly constructed townships. In 1974, the construction of Mitchells Plain commenced. It would serve as the largest outpost for uprooted coloured people, and would later become my home.

Amanda and I were sent to newly built Turfhall Primary School in Athlone. I was confused by the need to change schools but was excited, at six, by the independence of travelling to school by bus without any grown-up supervision. My Grade 2 teacher wrote in my report that I was 'a neat and excellent worker'. Something must have gone wrong as time passed since neatness was certainly never recognised as one of my strengths – at school or at home. My Grade 4 teacher would write two years later: 'he is still the best in class, I just wish he would write neater.' I was described as a 'diligent and constant worker' which made me sound awfully boring, but I guess I was getting on with what needed to be done.

Two years passed at Turfhall without incident, except for the new

---

* *The Cape Times*, 23 January 2013

trouble that beset me: girls. Suddenly, as if by sorcery, they appeared. I was no older than seven when girls started to attract my attention. I had a pen-drawn tattoo on my arm declaring my love for a girl named Abigail. I would wink at Andrea whenever I saw her and I enjoyed holding Zulpha's hand. Once I held her hand under our desk without knowing that our innocent clasping hands were in full view of my teacher. I tasted the cruel sting of my teacher's cane and was perplexed that something as wonderful as holding a girl's hand would lead to punishment.

My father was not the only one with ill health. I was constantly sick, either with allergies, asthma or chest infections. During my first five years at school I missed 80 days due to illness, an average of 16 days each year. In Grade 5, I was out of school for 23 days. Going to Red Cross Hospital seemed like a normal thing to do because we did it so often. My mother would gather Nick and me for the long journey by foot and multiple buses to Rondebosch. I would drive my mother crazy in the bus by reading out every word I saw as we drove by buildings, billboards or passing vehicles, clearly proud of my reading skills. I still enjoy doing this but I have learnt to do it silently.

I had shown early signs of promise at school despite the surrounding turmoil.

In 1979, I started Grade 4, but did not finish the year at Turfhall Primary. Soon I would change schools again, and again it would be because of apartheid. This time we had to pack up our home and relocate. Ironically, we were forced out of our home because Lansdowne was declared a 'coloured' area. This reclassification compelled the white owner of the house to sell. Even though my father was working again my parents could not afford to buy the house so it was sold to another family thus requiring us to move out.

When so much of your life is unstable and uncertain, home ownership can be a vital source of stability and security, so my parents were determined to buy a house. Wherever they looked they either could not afford the house or they were not allowed to buy in the area owing to our race. There was one area where houses were available, affordable and where we were allowed to live – Mitchells Plain.

Mitchells Plain is located about 32km from the centre of Cape Town. It was designed by the apartheid government to provide a designated area for the city's coloured population. These days it is a sprawling township – with an official population in excess of 400,000 that represents over 10% of Cape Town's population. This population is roughly equal to that of Coventry or Wigan in the UK, or that of Tampa or Cleveland in the US, although squeezed into a much smaller area. Today, roughly half of those households live below the poverty line and unemployment among the working age population is close to 60%.*

By design of the apartheid architects, Mitchells Plain is isolated from the rest of the city and those residents who are employed have to travel for long periods each day to get to work, not only burdening them with high travel costs but the social cost of being away from their families from early morning until late into the night. When my father travelled to work by bus he would leave home before 6am, and only return home after 7pm. We hardly saw him during the week, rendering him a ghost in our midst.

Before development, the area was covered in sand dunes and fynbos vegetation. The rapidly built homes on loose sand dunes meant that cracks frequently appeared in the walls of homes and gardening was nigh impossible owing to the unfertile sand.

In my nine-year-old ignorance to the grim context for our relocation, I was excited to move into our new area and new house. Home was a three-bedroomed, mid-terrace brick house at 12 Aarbeihof in Westridge, one of Mitchells Plain's ten sub-sections. The lower half of the house was plastered while the top half had exposed brick. We had a small 7m x 5m garden to the front of our house with wooden poles at the perimeter and a similarly sized backyard. We tried growing a lawn in front and my mother planted flowers but the

---

* 'Socio-Economic Profiling of Urban Renewal Nodes – Khayelitsha and Mitchell's Plain', The City of Cape Town, July 2006 (www.capetown.gov.za)

white dune sand was inhospitable to any life. Eventually, we paved both the front and back of our house.

Aarbeihof, or Strawberry Court, had 23 houses, all sharing side walls, arranged in a horse-shoe around a half-acre open common area, which we called the 'park'. The park, which went through multiple iterations of being covered in grass, sand or gravel, was where we played our neighbourhood soccer matches and other children's games.

Nick and I shared a bedroom which had just enough space for our single beds and a free-standing wardrobe, while Amanda had her own room. When Roscoe arrived a year later, he slept in our parents' room and would later have his own bed in Amanda's bedroom. The house was carpeted with a flat-grey industrial carpet. Our house may have been modest but my mother was exceptionally house-proud. Our house was always spotless and characteristically my mother polished the bronze garden tap, door knocker and the '1' and '2' screwed into the wall at the front of the house, every week. With her tin of Brasso and a *lappie* she would stand on a chair in the garden to reach the number of our house to polish it. These bronze items shone brilliantly and could be seen from afar as the sun reflected off their perfectly polished surfaces.

In Lansdowne, Nick and I only had each other for company, other than Amanda, but now there was as much as 20 children our age so there was always a group to play with which included games like hide-and-seek, rovers and *kennetjie*.

Amanda, Nick and I enrolled at the unimaginatively named Mitchells Plain Primary School No.1, affectionately known as 'Number One'.

My third primary school in four years. I was only nine years old.

The walk to school took under ten minutes, a vast improvement on the treks to get to my two previous schools. I settled in quickly and continued delivering good results. In the mid-year exams I was placed top in the class, shared with two others. 'Considering that he came to school in the second term, his work is really meritorious!' wrote my Grade 4 teacher, Mrs Rhoda. I would head the class again in subsequent exams earning an overall grade of 85%.

It was during Grade 4 that my handwriting emerged as a serious issue, earning me the only C that I ever earned at primary school. I was deemed to be untidy and negligent until it was discovered that I had weak eyesight, and that I needed to wear spectacles. This solved the handwriting problem. Now I could actually see the lines in my books, and though I was teased with the taunt 'four eyes', I thought it was rather cool to wear glasses.

I managed to maintain my good academic performance all through primary school. My teachers wrote comments in my reports that I was 'a hardworking and intelligent pupil' and that I had produced 'excellent work'. There were a few prophetic statements too. For example, Mrs Lawrence, my Grade 6 teacher, wrote, 'Athol is self-sufficient and knows what he wants. He is going to make his mark in life.' A similar sentiment was expressed the following year by Mr Josephs: 'Athol has the academic ability to achieve what he deserves' and 'Athol has got the intelligence to be what he wants to become.' Even if I was unaware of my abilities back then, my teachers certainly had confidence and high expectations.

My first entrepreneurial seeds were sown while still in primary school when I started a newspaper delivery route. The *Cape Argus* is Cape Town's daily broadsheet, published from Monday to Saturday. I would collect my 30 newspapers, at a delivery point not far from home, stuff them into a backpack and then walk my route. At each house I would knock on the door and hand over the newspaper when someone answered. When no one was home I would stick the paper under their doormat.

There were many sources of anxiety as an 'Argus boy', as we were called. Sometimes newspapers got torn and I had to make the awful decision about who would receive a torn paper. Those who were not at home were prime victims because I could just place the torn newspaper under their doormat. Rainy days were the worst. A few papers would inevitably get wet and I would have to face the wrath of unhappy recipients of rain-soaked newspapers. At some homes barking dogs were a menace – but they were nowhere near as scary as the angry customers who received torn or wet papers.

Eventually Nick too started a delivery round which was another activity around which we bonded. Earning some pocket money meant that we could buy the odd piece of clothing or have luxuries that our mother could not afford. When I started smoking, it was useful having my own cash to buy cigarettes. The greatest lesson Nick and I learned while earning our own money was to save. We had our eyes on new bicycles.

Neither of us had ever owned a bicycle. Each week we would give our father a few rands. He recorded our deposits in a book and kept our money safe. After more than a year of saving, Nick and I were able to buy our very own new Western Flyer bicycles. It was an overwhelming thrill. Mine was red, Nick's was blue. It was the first possession that I had earned and I cherished that bicycle. I continued to deliver *The Argus* well into high school.

I learned that having money could also be a curse. Mitchells Plain was over-run with gangsters bent on taking whatever they could by whatever violent means they deemed necessary. And I would often fall victim to their thuggery.

Gangs and baseball ◉

He had slapped me before, on more than one occasion, but this time he was brandishing a knife. I knew I was in real trouble.

Gang activity was and still is a severe problem in Mitchells Plain. In a country with one of the highest crime rates in the world, Mitchells Plain has a murder rate more than double the national average, and worse than America's most crime-ridden city, Detroit. Furthermore, the area tops the crime incidence list for attempted murder, common assault and robbery with aggravating circumstances – all crimes most frequently committed by gangs.

Cape Town has two faces – it is rightfully ranked among the most beautiful cities in the world and the most dangerous. Some only see the beauty. I grew up only knowing the ugly face and the insecurity and trauma of being constantly threatened by violent crime. All through my teenage years I had to deal with the daily threat of gangsters who were bent on taking from me whatever they could or just simply dishing out violence and terror. They were everywhere – in the streets, at the malls, on the sports field, at school and even in church. For most Mitchells Plain residents, coming into contact with gangsters was inevitable. Countless children from my social circle ended up joining one of the gangs. In our street alone, of the 23 homes, three had gang members. I was tormented by a number of gangsters through the years, but one in particular seemed to seek me out.

My first encounter with Klip was when I was 14 years old walking to church on a Saturday evening. Just as I approached a bus stop, he emerged from the covered bus shelter. He stood directly in front of me, 'Gee my jou geld' (Give me your money), he barked. I squinted my eyes, confused for a second about who he was and what he wanted. Before I could say or do anything, he slapped me viciously across the side of my face. I felt the pain flame across my face. As I held my cheek, tears streaming down my face, two more thugs appeared from the bus shelter.

There was no point in putting up any resistance. I reached into my pocket to retrieve the two rand that I had for the collection plate at church. This satisfied them, and with a dismissive push, as if I was bothering *them*, they told me to be on my way. I was angry and felt humiliated, but not as humiliated as my next encounter with him.

It was a Saturday night. I was on my way to fetch my date for a night out at Westridge City, the local club. As I crossed the field opposite her house, there he was with his two sidekicks. He took all the money I had so already I knew my night was ruined. Just as I was about to leave he grabbed me by the arm, 'Vat af die hemp' (Take off the shirt), he ordered. I was wearing my favourite shirt – a mustard-coloured, cheesecloth, long sleeve DQ* shirt with a button-down collar. I often received compliments on the shirt because it was so unique. When I resisted, he slapped me across the face as he had done before.

I stood there looking down at him with a mixture of hatred and fear. I was a head taller. I was sure that I could beat him up but not with his two cronies there. He seemed to read my mind and slapped me again, this time into the front of my face, almost sending my spectacles into my eye sockets. He began shouting and swearing. What was I to do? So I slowly unbuttoned my favourite shirt and gave it to him. There was no way that I was going to continue to my date's house – imagine showing up at her front door bare-chested – so I turned around and walked home. My face was still burning, fighting back tears, as I walked in shame, half-naked, agonising over what

---

* DQ was a popular clothing brand. Since my father worked at a clothing factory, he sometimes brought me damaged items that were rejected by their quality controllers. My DQ shirt was one of those items.

reason I would give my date for standing her up. 'I hate this place,' I thought to myself, wishing that I could get out of here and be rid of these bastards.

My most frightening encounter with Klip would come a few months later at a party. I was on the dance floor bopping to eighties disco music, probably sung by Wham or Mel & Kim, when he appeared. I hated the sight of him – his potato face with a vertical scar on the left cheek, his black hair cut short revealing his scalp. As he approached me I felt my muscles tense and my face scrunch. He went through his usual routine of wanting money but I refused. I felt emboldened by the fact that there was a crowd of people surrounding me. But he persisted and kept pestering me. I relented and gave him some of what I had but he wanted everything.

By now I was fed up with this thug and refused. He punched me in the face. My head swung to my right and I stumbled backwards. I could feel my eyes tear up as a result of the pain. I decided that I had had enough of this terror so took a step forward and raised my hands to grab him by the throat. That is when he pulled out a knife and flicked it open.

I stopped dead in my tracks. There were gasps all around us, as others realised what was going on. I was shocked to see the knife. I had no doubt that he would use it.

The music faded into the distance. Klip was holding the knife with the blade pointing threateningly at my face. With his left hand he grabbed the front of my shirt and yanked me towards the exit.

'Buite,' (outside) he shouted. Soon I was being pushed and shoved out of the party and into the street. There was a madness in the air. Chaos surrounded me. I was being shoved. People were mumbling. I felt heat rush to my face and I felt light-headed; my heart was going berserk in my chest. Klip was walking ahead of me and one of his goons was pushing my back.

'Loop,' (walk) he commanded.

We stopped outside on a street corner. Klip stood about an arm's length away, looking up at me with an arrogant smirk. About ten of his fellow gangsters were there too. A crowd formed, all curious onlookers, no one stepping in to help me. I felt lame with fear and a heavy sadness washed over me. For a moment I considered running. I knew they would chase me.

The world went silent, I could no longer hear the people around me, I couldn't hear the passing cars; all I saw was this gangster threatening me with a knife. Klip took a small step toward me and motioned to put his left hand in my right trouser pocket but I hit his hand away and in a flash he struck with his right hand, still holding the knife. I felt a sharp sting, right in the centre of my chest, an intense burning similar to what one feels when suffering a deep paper cut.

He had stabbed me.

I seemed to wake from a dream, and heard the shrieks and gasps from the crowd. Klip's pals lunged forward and pulled him away. The maroon shirt that I was wearing had an angled cut across the front, about 2cm long. I put my right hand to my chest. There was blood on my fingers. I felt no pain, just the burning sensation. Klip was being ushered away by his mates. My fear immediately turned to anger. A rage built up inside me. Enough was enough. I was not going to back down from this low life anymore. Out of the corner of my eye I saw a brick lying on the ground.

Rather than walk away as I should have, I picked up the brick, walked up to Klip, and called out to him. As he turned around I smashed the brick into his face. It was a stupid and needlessly violent thing to do. He stumbled backwards and let out a loud squeal like a wounded pig. He raised his hands to his face and seeing blood on his hands immediately went for his knife. I saw the long knife blade glisten, picking up light from the street lights. I just stood there, with the brick in my hand, facing him and his fellow thugs.

I knew I was in over my head. But I also knew that I would use that brick again if needed. Just as Klip started to lunge forward, his fellow gang members grabbed him and pulled him away. He was still screaming and was now swearing at me but they continued to drag him away. I stood there, stunned, watching as my tormenter was dragged away with blood streaming down his face. The other gangsters were shouting at him giving the impression that they were irritated with him for creating a spectacle. They treated him like a belligerent child.

As they walked away, people stepped forward to see if I was okay. I checked the wound to my chest. The knife had struck my chest superficially and although it was bleeding, the cut was not deep. I knew that I was lucky to escape severe injury that night.

Klip never bothered me again but I lived in fear of his retaliation. I was in my teens and I had woken up to the fact that I needed to fight to overcome the oppression of apartheid but I had also discovered that I needed to be willing to fight just to survive. I am amazed to meet people who have never suffered physical violence. I have been punched, slapped, beaten with a stick, shot at, stabbed and mugged several times. Living with violence just seemed normal to me.

If gangs were a dominant feature of life in Mitchells Plain, another was sport.

I started playing soccer at the age of ten, first as a central defender and then later, when my lack of speed became a handicap, goalkeeper. In my first year I was awarded the prize for 'Most Conscientious Player', which probably translates into 'Player who tries really hard but sucks'. My teams won a number of trophies over the years and I did achieve some recognition: 'Sportsman of the Year' at age thirteen and 'Most Improved Player' at fourteen. At high school I captained our team to the championship in 1987.

Athletics was prominent at high school coached by Mr Chippie Solomon, the stern, no-nonsense athletics teacher who was an inspirational figure to many of us. Mr Solomon would later manage the successful Western Province Stormers, the professional rugby club in Cape Town. I was selected to throw discus for the athletics team every year at high school. This culminated when, in Grade 12, I was selected as our school's athletics team captain, the same year that we won the A section competition among the top schools in the Cape.

Every afternoon, between delivering newspapers and doing homework, I would be on the school field practising my discus throws, improving my technique and measuring my distances which peaked at 38m, matching the provincial record. I didn't have access to a discus so I practised with an old weights plate used at the gym. I trained intensely. The best I achieved was third place, being beaten by the same two boys every year.

If soccer and athletics didn't deliver success and arouse my sporting passions, then baseball most certainly did. I hadn't heard of the sport until I was ten years old. Baseball was not prominent in South Africa, which was dominated then, as it is today, by soccer, rugby and cricket, but for me it became all-consuming.

I joined Dallas Yankees, later to become Westridge Yankees, in the newly formed Mitchells Plain Baseball Union (MPBU). I was petrified the first time a baseball was thrown at me – the hard, heavy ball came flying at a speed that would certainly have knocked out my teeth, if not caught. It was fear that led me to play in the catcher position since the catcher was equipped with a mask, padded breastplate, protective leggings and a glove with extra padding. It was an ironic choice: I was attracted by the protective gear to avoid injury, yet in the position behind the batter, I often got struck by the bat or the high-speed ball being pitched at me. A more sensible way of avoiding being hit by the ball of course would have been not to play at all but that was not an option.

I loved the sport and found no greater joy than holding a ball in my hand or swinging a bat. I loved the smell of the leather gloves and the dust that got kicked up during the games. And I loved the strategy and precision involved in the game.

As the catcher it was my job to size up the batter and give the pitcher instructions on what type of ball to throw and where to throw it. A curve thrown at the outside edge of home-plate would entice a batter to swing but miss as the ball swerved away. A fast pitch on the inside edge of home-plate would likely strike the bat near the handle if the batter swung, leading to a hit that was easily fielded. Catchers earned their worth by their ability to throw the ball from home-plate to second base which is the longest infield distance. A runner on first base would try to 'steal a base' by starting to run to second base as the pitcher starts to pitch. It is the catcher's job to catch the ball and to throw it to second base before the runner gets there. This required speed, strength and precision. I spent hours practising these throws either with friends or just throwing a baseball at a wooden board set at the correct distance. I became well-known for my throw to second base and only the bravest runners would dare to 'steal a base'.

In the batting line-up the strongest batters are placed at number three or four, positions I mostly held. Just as with my fielding, I trained relentlessly to improve my batting. At home I worked on strength with weights and I put a tennis ball in one of my mother's old stockings, tied it to the washing line in our backyard and with a broom stick practised the precision of my swings. I became a fearsome batter regularly hitting home runs. It was the utmost flattery for a batter to have the opposing team's outfielders go as far back as they could when you stepped up to bat. There are few experiences more pleasurable than feeling a baseball fly off the sweet spot of your bat and seeing it fly into the distance.

I didn't have access to any training videos or books but I could find baseball-related movies like *The Natural* with Robert Redford, *Field of Dreams*, *Bull Durham*, *For the Love of the Game* with Kevin Costner, and *The Rookie* with Dennis Quaid. I have watched all of these numerous times. The sport was definitely made that much more attractive for me since my music hero Bruce Springsteen was a player and huge fan. His music video for the song 'Glory Days' starts with him pitching at a sheet of wood much like I did for my throws to second base.

After my first year in the sport, I showed enough promise to be recognised as the 'Most Improved Player'. I started from such a low point, cowering behind my glove in fear, so anything was an improvement. I became the regular catcher for our junior team and for the 1985 season, at the age of fourteen-and-a-half, I was selected from a pool of 200 players for the MPBU Under-17 team to play in the national baseball tournament. I was elated – I felt a massive sense of achievement.

There was something peculiar about the 'national' tournament, which again was a feature of apartheid – there were no white players at the tournament. Since non-whites were barred from representing South Africa in sport, the anti-apartheid movement established an alternate sporting body in 1973, the South African Council on Sport (SACOS), which opposed racial segregation in sport. Baseball was played under the South African Baseball Association (SABA) which was affiliated with SACOS.

At the end of the tournament all teams were called to line up for the awards ceremony. There were speeches and handing out of trophies to the winning teams. The finale of this ceremony was the naming of the national team. Names were called out one-by-one and the players stepped forward to accept a small trophy. There were no surprises as the best players stepped forward.

And then I heard my name.

For a second I paused just to process exactly what I had heard. My name was repeated. *It was my name.* It was as if I suddenly awoke. Those around me started applauding with smiles on their faces. I was in a daze. I walked forward to accept my trophy. As I stood in front of the applauding crowd I looked around me, surrounded by the best junior baseball players in the country, all holding our trophies. I smiled in the knowledge that I was counted among them.

Selection for the national team was the first significant reward for tireless work and dedication to any sport. It laid important foundations for my future efforts to work toward goals.

At club level I switched to Woodlands Baseball Club in 1986 where I continued to play catcher. The following year, at 17, I was promoted to the senior team. One of the highlights that year was beating my old club Dallas Yankees in the cup final. An article in *Die Rapport*, an

Afrikaans weekend newspaper, shows me being run out on first base – just my luck that the one action picture of my baseball career shows me being run out. The caption read, 'Athol Williams of Woodlands being caught out on first base ...'

I was proud to be part of this winning team especially since it was my first full season playing in the senior ranks. On 6 May 1986, the *Plainsman* published a photo showing a very happy looking Woodlands senior baseball team. I was shown with a broad smile and a raised clenched fist. The caption mentioned our awards for the year including the cup final victory.

Even school sport was separated between white and non-white. Our school sport was played under the Western Province Senior Schools Sports Union (WPSSSU), which fell under the South African Senior Schools' Sports Association (SASSSA) that was formed in 1961 to organise national schools sport tournaments.

In my final year at high school we formed a baseball team for the first time which I captained. Just as in soccer and athletics, the Westridge High team won the Western Province Baseball League. I was honoured to have captained all three teams.

The year was topped off for me personally as I was selected for the Western Province baseball team to compete in the national tournament in Port Elizabeth. I had fantasised about being awarded my 'WP colours' and now I had them. I wore my navy blue Western Province blazer and blue tie with great pride. For many years I would be seen wearing my blue tracksuit with the letters WPSSSU boldly embroidered in white on the back.

As the tournament started, the *Sunday Times* published an article which described our team as a 'strong squad' – we were the clear favourites to win the tournament among most of the game's commentators. We proved them right winning every game and being crowned tournament champions.

It was the last season that I would play my beloved sport, a sport that had given me so much enjoyment and that I played with deepest passion. As the new club season started in October 1987, I made the tough choice not to play so that I could focus on my schoolwork, with final high school exams only weeks away. After the fall of apartheid, when non-whites could represent South Africa internationally, many of the players with whom I played would be selected for the national team to play at the Olympics or at international baseball tournaments. My closest baseball friend, Neil Adonis, represented our country around the world and is one of the national coaches today. I have often wondered how my baseball career would have taken shape had I not given it up to pursue my studies, but I don't wallow in those thoughts for too long.

For brief periods I also tried cricket, hockey, long distance running, table tennis, karate and boxing but baseball was my sport. Baseball gave my teenage years purpose and was a healing antidote to the trauma of gangsterism, poverty and political unrest. I never missed a practice and never missed a game. It was a great joy to be on the sports field playing or watching games. I remember rainy Saturday mornings looking out of my bedroom window in despair knowing that our games would be cancelled. I thrived on the competition. I loved to win. In my last two seasons of baseball I played 43 games and won 34 of them. I believe that these experiences flowed over into my drive at school. Sport certainly got me used to winning and I believe that winning does become a habit. It was a habit that I continued to develop.

Paths almost travelled ◎

Founded in 1849, Bishops Diocesan College is one of South Africa's preeminent schools counting among its alumni presidents, judges and leaders of corporations. A Bishops education virtually guarantees a child a successful career owing to the superior education and the strong network of powerful alumni. With tuition fees more than double the annual income of the average South African, the school was out of reach of everyone except the elite. Because it was an independent school, it was not subject to apartheid's segregation rules and so had greater admission flexibility. Despite this, it was still rare for a non-white student to be admitted.

In 1982, while I was in my final year of primary school, my father saw an advertisement in the *Sunday Times* newspaper for scholarships to Bishops. He applied and I was invited to sit for the entrance exams which tested English, Mathematics and Science knowledge, as well as general academic aptitude.

On one April Saturday morning, my father and I took two buses to Rondebosch and after an uncertain walk, found our way to the mighty Bishops. I had been bouncing with excitement during the bus trip. Once on the school premises, I was in awe of the grandeur of the school. It looked more like an exotic city to me than a school. My school buildings were plain, functional concrete slab structures whereas these were majestic and beautifully ornate brick buildings set in vast park-like gardens. Even though I found the tests to be more demanding than I was acquainted with, I enjoyed writing them. As always, Mathematics was my favourite.

A few weeks later, the school wrote to my father asking that he send my mid-year Grade 7 school report when it became available. My report showed that I had achieved 84% for both English and Science, and 98% for Mathematics so my father was only too happy to oblige. It wasn't long before we received a letter from Bishops informing us that I was not only offered a place at the school, but that I was also offered a scholarship as well.

At 12 years old, I couldn't fully appreciate the magnitude of this opportunity but I understood enough to know that my life would be incalculably better. Imagine, a boy from Mitchells Plain, the son of uneducated working class parents, would now be educated at one of the top schools in the country.

My parents were excited. I was over the moon.

But my excitement would be short-lived.

The scholarship would cover the cost of tuition but my parents would be liable for all other costs such as books, school uniforms, equipment, travel, sport and extracurricular activities. Based on the estimates from the school it was clear that my parents could not afford it. My father petitioned his employers for financial support but they were unwilling to help.

I was angry for weeks after they told me the miserable news that I would not be going to Bishops. I felt betrayed. I had done all that was asked of me – but the grownups at home and at Bishops had not kept their end of the bargain. So rather than attend the great Bishops, in January 1983, I started high school at the humble Westridge High in Mitchells Plain. The silver lining was that the school was a two-minute walk from our house which was a blessing for someone, like me, who hated getting out of bed in the mornings.

One of apartheid's most perversely oppressive policies was the creation of separate education departments for each race group with the goal of educating white children and dumbing down everyone else. What better way to subject millions of people to lives of inferiority than to deprive them of a meaningful education. Westridge High was a government school that fell under the Department of Coloured Affairs, later to be called the Department of Education and Culture, the pit from which apartheid's vipers administered the system to deprive coloured children of a proper education.

Every aspect of education differed by race, including the curriculum, books and school infrastructure. We almost never performed science experiments because we simply did not have the equipment. White schools had the luxury of small class sizes while our classrooms were overcrowded. Government spending was heavily in favour of white schools. Spending per white child was typically twenty times that spent per coloured or black child. In 1985, whites represented 14% of the population yet received 45% of the education budget. Teachers in our schools were grossly underpaid with extremely limited opportunities for career advancement or professional development.

Gross inequalities existed in the education of the races as far back as 1910, but it was in the 1950s that these inequalities became entrenched. 'There is no place for him [the Native] in the European community above the level of certain forms of labour ...,' the future Prime Minister, Hendrik Verwoerd explained. So education for coloureds and blacks was designed to prepare us for lives as manual labourers. As I started high school I was not aware that I was receiving a grossly inferior education. I found my Grade 8 classmates to be bright, intense and competitive. For the mid-year exams, I was placed fourth in my class, my lowest ranking to date. My position improved to first place in September and I ended the year in second place. My strongest subjects were Science, Accountancy and Mathematics; languages were my weakest subjects – this would not change throughout high school.

In Grade 9, at the age of fourteen, things deteriorated drastically. I found myself bored and disinterested with what was happening at school. I began misbehaving in class, being the class clown or behaving aggressively towards other students, and sometimes even the teachers. My behaviour was increasingly getting me into trouble, and on many occasions, I was ejected from the class. I began spending regular periods in after-school detention and paying visits to the principal's office. My parents were called to school often enough that the principal got to know them well. This was also the year that I began smoking cigarettes. It started out as mere curiosity with some school friends. Four of us would buy a cigarette and pass it around taking puffs. At first we coughed our lungs out, but we soon got the hang of it. Both my parents smoked, as did most adults who I encountered, so smoking was commonplace. But only the cool teenagers smoked and for a while, being cool was appealing. I would smoke for the next 19 years, thankfully managing to quit in 2003. I haven't touched a cigarette since.

There was an occasion when I was so bored at school that I decided to write rubbish on the History test paper instead of answering the questions. For example, a question asked, 'Who arrived in the Cape in 1652 with three ships?' and rather than answer 'Jan van Riebeeck', I wrote, 'Superman'. As had been happening frequently, my mother was called to the principal's office. My test paper had been pinned up on his wall. My poor mother cringed with embarrassment as the principal and teacher read out each of my answers.

School began to remind me of sleep-time at nursery school although escaping didn't require me to dig under the school gate. There were large gaping holes in the school fence for this purpose. Many were the afternoons that I would spend with friends at their homes watching movies or listening to music while drinking and smoking. The lines from Springsteen's song 'No Surrender' rang in my ears during these occasions – he sings about skipping school to go listen to music since music, he claims, offered him a better education than he could get in a classroom. At times I felt the same way.

At the age of 15 I had my first experience with marijuana. It was readily available, just as drugs continues to be in Mitchells Plain today. I started coming home late at night, drunk or high and having regular fights with my parents. These got physical sometimes, leading me to run away from home on more than one occasion.

Generally I became quite aggressive. After my regular run-ins with the gangster Klip and other incidents with gangsters, I began using violence as a way to settle disputes. I was in fist fights regularly, some of them quite brutal. One of my victims ended up in hospital with head injuries. I just felt angry and was out of control. By all accounts I was a school bully, even earning the nickname *Bull* which has stuck. Many of my high school acquaintances take great pleasure now in reminding me of my violent streak. It is a source of great embarrassment for me, although I do jokingly remind classmates of what led to some of my violent outbreaks, particularly theft of my homework and my lunch.

It became known that my mother packed delicious sandwiches for lunch. Mondays were best because my sandwiches would include leftovers from Sunday lunch so perhaps some chicken or if we were lucky some lamb with beetroot. Most days it was run-of-the-mill peanut butter and jam, sandwich spread, cheese or fish spread, but even then my mother managed to make it exciting by adding a variety of homemade salads, sauces or pickles.

My favourite was Melrose cheese spread. So mysteriously my lunch would disappear from my school bag. It was a conspiracy. I would be distracted while someone grabbed my sandwiches or someone would crawl under my desk to fish it out of my bag while I sat reading or listening in class. Can I then be blamed for my violent outbursts? Still today some of my friends thank my mother for the sandwiches they enjoyed, always attracting my scorn.

People who meet me anew refuse to believe that I could have been this aggressive in the past. It was a personal boulder that I had to push over the hill. Thankfully, just like the other vices, I have outgrown my violence as well, so much so that today I refuse to consume any animal products because of the violence that the animals are subjected to. It is an ethical stance I have taken to cause as little harm as I can to other beings as well as not take from animals what is not mine. So I eat no animal products, whether red meat, chicken or seafood, and consume no milk or eggs. Additionally, I wear clothes that contain no wool or leather. This can be a massive inconvenience, especially when it comes to finding good non-leather shoes, but I manage. This lifestyle is termed *vegan,* a label which I accept reluctantly because labels are always problematic.

Our family interactions revolved mainly around meals. In fact, most socialising happened in the kitchen rather than in any other part of the house. There was a strict rule that we should be home for supper every evening. My mother invested enormous energy in cooking and baking each day, spending most of her day in the kitchen. Every meal was made completely from scratch, nothing was pre-made or microwaved, or out of a can or packet. We rarely had meat or chicken during the week but Sunday lunch was guaranteed to have one of these.

I loved my mother's ou mense onder komberse (old people under blankets) which was a stew of frikkadels (meatballs) wrapped in cabbage, or her delicious tomato bredie (stew) or bean curry. Her soups were also all made from scratch, mostly vegetable soups with stamp en stoot (barley and samp) and on some occasions with soup bones which were meatless bones that offered the soup great flavour.

My father had a penchant for cooking the strange and bizarre so would occasionally prepare cow's or sheep's heart or sheep's brains. Eek! I didn't mind sheep or chicken liver and now and then didn't mind cow tongue. My mother made tripe and trotters curry occasionally (the stomach lining and feet of cows, pigs or sheep) which would stink up the whole house. We never ate out and very rarely got take-outs. As a treat, my mother would occasionally buy fish and chips from the local fish and chips shop, and on extra special occasions, we would get KFC. Our other local take-outs would be a chip roll, a white bread roll filled with fries, a real starch overload, or a gatsby, which is a large white oval bread, cut in half and filled with a choice of chips and polony, mutton curry or steak and chips. This was the staple diet when I was out partying with friends because a gatsby was cheap and could be cut into a number of pieces to feed all of us. My mother often cooked Cape Malay specialities such as bobotie or her range of curries. My favourite of her baked goods was chocolate cake and her chocolate eclairs were to die for. Sadly, my vegan lifestyle now precludes me from enjoying many of my mother's amazing culinary creations.

Unsurprisingly, my lack of interest in school began to show in my results and in Grade 9 my aggregate dropped below an A for the first time. My father was furious. He declared rules about how much time I could spend on leisure in the afternoon and how much time I could spend with my friends. I wasn't too bothered with these constraints but then he touched a sensitive area – baseball. He threatened that if my behaviour and results did not improve I would not be allowed to play baseball. He got my attention.

I survived this rocky patch. Even though I continued smoking, drinking and getting into the occasional fight, I was able to rise above the rage that burned within me and managed to dissipate it. I could have travelled a path much worse than I did had I continued along the path of disinterest in school, substance abuse and violence, a path that could easily have taken me in the direction of gangsterism. The boulder of socioeconomic context is often unacknowledged, yet has a pervasive effect on those in whose path it stands.

Or I could have taken the path to a privileged education at Bishops. I've sometimes wondered what my life would have been like or how I would have developed had I gone to Bishops. The folks at Bishops definitely dodged a bullet by not having me attend their school. Imagine the chaos this rowdy teenager would have caused at their school. Or perhaps, as I'd like to think, this teenager would have been challenged and inspired had he gone to Bishops rather than suffer the boredom and negative influences that he did in Mitchells Plain, and perhaps this unsettled period of his life would never have occurred. Of course we will never know.

The political whirlwinds around the country were rapidly becoming a hurricane as the anti-apartheid movement began taking to the streets. In 1985 this hurricane would blow into Mitchells Plain and my life with devastating force, compelling me to make some important but difficult choices.

I chose the pen ◎

I started keeping a diary from December 1984, and continued doing this all through high school. While our country stood on the brink of civil war, my mind was on a girl at school named Liesle Tobin. The first half of my 1985 diary is dominated with entries relating to the colossal crush and budding romance. We were in the same grade at school but in different classes. Her name appears sporadically at first but from February, with great dedication, I wrote something about her every day, providing an account of the rise and rapid fall of my first 'relationship'. I was saddened by the break-up. Months later a diary entry declared: 'Think about Liesle all the time, missing her.' But in true teenage fashion, it wasn't too long before I was onto the next romance, with an entry that read, 'Went to party with Collette, kissed her twice.'

In the background to my romantic endeavours the tide began to rise as anti-apartheid groups began mobilising and the government began tightening its grip on the country. Evidence of a regime's desperation to hold onto power and a leading indicator of its demise is always its use of widespread force against its citizens. The second half of my 1985 diary captures this rising tide of struggle against the apartheid regime and the devastating impact it would have on my schooling.

As a show of reform, in 1983 President P.W. Botha announced the creation of a Tricameral Parliament, which restructured the existing whites-only Parliament to accommodate two new houses of parliament to represent the coloured and Indian population. The black population would continue to have no representation. While opportunistic coloured and Indian politicians jumped at the chance to participate in this farcical parliament, the majority of South Africans rejected it.

Nelson Mandela was still in prison and most anti-apartheid political parties and movements were banned. Activists created the United Democratic Front (UDF), a mass movement that had affiliations to over 400 political, community, sport and religious organisations that opposed apartheid. The UDF was launched in Mitchells Plain on 20 August 1983 placing my hometown right in the centre of South Africa's renewed and reinvigorated struggle against apartheid.

While my attention was on the normal teenage boy concerns – schoolwork, sports and girls – violence started flaring up around Cape Town towards the end of July and into August. At 1:40am on 15 August I was woken by a loud bang. It was muffled and sounded a few blocks away, but the sound shook me like no other bang had before. I managed to go back to sleep but as day broke, news spread that the home of a schoolmate had been attacked with a hand grenade, which was lobbed through the window of their first floor bedroom. A 16-year-old fellow student was killed in the blast.

The violence reached fever pitch when, on 28 August, thousands of people marched to Pollsmoor Prison where Nelson Mandela was being held, as a symbolic act calling for his release. The police tried to prevent the crowds from marching using firearms and sjamboks.* By the end of the day, 28 people were killed, mainly children. A further 150 people were admitted to hospitals with severe injuries. Over 170 arrests were made.

High schools became centres of protest activity leading the government to shut down schools. Most of my diary entries for the following weeks start with 'no school' entry. In fact, we did not have any classes for most of the second half of the year. Closures were intermittent at first but eventually in September, the government closed 464 coloured schools, including mine. My daily diary entries had a similar theme – 'no school because of boycotts'. Everything at

---

* A heavy leather whip

school came to a halt – classes, exams, sport, even our talent show.

It was not uncommon to see armoured police vehicles patrolling our streets and with increasing regularity we could hear gunshots ring around the neighbourhood. Burning tyres blocked the streets around my school and a general unease filled the air. In my diary I wrote 'no school – lots of unrest – boycotts getting out of hand', as protests got increasingly violent.

There was an air of chaos at school, on the days when it was open, that is. There were voices constantly blaring over loudhailers – the voices of students, teachers or the police. Classes were disrupted and it became impossible for any learning to take place. My diary continued to capture events: 'lots of violence broke out in Mitchells Plain – shops smashed, schools burnt, cars smashed and people beaten.' School children were regularly killed at the hands of the police, which served as an agent of enforcement of apartheid rather than a protection service to citizens.

With schools and even public libraries closed I was bored out of my skull. Even my newspaper round was halted. 'Another day with nothing to do – walked around the whole day', my diary read. I leapt at opportunities that cropped up occasionally to join friends to watch porn movies, have a drink or smoke marijuana.

Protests continued countrywide. In Mitchells Plain, police shot and injured two women while they were returning home after watching street protests in the area. My father was insistent that we remain indoors during the day. With the number of deaths and injuries climbing, especially of children and casual onlookers, he didn't want us on the streets during protests.

By October 1985, schooling across the country had been comprehensively disrupted. There were periodic attempts by the government to open the schools but continued boycotts and unrest again resulted in closure. I remained on the periphery of the unrest, joining the marches when they were peaceful but retracting when it got violent. I listened intently to speeches because I wanted to understand what was happening.

On Wednesday, 23 October, I headed to school. We got word that morning that our school would be open. With order at school completely dissolved, children were constantly coming and going. It was a bright spring morning and the heat was already bearing down as I started the short walk to school. As I took the turn to approach the school gate, I froze in my tracks in shock.

I faced a scene of chaos. There were burning tyres in the street, police cars and casspirs* everywhere and students running in every direction. I was shocked to see that a casspir had driven through the perimeter fence of our school and now stood inside the school grounds. Policemen were shooting teargas canisters at the groups of students assembled and chasing and beating children with batons and sjamboks. Students were dragged by their hair, beaten and dumped into the back of police vans. I saw policemen shoving handcuffed teachers into vehicles. The violence was escalating – right in front of me.

As the crowd of students dispersed a number of children ran towards where I stood. An older boy ran straight at me, shouting that I should hide. I immediately followed him to where a neighbour had opened the side gate to her yard allowing us in. Within minutes of my peaceful walk to school I found myself right in the middle of a violent and frightening outbreak.

I was petrified.

I cowered behind the wall with approximately 15 other schoolmates. A police vehicle approached the area close to where we were hiding and the rocks started flying towards the vehicle from all directions including from my location. Without thinking I joined in the throwing. We grabbed whatever we could throw. The police shot a canister of teargas in our direction which wreaked havoc with our eyes and noses – it burned intensely and my eyes teared uncontrollably. This was my first, but certainly not last, experience of tear gas.

---

* Armoured vehicles used in urban areas. These became symbols of apartheid violence directed at citizens.

Anger swelled within my group and suddenly petrol bombs were being passed around. I was standing near the gate and one of these lit petrol bombs was handed to me. I stepped out of the gate and threw the petrol bomb as far as I could, not waiting to see where it landed. A whirlwind of emotions swept through me: terror shook me, anger that the police were acting violently towards us, and doubt that my violent actions were of any use.

I had already begun to feel a strong unease about my fist fights and in those moments hiding from the batons and guns of the police I felt an even stronger unease about my involvement in violent protest.

Within minutes the battle was over. The police had put out the fires and their cars and casspirs retreated. Children emerged from their hiding places, stumbling in a daze, recounting their experiences, checking on those with injuries and wondering aloud about those who were arrested. I walked home in a state of shock, unsure of what to make of it all and rather stunned that I had been so moved by the events that I joined in the action against the police.

The event got me thinking deeply for the first time about what role I was to play in our collective struggle against apartheid, and in my own personal fight for freedom. My diary entry that evening read: 'Lots of unrest at school – burning tyres and presence of casspirs' – quite an understatement, and perhaps due to the limited space in the diary, I make no mention of my involvement.

October was an extremely violent month. It was estimated that at one point 650,000 students were involved in the protests. On 26 October, three days after my petrol bomb incident, a state of emergency was declared in the Western Cape, which prohibited up to a hundred organisations from holding meetings and restricted the media. Four hundred people were detained in the first two weeks of the emergency: the death toll continued to rise at the rate of several deaths per week.

The townships in Cape Town remained in upheaval until the end of the year, with ongoing street battles with police and arson attacks on public buildings, shops and schools. Mitchells Plain was regularly sealed off by security forces and placed under virtual siege.

We were placed under curfew where no one was allowed on the streets between 8am and 3pm. Even my baseball training sessions were banned, because group meetings were banned and the bats were seen as weapons.

My parents were firmly opposed to any involvement in the protests, which led to many shouting sessions in our house as I insisted that we could not just stand by idly. I defied my parents, attending protests whenever I could. On one occasion a classmate, Larry Wessels, and I went to a rally at Mondale High, a nearby school. We joined the chanting and singing crowd. I was moved by the passion of the speakers who called on us to take a personal stand, to stand up and be counted.

As I listened, I suddenly sensed a panic in the crowd and everyone began scattering. Larry and I ran together heading for the gate but we then saw that the police had the entire school surrounded.

We were trapped inside.

'Oh shit,' I thought, as I stood in fear.

Students continued singing and the odd missile was hurled at the police. Over a loudhailer a policeman announced that if we left the school premises immediately we would go unharmed. The three gates of the school were opened. But, back inside the school voices from loudhailers urged us not to leave and a crowd continued to sing and taunt the police. Larry and I decided to leave along with many others who started filing out through the gates into the street. Then a wave of policemen rushed towards us.

I ran as fast as I could. Policemen were beating people with batons and arresting those who they could catch. I lost Larry in the chaos. I managed to escape by running between the surrounding houses. Larry and I spoke on the phone that evening, recounting the horror of the experience – we were lucky to escape unhurt – many others were not as fortunate. My life would have turned out so much worse if I had been arrested on one of these occasions.

When I think back on this period, I recall how scared and confused I was as I watched what appeared to be a war unfolding around me. However, a lot changed for me during this time. Even as I was throwing that petrol bomb a few weeks earlier, I knew that violence was not the path that I was to travel. I needed to decide if my freedom was going to be earned by the bomb or the pen.

I chose the pen.

Just as I had at nursery school and after the experiences with the gangster, I had a strong sense that I needed to 'get away'. I didn't know where I needed to go but I knew how I would get there – educating myself was the only hope I had. I did not care that I was receiving an inferior education at school, I was going to master it. I was going to do absolutely everything that it took to get into university. If I didn't get in the first time round I would reapply and reapply until they let me in. I was going to find ways of funding these studies – I would apply to every company, every organisation, and every institution to provide me with funding. I would get the best education possible.

As the end of the 1985 academic year drew nearer, the question of whether exams were to be written emerged. How were we to write exams when we attended school for only half the year? We were given the choice to either write exams or repeat the entire year. Many students chose not to write the exams either as continued protest or feeling that it would be pointless since they were likely to fail.

I decided that I would write.

I would rather fail trying than not try at all, even if the odds were heavily stacked against me. Many anti-apartheid leaders encouraged students to return to school, not as an acceptance of the inferior education but in recognition of the value of even an inferior education.

The police and army continued to have a heavy visible presence at our school and we even had an armed soldier in our classroom during all our exams. At the age of 15, I wrote my final exams with a soldier, dressed in brown and green combat gear and armed with an assault weapon, patrolling in the classroom. Was this guy going to protect me or shoot me? I was distracted by his presence, looking up at him every time he passed my desk.

My diary entries about the exams are bleak. For example: 'Wrote

Mathematics – a real nightmare, little hope of passing.' My Grade 10 report reflects the fact that I had no education for half of the year. It shows mid-year results, the usual good marks for Mathematics, Science and Biology,* but no marks for the September and November exams. We did not write September exams and despite me writing the November exams no marks were captured, just the words, 'Athol has passed'. So I had no idea how I actually performed in Grade 10 but I guess I didn't do too well based on how I struggled the following year.

At home my father decided to fill our education gap by instituting a dreaded Sunday after-lunch ritual of tackling general knowledge quizzes, crossword puzzles or playing Scrabble. Nick and I tried our best to escape but always failed. It did turn out to be fun, eventually. It instilled in me a discipline and a love for problem-solving which has endured.

My father was determined that we would be educated: 'No one can take your education from you,' he often repeated. In a country that seemed capable and willing to take away from me everything of value, it made sense to maximise the one thing that no one could take from me – my education.

---

* I had dropped Accountancy and replaced it with Geography.

My revolutionary plan ◉

My Grade 11 teacher, Ms Zubeida Desai, optimistically described my June results as 'excellent' and encouragingly wrote: 'He is definite university material.' However, the impact of missing half of Grade 10 was evident in my results and that of my classmates. My overall aggregate mark was 70%, the lowest that I had ever achieved. The class average was 48%. For Physical Science I got a disappointing 74% but again it was well above the class average of 28%.

It was a dismal year for everyone. I had given all I could to my studies and was sorely disappointed. While my results would still have been good enough for university entrance, I worried that they would not be good enough to be awarded a scholarship because no one would know the context of what happened at my high school over the preceding years.

While 'Liberation before Education' was the cry among protesters, I understood that we, as oppressed people, could achieve liberation *through* education. I simply had to succeed at high school and get into one of the top universities. This seemed like an impossibility given the disastrous grades I had achieved. The boulder of my oppression seemed to be growing in size. I felt like I first had to climb out of a deep hole before I could even begin to push this boulder.

The Roman poet Horace famously wrote over 2000 years ago: 'Adversity has the effect of eliciting talents, which in prosperous circumstances would have lain dormant.' The adversity that I faced during the last three years of high school certainly elicited many talents but none more than the talent of focused determination. I discovered in myself the ability to harness all of my energy towards a goal and drive towards it unwaveringly and at times maniacally.

I had a big dream, to study mechanical engineering, and I was prepared to do whatever was required to achieve that. It was a skill that had been developing slowly during my youth, one that I would call upon frequently in subsequent years. But in 1987, in Grade 12 it came to the fore with great force. We received no career guidance at school but I had read about engineering, and the incredible work that engineers did to solve societal problems by harnessing the forces of nature. Engineers applied scientific principles to transform natural resources to beneficial use by mankind. I liked the combination of theory and practice and I was attracted to the idea of designing and creating solutions to real-world problems. I fantasised about designing cars and spaceships, and imagined designing my own house one day where everything was automated and remotely controlled – all the curtains, gadgets, appliances, doors, windows, everything – probably influenced by something I saw in a James Bond movie. Engineering required strength in Mathematics and Science and strong analytical abilities. My research indicated that engineering had among the toughest entry requirements at university. Rather than scare me, this spurred me on.

But it was not a popular choice. There was no status in my community associated with being an engineer. No one knew what engineering was. Most people interpreted my interest in engineering as wanting to be a car mechanic. 'Why not become a lawyer, doctor or chartered accountant', was the comment I heard all too often.

One teacher who did appreciate the demands of engineering study said he admired my ambition, but suggested that I would be stretching myself too far, that our school curriculum did not adequately prepare me for the demands of engineering. He reminded me that one of the brightest students that my school had ever produced went to Wits to study engineering and had failed in his first year. He didn't want me to suffer the same fate and to have my 'spirit broken'. I was unmoved. I had career direction.

In 1960, the apartheid government established the University of the Western Cape (UWC) in Cape Town, a university for coloured people. The same was done for blacks and Indians, thus reserving the ten established universities for whites only. But UWC did not offer engineering. Going there meant changing my career focus. This was another example of the government seeking to write the script of my life, by narrowing coloureds' education options in terms of access to higher education institutions and the scope of available degrees.

Fortunately for me, the tide in South Africa was shifting sufficiently that some of the white universities, including the University of the Witwatersrand (Wits) and the University of Cape Town (UCT) began admitting limited numbers of non-white students. If I wanted to study engineering I would need to compete for one of the limited places at these white universities.

There were two cunning ways in which the apartheid racists ensured that non-whites did not gain entry to these white universities. The first was that there were virtually no coloured or black families who could afford to pay university tuition. This was certainly my situation – university tuition fees at UCT or Wits would have consumed 70% of my father's after-tax income annually. And we had no savings to draw on. The second way of keeping non-whites out was more macabre. Having separate education departments for each of the races ensured that the government could control the quality and content of education received by each race. So how do you ensure that no coloureds gain entry into the precious white universities? Give them an inferior education and then when it comes to the Grade 12 final exam, which is effectively the university entrance exam, you set the exams at a standard such that no coloured child would attain the required grades for university entrance.

Those bastards!

Even when coloured or black students did enrol in engineering few graduated confirming my high school teacher's fear. Wits engineering professor, Jeffrey Hillman, reported in 1996 that only 17% of black engineering students graduated from Wits and even then they took an average of 5.2 years to complete the four-year degree. This compared to 58% of white students and an average of 4.5 years. It scared me that even with their privileged education, 42% of white students dropped out. What chance did I have? I was not just suffering under the burden of an inferior education, but also the fact that I had missed so much of it because of the political unrest.

I had to overcome the two colossal obstacles that were designed to prevent me from getting into an engineering programme – firstly, I had to find the money to pay for my studies, and secondly, I needed to overcome my education deficit to achieve the required university entry grades. This became my sole focus, even as our country was still wrapped in the violent struggle against apartheid. I turned my attention to this seemingly impossible task. My parents encouraged me, only occasionally wavering to suggest that perhaps I should hedge and consider a broader set of academic options.

University prospectuses described the minimum entry require-ments for engineering and indicated that I needed to have English, Mathematics and Physical Science on higher grade.* I was most worried about English. For most of my school years I did not particularly enjoy languages and would never read a novel outside of what was required for school. All of my private reading was non-fiction – science, mathematics, technology or history. It is ironic that I would later become an award-winning poet.

My father was an avid reader and had a bookshelf of paperback novels which included classics such as John Steinbeck's *The Grapes of Wrath* and *Papillon* by Henri Charrière. Also on his bookshelf was a huge dictionary as well as a full set of encyclopaedias. The dictionary and encyclopaedias held sway over me at the expense of the novels. I enjoyed flipping through the dictionary to learn new words and to read the formal definitions of words that I already knew. The encyclopaedias opened many new worlds for me. There was a magic to just browsing through these books without looking for

---

* Schools offered subjects at two levels, higher grade and standard grade, with the former being the more demanding level.

anything in particular. This enabled me to develop a taste for a range of subjects that I was not exposed to at school; I remember reading about ecology and how volcanoes emerge, particularly drawn to listings that explained how mechanical and electrical gadgets worked.

These quiet moments of wonder immersed in books sowed the seeds for my lifelong thirst for knowledge and my firm belief in the liberating power of reading and education. In some nascent way, by liberating my thinking and developing in me this thirst for learning, books set me free.

In a fit of scientific inspiration I set out to disprove gravity, or the claim that a gravitational force existed. I refused to accept the claim that there was a force of attraction between objects and the earth. My readings in magnetism confirmed my suspicion since magnetism exists between objects, usually metallic, that have magnetic fields within them. A baseball didn't have any magnetic field, to my mind, and neither did the ground on which I dropped it. Myth busted! Or so I thought.

It was not until I understood the nature of gravitational pull between orbiting bodies like the earth, moon and other planets that I understood the nature of gravity and the force it exerts on all earth-bound objects. Even my idea of magnetism was a narrow one because there is an array of sources of magnetism and in fact every object does indeed possess some magnetic field no matter how weak. It was not the greatest moment of scientific insight or endeavour, but it was an early exercise of my curiosity and refusal to accept information as gospel.

Unexpectedly, Physical Science became a worry as well (or perhaps expectedly given my misguided foray into disproving gravity). Missing half of the year's curriculum in Grade 10 (in 1985 due to the unrest) had a double negative effect. Not only did I now suffer the deficit of missing the actual content of half the year, but Westridge High decided not to offer Physical Science on higher grade in Grade 11. This decision was in response to the poor preparation that students received in Grade 10. Without Physical Science on higher grade, I would not be admitted to an engineering degree.

This seemed grossly unfair.

I asked my Physical Science teacher, Mr Antooley, to write a letter explaining the situation – I would send the letter to the universities and to potential funders, hoping that they would understand my unique context that was beyond my control, and make an exception. In his letter, Antooley explained: 'School in our area was adversely affected by the boycotts of the previous year. For Physical Science teaching this meant that certain sections of the Grade 10 syllabus had to be repeated in Grade 11, thus increasing the volume of work covered in that year ... I remained convinced that the Higher Grade paper would be too demanding under the circumstances which prevailed.' Thankfully, the recipients of the letter accepted this explanation.

Yet this did not alter the fact that yet again another layer of disadvantage was being heaped upon me. Physical Science was offered on higher grade in Grade 12, so I would be taking that subject having learned Grade 11 on the standard grade. Again, the odds were stacked heavily against success. Again the boulder grew larger and heavier.

It began dawning on me that to get into an engineering programme I needed to make a monumental effort. I found encouragement in the words of some of my teachers who consistently acknowledged my potential despite the challenging environment in the country. In support of my applications for two engineering scholarships Ms Desai completed two reference forms. Excerpts from the first reference form shows the confidence that she had that I would succeed:

> Athol's achievements are exceptional in both the academic and sporting fields. He consistently achieves good results at school. ... Athol should go far in life. He has tremendous drive and knows his potential. A well-balanced young man who should be an asset in any normal society.

Ms Desai's reference to me being an 'asset in any normal society' would stay with me for many years as I struggled against the currents of an abnormal society that treated me as if I was a liability. In the second reference form she wrote:

> Athol is indeed a rare person. It is difficult today for students to give their undivided attention to studies. Uninterrupted schooling is a thing of the past. For Athol to fare so well despite these odds says a lot about him. Athol seems to excel at whatever he does ... He is bright and loves challenges ... That Athol is an intelligent young man cannot be disputed. What impresses me is his ability to find things out for himself. He loves challenging teachers and does not regard their word as gospel... He has the perseverance and acumen to make a success of whatever field he gets involved in... He is very confident about himself. This somehow makes him a popular person in class. His aura of confidence appeals to teachers as well... Nothing will deter him from achieving his goals.

I was not supposed to read these reference forms but I'm glad I did – Ms Desai's words validated my belief that I could overcome the boulder that stood between me and a mechanical engineering degree. She believed in me and it magnified my self-belief. When storms of self-doubt would rage, as they often did, her words served as an anchor.

As the year got underway, I turned my attention squarely to my studies. My days were spent studying with a determination that bordered on obsession. I cut down most social events and even stopped playing club baseball. The main thrust of my revolutionary plan was to get as much academic input as I could. My first step was to enrol in night school.

Entry to night school at Westridge High was initially refused since it was reserved for working adults. The irony of the situation did not escape me. Whereas most teachers were struggling to get their students excited about any learning, here was a student who was so keen to learn that he would attend day school and wanted to give up his evenings to attend extra lessons, but was being turned away. I pleaded with the teachers. The Physical Science teacher was determined to stick to the rules so I could not enrol.

However, in the Mathematics teacher I found a more sympathetic ear. Mr Wajiet Parker recognised my determination, and was willing to reward my effort by bending the rules to allow me into his class. I was the only teenager in those classes among the many adults. I had a good day-school Mathematics teacher in Mr John Scholtz, but I was looking forward to the extra tuition from Mr Parker. So twice a week, for two hours in the evening, for the entire year, I attended Mr Parker's class. I would come home after day school, do my homework, have dinner and then, while other teenagers watched TV or socialised, I went to night school.

In addition to night classes, I enrolled in every conceivable extra class that I could find and that my parents could afford. I gathered every study guide and past exam paper that I could. Our school principal, Mr Peter Petersen, recognising the effort I was making, made the generous offer to pay for me to attend Star Schools at UCT – these were classes taught by the TV celebrity William Smith and held during the school holidays. The classes were based on a different curriculum to mine so I had the challenge of constantly having to refer back to my books. However, I enjoyed the novelty of the content.

I could do nothing about the education department setting unrealistic questions in the final exam but I reasoned that the toughest exams that could possibly be set would be based on the more advanced curriculum taught at the white schools. The second part of my revolutionary plan was therefore to prepare for final exams based on the white curriculum.

My father's white boss had a son older than me. My father got from him his son's old textbooks which I worked through. With money that I had saved from delivering newspapers I bought myself a small desk that I managed to squeeze into the bedroom that I shared with Nick. It was a cheap desk made of chipboard, but it served the purpose. I wrote out formulas and summary notes on sheets of paper that I pasted onto the walls in our bedroom. These sheets covered the entire room, only leaving space for posters of Bruce Springsteen and the Arsenal football team.

It became a massive team effort at home – my family did all they could to create an environment in which I could study. There was little time for anything other than study. I had classes during the day and evening, plus homework and preparation for each class, with weekends and other spare time devoted to reading the additional books.

It was Henry David Thoreau who wrote: 'I know of no more encouraging fact than the unquestionable ability of man to elevate his life by conscious endeavour.' My endeavour was certainly conscious and I was determined that this endeavour would indeed elevate my life. I've always believed that when man is faced with a crisis, he invariably finds courage, innovation or strength from stores he was before unaware.

Many stories are told of people leaping over eight-foot-high walls when chased by a vicious dog or of people lifting crashed cars with their bare hands when a loved one was trapped underneath. I was faced with a similar crisis now and somehow I found stores of ideas and energy to deal with the crisis.

During my late nights studying I still felt that I was part of the struggle against apartheid, because I was going to break out of the chains that had been placed on me and I would inspire others to do the same. I was not allowing the government to dictate what I could know and what limits there were on my levels of achievement. I would not be relegated to being a third-class citizen. This was not just studying to get through exams, this was part of my fight for freedom.

I began achieving good results in Physical Science. For the March test, I earned 94% even though this was still on standard grade. At that point, finally, the school offered us a choice to continue on standard grade or to transfer to higher grade. I immediately switched. I obtained distinctions for English and Mathematics in the March tests and although my Physical Science mark dropped in the August test, my report card read 'Excellent results'. My hard work was paying off.

The most significant transformation happened in my enjoyment of

English and again the inspirational Ms Desai played a significant role. For the first time I began finding great pleasure in reading novels, plays and poetry. I saw the power and beauty of metaphor and imagery for the first time. My eyes opened to the richness in Shakespeare's *King Lear* and I became consumed by the drama in Harper Lee's *To Kill a Mockingbird*. I pored over study guides and even rented videos of the books that we needed to study.

I still needed to find a bursary if I was going to study at university. Corporate South Africa had begun to see the urgent need to educate non-whites to meet the growing demand for qualified skills. For many years, companies relied on European expatriates to fill our engineering roles but as the political situation began shifting and economic sanctions against the country began taking hold, the supply of engineers began to slow. For reasons owing both to need and nation-building, companies began thinking about investing in developing local engineering talent, and began creating bursaries for non-white students.

The career section of the *Sunday Times* proved to be a valuable source for lists of bursaries. Every Sunday I would earn the ire of my father as I tore into the newspaper searching for bursaries before he could even get his hands on the paper. I ended up writing letters to 29 companies enquiring about bursaries – some of these came from the advertisements but most were speculative letters sent to companies whose addresses I sourced from the telephone directory. All application forms required an ID photo so I had fifty ID photos printed, indicative of my intent to apply for every possible bursary that I could find. I spent many hours in the evenings and over weekends writing letters by hand and filling out application forms. It was a time of great promise and excitement as I'd send off a letter and then visit our mailbox every day hoping to find a reply.

A flood of rejection letters started. I received more rejections from companies to my applications than I received from teenage girls to my dance invitations at parties and clubs. Of my 29 enquiries, three companies, Sasol (the state-owned oil company), Eskom (the state-owned power company) and Anglo American (the mining corporation) invited me for interviews and tests.

Anglo American invited me to a second round of interviews in Johannesburg. It was my first taste of special treatment owing to my academic achievements. I got to take a flight by myself to Johannesburg and got to stay in a hotel for the first time – I had a room at the Johannesburger Hotel in Joubert Park. I felt quite important having this large company pay for my flights and hotel, and even collecting me at the airport. My family and friends were abuzz with this amazing news that a company was flying me to Johannesburg for interviews. This was unheard of in my circles. The interviews were at Anglo American's head office on Main Street in Johannesburg. The building was grand and intimidating. It was the first time that I had been inside a corporate office building and everything amazed me, the beautiful furniture, the wood-panelled walls, and the grand scale of the lobbies. I left Johannesburg feeling confident that the interviews went well.

Soon it was final exam time. I took them all in my stride, feeling well prepared and confident. All went well, except for Physical Science in which questions seemed to come from an altogether different curriculum. Even though I was as prepared as anyone could be I did not even recognise many of the questions. It was a disaster. There were rumours later that the person who set this exam committed suicide knowing that it had been set consciously to trip up coloured students. Even my later university Physics professor was surprised by some of the questions.

Despite all the setbacks I prevailed. My last year at high school ended successfully. I passed all my subjects and received offers of a place to study mechanical engineering at both UCT and Wits. Even more exciting was that I received offers of bursaries from all three companies that had interviewed me. Yet I was disappointed with my final exam results. I missed my target of earning a distinction overall. I felt that I had done absolutely all that I could do and deserved an overall A. Instead I ended up with a B aggregate. It felt like failure, especially after the colossal effort.

The day before Christmas of 1987, the *Cape Times* reported the Grade 12 results in a supplement. I was proud to see my name there and the inclusion of an 'x' next to my name indicating that my pass qualified me for general university entrance. The results showed the sad fact that only one third of my class had passed and only three of us had earned university entrance. The apartheid cretins must have celebrated that day, sitting somewhere drinking tea, since their plan had worked to stifle the education of many young people. To the credit of many of my classmates and friends, they chose to rewrite exams, or to repeat Grade 12 to improve their results.

I had to make two important choices – which university to attend and which bursary to accept. What a luxury! Although it was earned it was a luxury nonetheless. My research indicated that the mechanical engineering programme at Wits was a better fit for me than UCT. While the Sasol and Eskom bursaries were good for study at either university, the Anglo American bursary was only valid at Wits. In addition, Wits offered something unique.

To address the high failure rate of black engineering students, in 1986 Anglo American collaborated with the Wits engineering faculty to create the Pre-University Bursary Scheme (PBS) for black students. It was a year-long programme that combined academic study at the university with exposure to the engineering environment at a host company. Anglo American offered me a choice – I could go directly to first year of the engineering degree or I could participate in the PBS programme which offered excellent preparation for engineering study. Aware of the gaps in my high school education I figured that the PBS programme might be to my advantage. Besides, I had a year to spare since I had started my schooling a year early. Choosing this option meant that I had five years of full-time study ahead of me – one year for PBS and then four years for the degree. The Anglo American bursary was far more lucrative than the others, offering full tuition, accommodation, travel between Cape Town and Johannesburg, a clothing allowance, book allowance and spending money.

I was sold.

And so I accepted the Anglo American bursary. Of course, studying at Wits meant leaving home for Johannesburg. I'd always had this sense that my path to success would lead me away from home. *Away* somehow seemed better than *here*, even when I didn't know where *away* was. This wasn't hard to understand when home was dominated by gangsters, poverty and hardship. Despite the sadness of leaving my best friend Nick, the rest of my family and baseball behind, I knew that I was making the correct decision.

Despite all the setbacks of political violence and an oppressive government that tried to force me into a life of mediocrity through its inferior education, I had overcome. Despite the socioeconomic factors that made me lose my way briefly and that limited my access to education, I had prevailed. I had achieved my dream. I had managed to push an enormous boulder up the hill, and despite it frequently crashing back down, I had managed to get it over the top of the hill and push it away into the depths of the ocean. Little did I know that there would be many more boulders to face but for now I had my ticket to freedom. I was going to university. I was going to Wits!

1988 ⊚

1988 promised to be the year that marked my victory over the old injustices that sought to prevent me from gaining a higher education. I had overcome great odds to fulfil my dream to be at Wits and would be seeing the fruits of my intense work and sacrifice at high school. My whole family was at the train station as I left Cape Town for the 24-hour journey to Johannesburg. My mother, father, Amanda, Nick and eight-year-old Roscoe wished me a sad farewell. I was happy to be on my way and excited about what lay ahead.

I arrived in Johannesburg with a sense of destiny. I felt that greatness awaited me. I was the first member of my extended family to enrol in a degree programme at a university. As far as I knew, no one from Mitchells Plain had ever graduated from Wits and no one from Mitchells Plain had ever graduated with an engineering degree. As it turned out, I would be one of the first coloured engineering graduates in the country.

Wits University is located in Braamfontein, near the centre of Johannesburg. My one-year PBS Programme was housed in a building on Yale Road, on Wits' West Campus. We were a class of 55 students from across the country, 53 black and two coloured. We were all fully funded, either directly by the Anglo American Corporation or through one of their group companies. I fell into this latter category, receiving my bursary from Boart International, an engineering company that manufactured mining equipment. Boart was headquartered in Sandton, Johannesburg and had research and manufacturing operations across the country and sales offices worldwide. I was allocated a room in Braamfontein Centre, a university-owned apartment block, located across the road from the main campus. I shared Apartment 305 with classmate Pakiso Mokoena, who grew up in the apartheid-created homeland of QwaQwa in the Free State. He was a quiet, gentle person who did not drink or smoke, unlike his rowdy room-mate.

The academic component of the programme was intense and comprised nine full-year courses covering the spectrum of the sciences and engineering. The first semester started with a review of material that we should have covered in high school – much of it was new to me. The lecturers were engaging and the material came alive for me for the first time. I loved being at Wits. I was on a high.

In April, I started my first period of practical training, a requirement of my programme, at a Boart manufacturing facility in Roodepoort, an industrial town west of Johannesburg. I was dressed in my best outfit as I waited expectantly at the bus stop ready for my first day of work. I was told that the buses to Roodepoort were easy to spot owing to their distinctive design of a dark blue bottom half and white top half with the word 'Roodepoort' in blue capital letters on the front and sides.

Exactly as described, the blue and white bus arrived and stopped where I was waiting in line. I proceeded up the steps and held out my fare to the driver as I reached him. He refused to take the money. He just stared at me. 'You can't use this bus,' he eventually said. I was confused. *Did I board the wrong bus?* He spoke again, more sternly this time, in an Afrikaans accent: 'Listen, you can't use this bus!' I had no idea what to do. I looked around the bus and saw that the passengers were staring at me. It was probably only ten seconds but it felt like forever. Then the realisation dawned – everyone seated in the bus was white, the bus driver was white, the irritated people standing in the queue behind me waiting to board were white. I looked back at the driver and he nodded as if to say, 'Do you get it now?'

'Please leave the bus,' he spat, sounding irritated, and gestured with his hand towards the door. The person behind me, a white woman, shoved past and handed over her fare. My confusion turned to embarrassment and then I felt a pain rise in my chest. His words –

Please leave the bus – felt like daggers in my chest.

The boulder came crashing back down the hill. That boulder that I had been pushing up the steep hill for years, to earn dignity, to be recognised as a person worthy of mutual respect, came crashing back down the hill and rolled right over me.

With a heavy heart I made my way awkwardly down the steps of the bus. People on the bus stared at me as though I was a criminal or a leper rather than a teenage student trying to fulfil his dream of becoming an engineer. The door closed with a deafening thud and the bus pulled off leaving me staring at it. I felt the saddest that I had ever felt in my life. My legs felt like jelly so I sat down on the kerb, tears running down my cheeks. This was supposed to be my time of greatness. I recalled my high school teacher's words, 'Athol should go far in life.' Perhaps not. I sat there on the pavement crying like I was mourning a death.

The reality of living in South Africa in the late eighties hit home that day and it hit hard as I discovered that some things were closed to me because of my race. I had stepped onto a whites-only bus as all Roodepoort buses were. Until then apartheid had been an abstract concept. I had seen state-sanctioned violence, but never the ugly face of racism practiced by the likes of a bus driver or other ordinary people. But that day I saw it: it stared at me, it slapped me in the face. It stabbed me in the chest far worse than that gangster at home. I felt stripped of my humanity. And I was only eighteen.

After a few minutes I stood up from the pavement, from the spot where the bus driver had driven off. I refused to be discouraged. I would not quit and I would not let these small people, who lived in ignorance and with prejudice, break my spirit. I wedged my shoulder firmly under the weight of the boulder and started pushing again.

I walked from Braamfontein to the centre of Johannesburg, a thirty-minute meandering walk because I didn't know my way around. I eventually found the train station and took a train to Roodepoort. The delays meant that I was late for work. Rather than receive sympathy I was chastised by my boss for being late and given a lecture about professionalism. I kept my mouth shut.

But I wouldn't keep my mouth shut for long.

The facility where I worked was split in two – the office building on one side of Main Reef Road and the factory on the opposite side. I had been working in the office for a few days when I experienced my first racist incident at work. It was in the toilet. As I was standing at the urinal, the white guy using the urinal next to me spoke, 'You people can't use this toilet,' he said. *You people?* I wondered what he meant by that. I looked at him briefly but kept quiet.

'You must use the toilet for blacks,' he continued. *What did he just say!*

'What's wrong with me going here?' I retorted with anger in my voice. He explained, with a calm arrogance, that I had to go out of the office building, cross the road and go all the way to the back of the factory to use the toilet there. 'That toilet,' he continued, 'is reserved for you blacks.'

Another boulder to push.

I was incensed and marched over to the office of the human resources manager where I explained what had happened. His response almost knocked me over but it was something I would hear many times over the coming years. He explained that this was 'just the way things are', and recommended that it would probably be best if I didn't use the toilet in the office again. Despite my protests, he was adamant. A mixture of anger and sadness came over me. It felt like I was being drained of blood, of life. *How can this be happening?*

As a teenager, I had the impression that apartheid and racism was the work of politicians and policemen. I now discovered how mistaken I was. I was experiencing what millions across the country experienced every day – humiliation and disrespect at the hands of ordinary white people going about their ordinary lives. This was not about politics, this was about one person looking upon another with contempt. I was being subtly reminded that regardless of my academic potential, I was seen as inferior, that I did not belong. The boulders grew larger. For the remainder of my time there, every time I needed the toilet, I would leave the office, cross the busy road, go to the back of the factory and use the toilet there.

1988 was not delivering the greatness and victory that it had promised at the beginning of the year. The challenge of studies and the horrible racist experiences took their toll. I missed home. I was, however, comforted by a steady stream of letters from Cape Town, mainly from my family and a number of friends. I was able to telephone my family periodically from a payphone – a real highlight.

I found a supportive community in the Catholic Society on campus which was attached to Holy Trinity Church in Braamfontein. There were regular lunch-time events, retreats and I attended mass every Sunday. As I became increasingly involved in the church, I eventually decided to follow a programme to becoming a eucharistic minister. I was commissioned in October. My duties included planning mass, serving communion and doing bible readings.

I was committed to my studies and engaged in events at church but the struggle between my angels and demons was relentless. I was a regular at parties on campus and often the key protagonist in binge-drinking episodes that went long into the night. I frequently took the long walk from Braamfontein to Hillbrow to a club called Why Not which was one of my favourite hangouts. Even though Hillbrow was quite cosmopolitan, Why Not club attracted mainly black patrons. I enjoyed the vibe – the music was a unique mix of African beats, Kwaito and eighties disco.

Apparently, Why Not was a meeting place for ANC members. On a Thursday night in September, the security police detonated a bomb in the club as an attack on the ANC. The blast injured 13 people. Thankfully I was not at the club that night. At the Truth and Reconciliation Commission (TRC) years later the four policemen involved in the bombing also admitted to being involved in bombing the headquarters of the South African Council of Churches a month earlier. I was back at the club with my friends soon after it was refurbished and re-opened; we were determined not to let those assholes spoil our fun.

Anti-apartheid activity on campus increased as the year wore on. I attended as many public meetings and protests as I could. These meetings were often broken up by the police who used tear gas to disperse crowds of students. One of my diary entries states: 'I ended up with tear gas in my face, which was shot by policemen. This caused my eyes to tear and burn and caused me to cough.' I also wrote about helping a girl who had fallen and who would have been 'stampeded by students fleeing the police'.

At one rally on campus I got to hear Winnie Mandela speak for the first time, calling on students to be resolute in our opposition to apartheid. I would see her often on campus – she was studying towards a degree which had lectures in the Richard Ward building where I too had a lecture once a week. I couldn't help but stare at her – she *was* the wife of Nelson Mandela after all. She was always dressed in dark colours and seemed to keep to herself. I thought of approaching her on occasion but could never think of anything worthwhile to say.

With final exams just days away, I cleared my desk in the apartment and designed my revision timetable. I was worried about exams but I was sure that 1988, the first year of my university studies, was going to end on a high.

But I was wrong. The agents of apartheid were not yet done with me.

It was around midnight on 17 November. Loud banging on the apartment door woke me. I was annoyed by the banging, it was late and I had just gone to sleep. I thought that it was probably a neighbour who usually banged on the door rather than knocked. I was in a daze as I walked into the kitchen to open the door wearing nothing but my underwear. I had barely opened the door when I was overwhelmed by the rush of heavily armed men pushing their way into the apartment. All I saw was a blur of guns, helmets and lights. I let out a scream as they overpowered me. Three or four men grabbed me and violently turned me around and bashed my face into the wall. I could feel the force of someone leaning into my back and I felt the hard metal of a gun against the back of my head.

'Staan daar, staan daar!' (stand there, stand there!) one of them was yelling. Simultaneously, men rushed in and ripped my roommate from his bed.

With my face pressed viciously against the white kitchen wall I felt something inside me collapse, *Oh God, I am going to die.* At first I resisted the grip that my attacker had on me but this earned me fist blows to my lower back. I couldn't breathe. After a while, the intruder pressing against my back released me while the other moved his gun down to the middle of my naked back, the cold metal pressing deep into my muscles and grinding against my spine.

In those first few moments, I was absolutely convinced that the intruders were going to kill us. This was South Africa and they were white men with guns. We were black kids and they had forced their way into the apartment to kill us. There were about ten of them, armed and dressed for battle with helmets and bulletproof vests. Although I had screamed once when they entered the apartment it felt as if the screaming in my head continued – loud, piercing shrieks echoed all round my head. My first guess was that they were the Wit Wolwe (White Wolves), a white-supremacist group allegedly travelling the country killing black people. The Wit Wolwe were top of mind because just two days earlier Barend Strydom, who claimed to be their leader, went on a shooting spree in Pretoria, killing seven black people and wounding fifteen more.[*]

People say your life flashes before you when you're facing death; my life didn't flash before me. I was consumed with terror and fully believed that these men had come to kill me. Within a few minutes it was all quiet. I was still pinned to the wall, at their mercy. All my visions of doing great things, of breaking free from the chains of apartheid were gone. That feeling of aloneness came over me again, the same way that I felt that morning when I was told to leave the bus, only this time it was with fear thrown in. *Please let me live, I don't*

---

[*] It is disputed whether the Wit Wolwe actually existed or whether reports of their existence was government fear-mongering propaganda.

want to die, I prayed, quivering in silence.

There was constant talking amongst the men, in Afrikaans. After a few seconds, the bearers of the guns stepped away from me. I was grabbed by the arm and pulled around and shoved with my back against the kitchen wall. For the first time I could see the faces of my assailants. Some of them didn't look much older than me. They kept their guns trained on me with looks of venom in their eyes. I felt lame and my breathing was laboured; I worried that I might have an asthma attack. One of the intruders explained that they were from a special unit of the South African Police 'acting under state of emergency regulations'. This was a serious statement. It implied that they would treat us as a threat to state security, giving them complete latitude to do with us as they pleased. The government had become notorious for its use of emergency laws to violently repress resistance to apartheid and to intimidate citizens.

The men began to search our apartment, causing havoc. Everything was overturned, clothes were thrown out of the cupboards, books and notes were paged through and just dumped on the floor. They went through everything – my letters, my diary, photos, my personal belongings. They demanded to see our identity documents and our student cards. Questions were barked at us:

'What are your names?'

'Who lives here?'

'Who's in charge?'

'Where are you from?'

They all looked like killers to me except one. He was young, with light brown hair and pale blue eyes. He stood frozen, looking more frightened than I was. I looked into his frightened eyes and for a moment our eyes met. Even though he stood there pointing a loaded gun at me, I felt sad for him. We both seemed to be in agony. It was the first time that I realised there are victims on both sides of every man-made atrocity.

The policemen seemed more interested in me than my roommate. They spoke on their radios, flipped through a mug-shot book looking up at me periodically. I noticed that they looked confused. Then they decided to leave.

The whole ordeal lasted about 30 minutes. When they left the leader, who had been barking instructions, turned to me and said, 'Good luck for the exams.' It was as if they had popped in for a chat. *No hard feelings!* I stared at the door left open as they filed out. After a while, I staggered to the door and closed it as I tried to come to terms with what had just happened.

I didn't sleep that night. I couldn't. I shook uncontrollably.

After a while I took out an audio cassette recorder and recounted what had happened. I ended the recording with, 'It's a mess, our room is a mess, I'm a mess, South Africa's in a mess, South Africa's in a mess, definitely.'

A few hours later I wrote in my diary: 'It's now 3:30am, three and a half hours later and we still can't sleep. I'm so terrified, I can't sleep, I can't close my eyes, I still keep seeing the vision of the men barging in. It is something that I will never forget; I think this will plague me for the rest of my life. ... I just thank the Lord that we are safe now.'*

The next day I reported the incident to the university.

'I cannot even think straight, let alone study and I've got exams in four days,' I wrote in my diary.

The raid was obviously planned. I knew, as did most others, that there were apartheid spies on campus. It was an unnerving thought that someone I knew was possibly feeding information about me to the police. It was frightening to think that I had been watched. I would never find out what or who they were looking for. Perhaps it was a mistaken identity. Perhaps they recognised me from Why Not club or the protest marches on campus. Or perhaps the spy had heard me express my strong views against apartheid. I would never know. I just had to live with the effects of yet another violation, and try to get on with my life.

When Boart heard about the incident they sent me a letter: 'We

---

*   I still have the audio cassette and the diaries which capture the horror of this ordeal.

share with you your anxiety resulting from the ugly raid on your residence and the threats made on your life last month.' (What I was feeling was far more intense than mere 'anxiety'.) 'But life goes on and with time the memory of bad events dims,' the letter continued, which really irritated me. What I had been experiencing since I was born and would continue to experience for years to come was significantly more than mere 'bad events.' These scars would not dim with time.

My anger returned. I was angry that the police could dish out such terror, terror that fractured something within me. Angry at the indignity. I hated the way I screamed and the way I shook. I hated the fact that my eyes filled with tears. I hated how docile I was. I wished I had been bolder, braver, that I had said something strong and challenging rather than stutter and whimper like I did. But I was afraid; I was filled with fear ... just like the men who stood there threatening, my life were filled with fear, just like the men and women who had sent them.

Friends pointed out to me that my experience was exactly why we needed the armed struggle. They urged me to get more involved with on-campus political groups. I was angry but I did not feel that violence was the answer. Again I had to make a choice whether to earn my freedom through the bomb or the pen. Just as in 1985, I chose the pen.

Two days after the raid I wrote in my diary: 'Worked at the library for a while, but couldn't get much done. I am still paranoid and scared.' I was still shaken up when the day of exams arrived. The university offered me the option to postpone my exams but I decided that I would write them. Not for the first time I sat for exams after a period of violent encounters. My resolve hardened. Just as a bodybuilder needs the resistance of his weights to build muscle, the adversity that I experienced spurred me on. I was determined to succeed. My focus returned.

Despite the trauma and hardship of the year, I passed my exams with distinction – I got the 'A' that eluded me in my final year at high school. This was the best way to respond to the year I'd experienced.

I received a letter from Boart congratulating me on my results that 'indicates both ability and application'. I had passed and would now enter the first year of the BSc Mechanical Engineering degree.

It is terrible to be born with a deficit, particularly when the deficit is created by human beings. For most of my childhood I was not aware of the disadvantage into which I had been born. If my struggle to date had been an unconscious struggle for freedom, the next phase of my life was certainly conscious and deliberate. It was a struggle for my place in society, a struggle for recognition and a struggle for me to fulfil my dreams. I had no idea just how concerted the resistance would be to my efforts, just how much more I would have to overcome.

From the valley
to the mountaintop ◎

The bursary from Boart would be renewed annually subject to satisfactory results. It came with a few conditions, none more frightening than the condition that required my father to sign a deed of suretyship, which stated that if I did not pass, he would be liable to repay what Boart had invested. There was no way my father could repay, yet he signed that deed. I can only guess the anxiety he must have suffered signing that document and putting our family at such grave financial risk. Financial insecurity like this is one of the unseen struggles that is unique to those who had suffered under apartheid or those who live in poverty around the world. The level of risk required to take even the smallest step forward is so much greater than those who are wealthier.

In stark contrast to PBS where all my classmates were black, in my first year virtually everyone in my class was white; I stuck out like a sore thumb. In my usual bullish style, I settled in quickly and made friends. I didn't experience any racial hostilities from classmates, rather I found it a deeply rich experience to engage with classmates across racial lines. For most of us, this was the first time that we had peers of a different race, and despite being told all our lives how different we were, we came to recognise our similarities.

Occasional tensions arose during political protests on campus. An example was the outcry on campus after the assassination of David Webster, a Wits lecturer and long-standing anti-apartheid activist. Webster was gunned down on 1 May 1989 outside his home by government assassin Ferdi Barnard. The continuous rallies, marches and disruption of classes drew the anger of many in my class. I was treated with some suspicion after returning from the rallies but even though we had some right-wing hardliners among us – including someone who openly campaigned for the AWB, a white supremacist paramilitary group – the situations never flared up.

I moved to an on-campus male-only residence called Men's Residence or Men's Res. Men's Res had two buildings, College House and Dalrymple House. I shared room 158 in College House with a coloured student from Kimberley – hardly a coincidence that the only two coloured students in the residence were assigned to the same room. It was 1989, and while some racist rules were loosening, apartheid was still in full swing.

Other than a handful of black and Indian students, the residence was made up completely of white students as would be expected given the student population of the university. The social culture was dominated by excessive drinking, elaborate tales of sexual conquests, mischievous and dangerous quests (like stealing traffic lights), and of course, rugby. I had never played rugby before, not even having participated in a friendly game. I rarely watched rugby on television and, as my team soon came to realise, I didn't even know the rules of the game. But that did not stop me from attending trials for the Men's Res team for the traditional annual grudge match against our arch rivals, EOH or Ernest Oppenheimer Hall, the other all-male university student residence.

At our first training session we played *touch rugby*, something I had never heard of. In touch rugby, as the name suggests, merely touching an opposing player constitutes a tackle. Instead, for my first tackle, I delivered a WWE-style clothes-line tackle that knocked a player out cold. This incident instantly earned me notoriety as a mean tough guy not to be messed with. The nickname 'Bull' became institutionalised. I was assigned the position of tight-head prop which meant I took up a position at the front of the scrum. I could think of nothing worse than crouching with someone behind you putting their arm between your legs, reaching up to grab your jersey, squashing your genitals with their forearm while you bent forward ramming your head, neck and shoulder into that of an opposing prop in a scrum. It was ridiculous. It was painful. Sometimes it was just plain scary. But there was no way that I was going to let on that I was freaked out of my mind; after all, I was Bull. Our triumph in the inter-residence duel made instant heroes of our team members and added to the long history of Men's Res victories.

It was at Men's Res that I met Bert Frahm, with whom I've remained friends to this day. Bert tells the story of how he strategically chose to befriend me because I was seen as the most dangerous guy on campus. To his thinking, being friends with the most dangerous person would ensure his safety. Bert and I were both studying engineering and that was where any similarities ended.

He enjoyed the music of Prince and I was a fan of Bruce Springsteen. He preferred going to jazz clubs, for me disco was the thing. He had attended a private school, I had gone to a township government school. He was white, I was coloured. Yet we developed a close friendship. He was eccentric like me which did help. We did crazy things like throw baseball on the library lawns in our underwear or try to invent a new recreational drug by soaking cigarettes in alcohol – leading to us coughing violently and getting sick. Bert and his family were good to me, always welcoming me warmly to their home. For the first time I felt that I had found a friend in Johannesburg.

I found the year tough academically but I passed. Bert did not. He joined the army the following year and now runs a successful tango dance studio.

I had beaten the curse of black engineering students failing first year.

At the start of my second year, I moved into an apartment off-campus with a friend, Gillian Adams, who was a medical student. We moved into 306 Quartz Hill, a furnished flat located at 5 Bruce Street in the dodgy suburb of Hillbrow.

Hillbrow was a densely populated suburb adjoining downtown Johannesburg which consisted mainly of high-rise residential blocks. In bygone days it was a highly sought-after area and a popular spot for nightlife entertainment. These days it sports one or two decent cafés and clubs but mostly is seedy, over-run with drug-dealers, gangsters and prostitutes. I frequented Fontana Chicken, famous for its roast chickens but more famous because it was open 24 hours a day. It literally never closed and in fact had no front door. The place was like an oasis to late-night partygoers and residents alike. I made the odd visit to Café de Paris on Pretoria Street which served large slices of cake and a range of hot drinks and occasionally went for a drink at the seedy Hotel Quirinel, which had a bar downstairs. I left my mark in Hillbrow, writing my name in wet cement in the street at the intersection of Bruce and Quartz streets. Years later I drove into the area to see if my name was still there but I was too scared to get out of my car ... Hillbrow has become a frightening place.

Hillbrow certainly encouraged the eccentric in me. For a while I would attend lectures wearing brightly coloured shirts, floral waistcoats and I even painted my fingernails black. As if I didn't already stand out from my conservative white engineering classmates. The black nails precipitated a period where everything was black including my clothes, and I refused to write with a pen if it didn't have black ink. The word 'black' dominated my poetry, not always in a negative sense but in the sense of rebellion. A 1990 poem includes the line: 'The black nails, the black clothes ... My black mind. Even my pen is black' and another 'Much richer is a blind man for his wealth is in his heart, not his eyes. Happy are the blind, for they and only they, see life as it really is ... black.'

It was a thirty-minute walk from Quartz Hill to Southwest Engineering Building where most of my lectures were held. I would take the long walk down Empire Road in deep thought on some days and on others in complete wonder at the world around me. There were many days when I just did not feel like walking. Since there was no public transport running from Hillbrow to Wits, I would hitchhike. I became easily recognisable along Empire Road by my black notepad folder which I held up to passing motorists containing the word 'Wits' written in Tipp-ex on the one side and 'Hillbrow' on the other.

Nelson Mandela was freed from prison on 11 February, ending his long walk to freedom and setting South Africa on course towards democracy. I was sad that I could not be in Cape Town that day when he addressed the cheering crowd as I was still studying in Johannesburg. I did, however, get to join a large group of students on campus to celebrate the occasion. It seemed so unreal that Mandela was free. For so long we had been singing and chanting and marching, calling for the release of Nelson Mandela and now he was free.

The political changes inspired many poems. I started writing poetry more seriously, something unusual for an engineering student. In 1991, I penned the poem 'New South Africa' which was published in the August edition of *Wits Student*, the university newspaper. It was my first published poem. The poem reflected the newfound optimism and hope in the country after the unbanning of the ANC and the release of Mandela. The poem urged South Africans to rise above its differences and to be an example of reconciliation to the world. The same newspaper carried a story of students being arrested for a political protest and an article about the awarding of an honorary doctorate in law for Mandela.

A landmark event in my development as a poet was my encounter with the South African poet Lionel Abrahams during a reading at Wits. Abrahams made an indelible impression on me. He was in a wheelchair and could barely hold the book from which he read owing to cerebral palsy. He read from his book *The Writer in Sand* and shared thoughts on being true to oneself and that we need to find our own voice. These sentiments resonated powerfully with the 20-year-old rebel that was me. I had never been to a poetry reading before, so this was a profound experience. Hearing him speak watered the seeds of poetry that would seek to challenge conventional societal thinking and my role in modern society. It would be many years before I would call myself a poet – but poetry came to be a significant part of my life from then on.

Second year proved to be a year of extremes academically. I earned a distinction and the highest mark in the class for Materials Engineering and the lowest mark of my academic career for Fluid Mechanics.

The words 'Fluid Mechanics' still make my skin crawl. The course was presented by a professor who seemed to loathe students. The fact that 'Fluids', as we called it, was complete gibberish to me, didn't help. The course combined advanced mathematics with the behaviour of non-solids (gases and liquids) under varying conditions. I was lost from the first lecture. And though I read the textbook and notes repeatedly I just could not understand the subject. I even mustered the courage one day to enter the professor's cigar-smoke-filled office to ask him a question. The blank look on my face in response to his explanation must have scared the poor man leading him to ask me to leave his office while mumbling something in irritation.

My end of year result for Fluids was 16%. *16%!* It was the first course that I had ever failed, and boy did I do a proper job of it.

How could I get a distinction for one course and fail another so dismally? I remember writing the exam and going from question to question without a clue of how I would answer them but hoping that each subsequent question would be easier, until I got to the end of the question paper. There were none that I could answer beyond writing down some basic formula. I looked up at the other students and they all were writing away feverishly. It was the longest three hours of my life! I tried to squeeze every iota of understanding of this incomprehensible subject out of my head. And all I managed was 16%.

Again it felt like the boulder that I had been pushing up the steep hill had now come crashing down. Like mythological Sisyphus I would have to go back down the hill to start pushing the boulder back up.

I hit a low point. For the first time thoughts of quitting entered my mind. I felt overwhelmed and worried that I would continue to struggle. Perhaps I would never get the boulder of engineering over the hill. Perhaps it was time to switch to a less demanding degree. But I couldn't quit. The financial consequences for my family would be devastating. This fact kept me going.

Fortunately for me, because I had passed all of my other courses, the university gave me a chance to rewrite the failed exam ... as if I really wanted anything more to do with this subject. After a December vacation ruined by having to study Fluids and the horrific thought of having to write a Fluids exam, I rewrote the exam in January and finally passed. It was a grinding experience, but it gave me a massive lift. Second year was the low point for me, but I got through it.

With renewed vigour I entered third year. Like one of those movies where the bad guys keep attacking the hero and as he defeats the first group more appear, more nightmarish courses kept coming at me – Thermodynamics, Instrumentation and Control, Mathematical Topics, Mechanics of Solids, Properties of Materials, Mechanical Engineering Design, Mechanical Engineering Laboratory and ... *Fluid Mechanics II*. The Fluid Mechanics curse would never end. The engineering curriculum was pre-set so I had no course choices. I braced myself for another tough year.

To reduce costs Gillian and I relocated to apartment 86 in Da Gama Court at 16 Catherine Street, still in Hillbrow. It was one of the few well-maintained buildings that rented apartments to non-whites. It was a studio apartment. She lived in the main room while I squeezed into a small enclave into which I managed to fit a single bed and desk.

The wall above my desk was covered with A4 sheets carrying

motivational slogans that I had written. One dated 2 February 1991 read, 'Everybody has got to be somebody, someday!' and another dated 21 February read, 'Every professional was once an amateur.' It was a time where I began to refocus my energies. Gone were the days of drunken parties with the boys; I had come to Wits with a mission and I was going to fulfil it.

To earn some extra cash I took on a few mundane part-time jobs like doing stock-taking at a supermarket and a bookstore, as well as tutoring Mathematics to a lazy teenager. I had a soul-destroying job as a proverbial vacuum-cleaner salesman. Thankfully I did not have to go door-to-door, I was based at a Game store at Bruma Lake, east of Johannesburg. I would spend all day Saturday in the store, hoping that someone would stop long enough at my display for me to demonstrate the magical sucking powers of the machine I was selling ... or *trying* to sell.

I had a dramatic sales pitch where I threw sand and stones onto a piece of carpet and then showed how the vacuum cleaner sucked it all up. I would then pour ketchup onto the carpet and show how the machine washed the carpet perfectly clean. I would dazzle the audience (usually consisting of a lost child or a bored husband waiting for his wife) with the different attachments that enabled cleaning of every household surface whether tile floors or upholstered furniture. I demonstrated how indestructible the machine was because the shell was made of the same materials used to manufacture motorcycle helmets. On and on I would go in the hope that someone would say those magic words, 'I'll take one.' Few did. The job sucked more than the vacuum cleaner did.

I once had a fun job as an usher for the legendary Hugh Masekela's homecoming concert in 1991 after his many years of exile. My most interesting (and frightening) job, however, was working as a personal bodyguard. A Wits researcher was conducting research among victims of gang violence and needed someone to join her for visits to their homes. I seemed destined to encounter gangs. I entered some horrific homes and saw some frightening people who seemed to live in a parallel universe of crime and violence.

Most of the victims of gang violence were gangsters themselves. At one home, two men stood with assault rifles in the room where we conducted the interview and another armed man stood at the door. *What the hell was I doing in this place?* What the researcher didn't know was that if ever we got into any trouble I would be the first to run.

After much begging I managed to convince my father to help me buy a car to get to campus. He matched what I had saved. By 'car' I meant something that could barely drive. All I could afford was a severely dilapidated two-door 1972 Ford Escort. The car looked like it had been used as a prop in multiple crash scenes in movies. The body was a patchwork of different colours, and had dents, scratches and rust on every surface. The driver's seat rested on two bricks to hold it upright and the gear lever got dislodged from the gearbox regularly while driving. The entire electrical system was blown so the car had no lights, indicators, windscreen wipers or hooter.

Needless to say, the car was not roadworthy. The greatest defect of the car was that the radiator was cracked causing water to pour from it freely. I drove with five two-litre Coke bottles of water in the boot so that I could top up the radiator when needed. As the car's temperature gauge moved into the red, I would jump out of the car, get a bottle from the boot, run to the front of the car, lift the bonnet and fill the radiator. Not cool at all!

Surprisingly I didn't battle too much with Fluid Mechanics II. I had a new nemesis – Properties of Materials. I had scored poorly on the first test and was sitting right in front of the lecture room when our test papers were returned at the end of a lecture. As other students filed out I remained behind, sitting with my elbows on the desk and my head in my hands staring down at the paper. Just as I was about to get up, I felt a tap on my shoulder.

'How did you do?' the friendly voice asked.

'Ag, terribly,' I replied, 'and you?'

'The same,' he replied, 'I am really struggling with the subject.'

'So am I,' I replied, comforted to know that I was not alone. This is how I met Tudor Maxwell, who would become a close friend. Tudor was a soft-spoken, thoughtful and sincere person. He was unlike anyone I had met before. He was my first experience of someone living consciously. He came from a wealthy family, yet he rejected the comforts of his family's wealth choosing instead to live a frugal lifestyle. He was a devout Christian and took a year off from his studies to join a missionary organisation. He was also a conscientious objector who, like a growing number of white young men, was refusing to serve in the South African army in protest against apartheid.

We decided to study together. I was slightly sceptical at first – how could we possibly help each other if we were both struggling, but just having someone with whom to discuss the work was a massive help. In addition to studying together, we also prayed together on campus. We found a disused entrance to a building which offered us a little nook in which we both could fit. There we would pray at least one a week, and earn the squints and frowns of students who saw us sitting there. I wonder what they thought as they walked past two young men sitting huddled in the dark doorway at the back of a building ...

One Friday afternoon Tudor suggested that I join his family for dinner. The Maxwells lived in upmarket Sandton, and since I hadn't been there before I needed extensive directions.

I loaded up my Escort with water bottles, never mind petrol. The car sputtered noisily along tree-lined streets with majestic homes, and made it to the Maxwell home before it choked on its own fumes. Tudor greeted me at the door. We walked into the dining room at which point everyone in the room stopped the words in their throats and spun their heads to look at me. Firstly, I was late and secondly, little did I know, it was a formal dinner. Ladies were in gowns, with their hair done to perfection and the men were in suits.

I was wearing a pair of worn sandals, a pair of old shorts and a bright orange paisley T-shirt that barely made it past my belly-button. I was grossly underdressed for a casual dinner let alone a formal event. I looked like I was there to collect the garbage. After everyone managed to catch their breath, Tudor's mother, Wendi, welcomed me warmly. I leaned over to her and whispered, 'I might be just a tad underdressed,' to which she let out a hearty laugh. This endeared me to her and this encounter is retold whenever we're in the same company.

I would spend many hours studying at Tudor's family's home, during the day, evenings and over weekends. I enjoyed the warmth that his mother showed me and enjoyed the conversations with his father immensely. Ken Maxwell had also studied Mechanical Engineering at Wits. He was the CEO and later chairman of the leading mining corporation JCI and Chairman of the South African Chamber of Mines – which made him an extremely influential person in South African business and politics. I was amazed by the statistic that he had flown to Japan 25 times on business. I enjoyed our conversations which opened a window to business and engineering that I hadn't seen before. Ken Maxwell would surface again later in my life, at my time of great need.

Finally the last stretch of my studies arrived; the fourth year of my degree. I was so close now and I was buzzing with excitement. The first half of my final year consisted of coursework while the second half was dedicated to two projects, a research project and a design project. I had become interested in biomechanical and biomedical engineering, areas of engineering which were applied directly to developing solutions to support people with disabilities, injuries or other medical conditions. For my research project I decided to study the forces exerted on the human leg joints during a vertical jump. This insight would contribute to the design of prostheses. For my design project, I settled on modifying a public transport bus to allow wheelchair access. But before I could get there, I needed to get through my coursework.

I had worked relentlessly since the beginning of the year but I always seemed to be on the back foot. When I look back at my education journey, my cumulative disadvantage in Mathematics becomes obvious which impacted not only my performance in Mathematics courses but also courses that depended on Mathematics like Fluid Mechanics and Properties of Materials. I just could not manage to regain the performance I had in Mathematics before the crisis of Grade 10. Whereas I consistently earned As then, I was now battling with Cs and Ds.

Advantage is also cumulative, something which seems to escape particularly those who would deny the advantage gained from privilege under apartheid. We do not start each year with a clean slate and on a level playing field. In education, as in life, we carry every advantage and disadvantage with us every step of the way.

The country's political transition had begun with the first plenary session of the Convention for a Democratic South Africa (CODESA) in Johannesburg. The government's lead negotiator was Roelf Meyer and the ANC's was Cyril Ramaphosa, both of whom I would have direct dealings with later. CODESA began the negotiations for the transition from white minority rule to democracy. The talks continued into 1992 with everyone watching and hoping for a peaceful transition. In February President F.W. de Klerk announced that a whites-only referendum would be held in March, to determine levels of support for the continuation of the reform process.

I didn't trust De Klerk. It was during his tenure as Minister of Education that the government clamped down on universities such as Wits during student protests. Furthermore, I didn't like the idea of a whites-only referendum – it would be yet another example of whites determining the fate of all South Africans – in fact I found it offensive.

I worried that whites would vote against continuing reforms and thus stall progress towards democracy. In the end close to 70% of voters voted 'Yes' and so the wheels of change began moving apace. I was elated.

Even as the ruling National Party saw the writing on the wall for its tenure in power, De Klerk used the opportunity of the opening of parliament in January to assure his supporters that they were still firmly in control. Many of his supporters took comfort from his speech, and one of these supporters wrote the President a letter of support. The supporter was my father.

It is bizarre to think back on this time, for while I was protesting against the government in Johannesburg, in Cape Town my father was writing a letter of support to the leader of the apartheid government, the very government that had been oppressing him all of his life. It seemed completely insane to me, yet my father insisted that life would be worse under ANC rule and seemed to adopt a 'better the devil you know' approach to politics. My father received a reply on the letterhead of the State President's Office on 6 March 1992:

Dear Mr Williams

Thank you for your letter dated 28 February 1992 addressed to the State President.

The President appreciates your words of support. He wishes to assure you that this task would be much more difficult without the backing and friendship he experiences in such a generous measure.

My father was offering De Klerk 'words of support' and showing 'backing and friendship'. My father did not tell me about the letter at the time. I have not seen what he wrote but I am sure I would have expressed disgust. My father was not alone in the coloured community in supporting the National Party; in fact, coloureds have shown overwhelming support for white parties since democracy rather than support black parties – a sure indicator of apartheid's success in creating distrust between the non-white race groups.

Negotiations started in earnest to craft the new constitution but by May it had stalled. With talks deadlocked, the ANC withdrew from CODESA and all seemed lost. Political violence escalated sharply across the country as parties began blaming each other and as people began losing hope. Rolling mass action spread countrywide as ordinary citizens took to the streets to vent their anger while our leaders were deadlocked. Then tragedy struck. In Boipatong, a township in Gauteng, 49 people were killed when groups opposing the ANC attacked ANC supporters. Eye witnesses reported that members of the security forces were part of the attack. The ANC accused the government of 'a cold-blooded strategy of state terrorism'.[*]

While the stand-off between the government and the ANC continued with cutting public statements, I wrapped up my coursework and exams, and started my two projects in earnest. I spent hours in the library doing theoretical research and in the computer lab doing modelling for my research project. I found myself driving around to engineering firms getting technical specifications for components for my bus modification project.

Engineering finally came alive for me and I was in my element. I had two supportive supervisors in Dr Mel Siff for my research and Dr Danny Cipolat for my design project. Cipolat was a tall, gruff Italian who taught me during my third and fourth year. We had a few run-ins mostly relating to me arriving late for class. On one occasion I arrived late because my car had broken down ... yet again. My hands were covered in grease from my attempts to patch it together, but he was hearing none of it, refusing me entry to the lecture.

As a supervisor however, he was a different person. He was patient and seemed to genuinely care about my progress. My discussions with Cipolat were the first where I felt that I belonged at Wits. He is the only one of my engineering professors who I visit whenever I am at the university.

---

[*]   Lauren Segal & Sharon Coot, *One Law, One Nation: The Making of the South African Constitution*, Jacana Media, 2011, p.98

I ended the year and my engineering degree on a high. My final year mark was the best I had received throughout the degree, placing me somewhere in the top quarter of the class and earned me an offer to continue to do postgraduate research at Wits. A professor in the Civil Engineering faculty saw applications of my research in the design of floors for multi-storey buildings. Unfortunately, I could not accept the offer to continue full-time studies because I had a work obligation with Boart. I did, however, register for a two-year part-time Graduate Diploma in Engineering (GDE) which was a stepping stone to a Master's degree.

And then the day arrived, 8 December 1992. As much as I believed in myself and believed in miracles, the arrival of my graduation day seemed unreal to me. There had been so much running around in the days leading up to the day that it caught me off-guard. I was in tears as I got dressed that morning. It had been such a long and bumpy road that required me giving everything that I had. And now there I was graduating as a mechanical engineer from Wits University, one of the first coloureds ever to do so. Of the 110 graduates in my class only five were black and only two of us had completed the degree without repeating a year.

I had made it. As deep as the valley was I was now at the mountaintop. As large and as numerous as the boulders were I had pushed them over the top of the hill. While the groans and cries of my slave ancestors echoed in my blood, and the agonies of my parents pulsated in my chest, I would walk tall in the knowledge that we had overcome. It was the absolute pinnacle of my life. Dreams could come true. And while South Africa was still in the throes of apartheid, for the first time in my life I felt free.

Gillian threw a small party in our flat. It was wonderful sharing the celebration with her since we had been flat-mates for most of my time at Wits. She also joined me at the graduation ceremony. My parents came up from Cape Town for the ceremony. They rightly beamed with pride. We had a celebratory dinner with Tudor's family on the night of the graduation and a party at Bert's parents' home the next day. It was fantastic to share the celebrations with the two families in Johannesburg that had 'adopted' me, and with my closest friends including Cate Arenstein who had become a close friend.

It had been a long, tough road for me to get to the point where I would graduate with a Mechanical Engineering degree. The odds were stacked heavily against me. I had to rise above the apartheid education system that sought to hold me back. I had to overcome racism in all its physical and psychological forms. I had to live through the most tumultuous and violent time in our country's history as we battled to overthrow apartheid. And I had to overcome my personal demons and doubts. But I had made it. As large and as varied as the boulders were that blocked my path to fulfilling my dream, I had pushed them all over the hill.

As I held my degree certificate in my hand that warm December evening, I felt ten feet tall. I had made it!

Old South Africa
firmly rooted ◉

I owed Boart two years of service for having funded my studies. This was not a bad deal at all. They had funded five years of my studies and required that I only commit to two years of service. I was excited about this new chapter, to begin to put into practice what I had been studying for five years and to earn an income.

I reported for work at Boart's head office in Sandton in January 1993. I was informed that I had been seconded to a subsidiary, Strata Control Systems (SCS), which was located in the homeland of KwaNdebele, located 125km outside Johannesburg.

KwaNdebele was created in 1979 under apartheid as a homeland for the Ndebele people. The government had established a number of these homelands for blacks as part of its plan to deny blacks citizenship of South Africa, leaving South Africa with majority white citizenship. The homelands were located close enough to urban centres, industrial areas or mining towns so that they could provide a source of cheap black labour. This made KwaNdebele's buses the only real growth industry, with 300 leaving in the morning to take the homeland's only export, black labour, to Pretoria and Johannesburg and return with them at night, usually well after dark. In its attempts to create local employment in the homeland, the apartheid government created Ekandustria, a patch of shiny shells of factories where labour-intensive, low-technology manufacturing took place. The government lured South African businesses to the homeland with grants and tax breaks. All the businesses were run by white South Africans, who drove in each day from surrounding whites-only areas like Bronkhorstspruit, while all the manual labour was performed by blacks.

It was into this cynical and oppressive environment that I arrived as a young enthusiastic black graduate engineer. It was not what I had in mind as my first engineering job but I was excited nonetheless. I contacted a few local property rental agents to find an apartment near the SCS facility. KwaNdebele didn't have suitable accommodation. Where there was suitable accommodation, like in Bronkhorstspruit, I was told I could not live in the area because of my race. *This same old shit*. That familiar feeling of rejection, of being treated as something less than human, returned. It always brought a sense of sadness.

My options were to relocate to Pretoria, or to stay where I was in Johannesburg. When I communicated my dilemma to head office they arranged that SCS make a car available to me at no cost if I stayed in Johannesburg. So each day I drove for about two hours to work and two hours back, covering 250km. I did this every day for a year. The drive alone would wear me out – driving in peak-hour traffic for two hours every day took its toll.

The commute wouldn't have been as awful if I was driving to a job with meaningful work. At SCS I reported to the production manager, whose main credentials seemed to be that he had served in the South African army. He enjoyed lecturing me on how he had served our country. Mistakenly he thought I'd be impressed by his acts to uphold apartheid.

It soon became apparent that SCS didn't know what to do with me. Being a black engineer upset their simple world where jobs were decided by race. In their world, as in the South African economy, regardless of skill or application, white people were professionals and managers who worked in offices, while blacks were labourers who worked on the factory floor. What were they to do with a black engineer? I couldn't sit in their offices. But what would an engineer do on the factory floor? Their solution: they offered me a desk in a portable hut placed opposite the factory entrance.

I was given menial tasks, none of which required any engineering knowledge or education at all, and basically told to stay out of the way. This was South Africa at the cutting edge of its transition to non-racialism and I was one of the experimental guinea pigs. These were the days before affirmative action policies and before diversity programmes were in vogue. Black professionals were simply not welcome into the cosy world of white privilege. Corporations like Anglo American and Boart may have had the foresight to begin educating black engineers, but they certainly did not have the foresight to design programmes to ensure the smooth transition of black professionals into their businesses.

Each day I would leave my apartment at 6am, drive for two hours to work, sit in the hut pretending to be busy and then drive for two hours again back home in the evening. It was soul-destroying. I was so frustrated, and angry. Eventually this frustration led to depression and even suicidal thoughts. I would drive along the busy highway to work with my foot flat down on the accelerator, almost hoping that I would crash into a truck or a wall. I was miserable beyond comprehension. While I was meant to be celebrating the great breakthrough into the world of a degreed professional, I felt stupid and small. I was embarrassed to tell my friends and family what I actually did at work. I picked up speeding fines so regularly that I began budgeting for them. My health began to suffer. I began getting acute heartburn and acid reflux. After a few visits to a specialist, which included a colonoscopy, I was diagnosed with early stages of an ulcer. At the age of 23 I was on my way to getting a stress-induced ulcer and had to take medication for it.

My poetry had always been about love and hope but now, for the first time in 1993, anger started to appear in my poems. My anger had overflowed into that special space that I had created in my poetry, where I could dream and fantasise, where the world was still idyllic.

I am often asked derisively why I am so angry. I suggest to my challengers that perhaps if they have suffered what I have perhaps they too would be this angry. I encourage enquirers to rather ask themselves, with all the injustices around us, why *they* aren't angry.

'What does it say about you that *you* are not angry?' When you are born into oppression your life becomes one of resistance, you are born into a fight whether you like it or not. We all choose to fight in different ways but you come to know that nothing you dream of is going to be handed to you, you come to know that everything you want to achieve will face opposition forces and thus require a fight. Ultimately my anger sits alongside compassion. I must be angry at injustices. But I also have great compassion and love for others. I believe that it is through love that we all heal and have hope of a harmonious future.

Despite all the progress that I had made, it began to dawn on me that my ambitions would not be fulfilled in South Africa and that I needed to go elsewhere if I wanted a meaningful career. It was a familiar feeling. I thought back to my time at nursery school, how desperately I wanted to get away from that school because of the mindless tasks we were asked to do. This felt a thousand times worse. I had educated myself as a way to break free from the chains that dictated that I be a manual labourer, a cheap factor of production in someone else's profit-making machine. But still I felt stuck and trapped.

Just as I had known at the age of five, I knew I had to get away.

It was then that I began planning to go study in the US. If digging under the school gate was my solution at the age of five, studying in another country would be my way out now, and would offer me another chance of a meaningful career. I had started the GDE at Wits, which focused on Industrial Management and had also enrolled in Economics and Accounting courses at UNISA, the distance-learning university.

I needed to escape the mining-related racist environment which, in South Africa, meant leaving engineering. My path to a meaningful engineering career in South Africa was blocked by what turned out to be an immovable boulder. It was a tough lesson – sometimes certain paths need to be abandoned, sometimes certain boulders cannot be pushed and instead we should create a new path around them. This is exactly what I did. I turned my interest to business.

Once I had made this decision, I chose to use my time at work more productively. If my employers did not want me to work, then I would use the time at work to study. I brought all my course books to work and spent the time studying. I subscribed to the *Financial Mail*, South Africa's business magazine and bought myself a copy of the *Oxford Business Dictionary*. There I would sit, working my way, line by line, through the *Financial Mail*, checking the definition of every word that I did not understand and making copious notes.

This was my introduction to business. I taught myself how to read the financial pages and began analysing companies' performance. I started taking more management-orientated courses as part of my GDE. Back home, I cut out an advertisement for a Master's in Business Administration (MBA) degree and stuck it on the wall above my desk.

My plan: to go to America to do an MBA!

Using my newfound knowledge of quality management, which I had been studying at Wits, I designed a simple quality control methodology that would not only improve product quality but also improve productivity in the factory at work. I presented my design to the quality assurance manager, Don Dunkley, who liked it. I started working more closely with Don who took me under his wing. Don was a tall, friendly Englishman, with bushy hair who wore large 80s-style tinted spectacles. He loved chatting and was the most passionate person about quality management that I had met. A light in the darkness that surrounded me.

Work began to have some meaning. We implemented different programmes and saw great results. Don showed me a machine that could not be repaired because we could not obtain spare parts so I designed a completely new machine from scratch. I was creating things. The human spirit thrives when we are creative.

I learnt about the Education Opportunities Council (EOC) which offered scholarships for South Africans to study in the US. I submitted an application as soon as I could. Don wrote a letter in support of my application:

Although I have known Athol for less than six months, it is clear that he is a mature individual well beyond his years. He displays first class situation assessment skills which indicate management material, coupled with an affable nature. It is clear that he is quick thinking and responsive to anything he is challenged with, and is very eager to extend his knowledge.

Don's comments were a huge boost for me. Finally someone at work recognised some value in me. It would be many months before I would hear from the EOC so in the meantime I put my head down and got on with my part-time studies and my self-driven projects at work.

Political negotiations resumed after a hiatus, even as the country suffered under waves of violence. On 1 April, 26 political parties gathered in the World Trade Centre in Johannesburg to start what was called the Multi-Party Negotiating Process (MPNP). Again negotiations were halted by violence, this time it was the assassination of Chris Hani, the leader of the South African Communist Party and former commander of uMkhonto we Sizwe, the ANC's military wing.

The assassination plunged the country into more violence. I remember seeing Tokyo Sexwale on TV crying outside Hani's house, the cry of someone who had lost a loved one. I was shocked. People began talking about civil war. At a dinner where I got to meet prominent anti-apartheid politician, Frederick van Zyl Slabbert, he talked about how the head of the South African Defence Force had recruited 3,000 soldiers who were committed to taking the country by force, giving a real sense of just how close we had come to civil war.

What the violence showed was that negotiations were our only hope of a peaceful future. Still white racists resisted change. The very people who I was reporting to at work and who had control over my career were the ones putting up fierce and violent resistance to democracy.

In June, several hundred armed AWB supporters, dressed in military uniform, invaded the negotiating venue demanding an end to negotiations. A month later, five members of the Azanian Peoples Liberation Army (APLA) kicked their way into a church in Cape Town, and opened fire and tossed hand grenades into the congregation of 1,400 people. Twelve people were killed and 56 were injured. This attack struck close to home as this was a sister church to Christ Church Hillbrow, where I was a member and served on the council.*

Despite all the opposition and violence, Mandela, Ramaphosa, De Klerk and the other negotiators persevered. On 18 November 1993, the headline on the front page of Johannesburg's newspaper, *The Star* read, 'Birth of the new SA', as word got out that agreement had been reached on a new constitution that was passed four days later. *The Star* continued, 'The new South Africa was ushered into being in the early hours of this morning signalling an irrevocable loosening of the centuries-long white grip on power.'

Nelson Mandela described the day as the 'beginning of a new era', and F.W. de Klerk was quoted as saying: 'It was on this day that we created a basis for good hope for this and for future generations of our people.'

I was living through some of the most significant days in South Africa's history.

On 22 November *The Star* reported that the 'last white parliament has finally arrived'. This would be the last sitting of a government that effectively retained all significant power exclusively for whites. Indeed, it was a day to sit back and reflect on the dramatic changes that had occurred in recent weeks, months and years. It was the end of white rule and the end of Apartheid. How many of us thought

---

*   I joined the Church of England in South Africa (CESA) a few years earlier, serving
      on the Council and leading a bible study group. It was a profound experience for me
      at 23 years old to play such an important role in the leadership of the church and
      leading bible studies with people who were much older than I was.

we would ever see this day? In December, Mandela and De Klerk were jointly awarded the Nobel Peace Prize – a fitting award for a remarkable accomplishment with the promise of peace. I say the 'promise of peace' because it was clear to us at home that peace and freedom had not yet arrived, but we had high hopes of their imminent arrival – definitely much higher hope than we had ever held. I was still not convinced that De Klerk was the great reformer that he was claiming to be, but that didn't matter: he was part of the journey to rid South Africa of apartheid.

I had not heard from the EOC, but continued to hope that I would be awarded a scholarship. In October I wrote to the HR director at Boart's head office, Paul Falla, to enquire about the possibility of the company deferring my work obligation so that I could pursue full-time studies overseas. I got no reply. Again in November, I enquired about 'the possibility of allowing me to study full-time in the USA'. Again I was ignored. My frustration was growing. As 1993 drew to a close I knew that things would come to a head soon. Just as 1994 would be a landmark year for South Africa's freedom from apartheid, I sensed that 1994 would be a watershed year for me as well.

Larger boulders to push ⊚

The prospect of our first democratic election had the country delirious with optimism. My one year secondment to SCS was over and I was now posted to Boart's head office in Sandton so the long daily suicidal drives to work and mindless days in a hut were over.

Rather unexpectedly, I had fallen in love. I met Michele Carroll while she was visiting Johannesburg from Cape Town. She was breathtaking and a gentle soul. We spent long hours hanging out at my apartment, chatting and laughing. I had moved again and was now living in Bellevue, a small suburb sandwiched between the horrible Hillbrow and the high society Houghton. Over the Christmas holidays I went to Cape Town and met up with Michele again. We had a wonderful time strolling through the paradise of Kirstenbosch Gardens, walking along the beaches of Noordhoek and climbing Table Mountain. We sat with our feet dangling over the edge of the majestic mountain as the hot summer sun began to set. It was the stuff of movies and there we shared our first kiss.

At first I was excited to be working at head office. I was hoping that I could get involved in some of the project evaluations or new product designs. Instead, my first task was to sort the Christmas cards that the HR director* had received the year before and to compile a list of the senders. Yes, this is what they would have a graduate engineer doing. *I was not a high school intern or someone who walked off the streets looking for an odd job, I was a bluddy engineer!* I sucked up my pride and completed the Christmas card list. The following days

---

* Paul Falla was the same man who had ignored my faxes the year before.

were filled with punching holes in documents, filing the documents and arranging the files in cabinets. This carried on for a few weeks. I was basically doing the tasks that his secretary didn't feel like doing.

My resolve to leave South Africa grew stronger. I researched business schools in the US and looked closely at the top-ranked universities including Harvard, Stanford and Chicago, but I was most drawn to the business school at the Massachusetts Institute of Technology (MIT) located in Boston. The MIT Sloan School of Management was among the top five business schools in the US and ranked similarly worldwide. MIT boasted 81 Nobel laureates and was ranked top globally in the overall university rankings by most ranking agencies.

An MIT education would all but guarantee a successful career. The university emphasised an analytical approach to business which appealed to me and had a particular strength in finance and strategy that was of interest to me. 'MIT Sloan' I said out loud, the words echoed beautifully, as though spoken by angels. For a long time I had a vague notion that I wanted to study at Oxford but for now MIT made more sense. From then on all I could think about was MIT.

At church I met a wonderful older couple, Neil and Hazel Fraser, who showed me incredible friendship and warmth. There was always delicious food to eat in their home, a major selling point for me, and they had the most comfortable sofas to lounge on. Hazel had a marvellous way of making me feel welcome. Her infectious smile lit up her face and filled the entire room with colour. 'Come here you rubbish,' she would say while giving me the warmest hug.

As I was going through my roughest patch at work, Hazel managed to lift me out of my darkest gloom because she believed in me. She really thought I was amazing and I could feel her sincerity. She thought it was absolutely ridiculous that I was being made to work on Christmas card lists. 'You are the most brilliant person I know, after Neil of course, how can they make you do this?' she shrieked in disgust, throwing her hands in the air. I needed to hear this because just as I was beginning to doubt my own abilities, she fanned the flame of self-belief. What a blessing to have a person like Hazel in my life.

Neil had been a senior executive in the construction industry. He now played a pivotal role in the regeneration of downtown Johannesburg through his role as Director of the Central Johannesburg Partnership. Neil too thought my treatment at work was unfair and offered me valuable advice in dealing with the challenges including the letter that I would write to the Boart CEO a few months later. When I learned that Neil had studied at MIT on a senior executive programme, I peppered him with questions about the university. He spoke with great admiration of the university and described the value that his experience there offered him, which further confirmed to me that it would be the target for my next degree.

One day towards the end of 1993, in casual conversation, Neil asked me if I wanted to apply to MIT. I almost choked. The words hung in the air for a few moments without me saying anything. He said he may be able to help. Was this some sort of practical joke? I may have mentioned to him that I had applied for a scholarship to study in the US and I guess he figured from my questions that I was keen on MIT but we never discussed it directly.

'Of course I want to apply to MIT,' I replied, 'Going to MIT has become a dream, it would be a dream come true!' And so began an unbelievable journey of submitting an application and seeking funding, a journey filled with belief and possibility, plus many enormous boulders and the odd miracle. If I didn't experience the events of the following months first hand, I would not believe that they actually happened.

Neil had received a letter from Professor Willard Johnson at MIT asking him to encourage high-potential students to apply. When I started questioning Neil about his experience at MIT, he remembered the letter. What miraculous timing. On 5 January 1994, Neil replied to Johnson indicating that 'there is a potential candidate for postgraduate study, whom I can highly recommend'. Johnson replied enthusiastically a few weeks later. Johnson replied that the deadline for applications to the business school had already passed, but they were willing to consider a late application. There was no guarantee of funding should I be offered a place but Johnson did ask for my CV which he would use to 'start to identify possible financial support sources'.

While lofty dreams of MIT filled my head, I had to deal with the mundane and frustration of life at Boart. A manager in HR told me that I was being characterised at the firm as 'not a mixer', in other words, I complained too much and was not fitting in. I didn't care what they called me. If they were going to insult me with the work that I was being asked to do, I would continue to complain.

Those who resist oppression are always seen as troublemakers to the oppressor.

From this point on there really would be no progress at work. The worse they treated me the more I complained and the more I complained the worse they treated me. The tragedy for me was that I couldn't quit because I was still under the bursary contract. I was trapped there and they knew it. Rather than earn my freedom, my education had trapped me. They used my huge debt as a threat – if I resigned I would have to repay it. This was slavery of a different kind.

Soon I was shipped off to another Boart subsidiary Osborn MMD, located in Boksburg, east of Johannesburg, another Afrikaner stronghold that resented the very idea of a black engineer. It was a miserable place. This time there were no illusions – I was issued with overalls and safety boots and directed to work on the factory floor. I had dreamed of designing solutions to improve people's lives yet there I was working with a blow torch, metal saw and hammer.

On a few occasions I got to accompany colleagues on visits to mines to observe our machines in action to determine causes of failure. Gold mines are extremely deep, often exceeding depths of a kilometre below the earth's surface. The deepest that I descended was 2km underground, that's equivalent to *five* Empire State Buildings stacked on top of each other. It was not a pleasant experience. It was hot and humid underground which made breathing very difficult for me, especially being asthmatic. It was also incredibly noisy with the constant rattling of machines and drilling into rock. It was as though another human species lived down there, they even had their own language, *Fanagalo* which was a mixture of isiZulu, English and Afrikaans.

It was unnatural being that deep underground. It felt wrong being there. But there was a familiarity – just like the human species that lived on the earth's surface, down there whites ruled and blacks laboured.

If work was dismal at least there was good news on the romantic front. Michele had decided to transfer to the Johannesburg office of her employer. I was overjoyed – no more phone calls and letters, now we would be able to spend time together. I needed this good news to get through the difficult patch.

By March of 1994 I could not remain silent about my work situation anymore. I might have been born in a cage but I knew I didn't belong in one and I certainly was not afraid to rattle it. I decided to write to the CEO of Boart, Colin Wood. As many South Africans have discovered during the years of freedom struggle, getting heard required bold action. I laid it all out in my letter. I described my situation from the experiences in KwaNdebele to the Christmas card list at head office to the issues at Osborn and how the futility of my work was causing me stress-induced stomach problems. I ended the letter saying, 'I am just starting my career and all I want to do is get involved in constructive, challenging work where I can make meaningful contributions to an organisation and to South African industry.'

Three weeks later, I received a reply in which the CEO said that my experience reminded him of his son's experience. It was extremely unlikely that his white son experienced anything remotely close to what I had endured. This comparison belittled my grievance. He offered no response to any of the points in my letter. 'Inevitably,' he wrote, 'there are irritations on both sides, as in all these cases.' In all which *cases*? Trapped employees asking for meaningful work? He dismissively concluded his letter writing that 'we put the past behind us and look to the future'. I was seething after reading his letter.

Management at Osborn were furious that I had 'gone over their heads' by communicating with head office. I was called in by the managing director who gave me a tongue-lashing. The abuse was now starting to affect me. I would drive in my car screaming and banging on the steering wheel in anger and frustration. I came to realise that no matter what I did or said they would not relieve me of my work obligation. I would have to endure this demeaning work environment just like my father did and just like millions of my black brothers and sisters did around the country. It felt as though I had failed in my lifelong efforts to achieve my freedom through education. There were just so many more barriers, so many more boulders than I could have imagined.

My health started deteriorating again. My stomach ulcer problem resurfaced and I was back to consulting a gastro specialist who prescribed Zantac. Too many balls of stress swirled around me – work stress and the future of my career, evening engineering studies, part-time economics and accounting studies, decisions about studying in America, violence and political uncertainties in the country. Added to this whirlpool was uncertainty about my relationship with Michele. What would happen to our relationship if I went to America? Perhaps I should wait out my time at Osborn and then find better employment in South Africa rather than go overseas. I wondered if better employment existed for me.

One morning I was called to a meeting at Boart's head office to meet with the CEO, the HR director Paul Falla and Osborn's HR manager. I went with the expectation of good news – perhaps a transfer to a better job? Or news that they would allow me to go to the US to study and postpone my work obligation until my return? Or even better, forgive my work obligation. Why else would three senior executives make the time to meet with me?

How naïve I was.

They dismissed my claims, implying that I was lying about the tasks that I was given. They painted a picture of me as a trouble-maker and spoke to me in the tones that I had come to recognise when whites spoke dismissively to blacks, as the Roodepoort bus driver had spoken to me, and the guy in the SECO toilets and the state security policemen who invaded my apartment at Wits. I stopped trying to explain myself because they were not listening. They were subtly reminding me that as a coloured man I was 'entrusted to their care' as the architect of apartheid, Hendrik Verwoerd had pointed out all those years ago, and that I ought to show gratitude for their generosity and benevolence in offering me study and work opportunities.

I remembered my father telling me many times how he had to grovel before his white bosses even when they belittled him or swore at him. I never understood why he accepted this abuse. He explained in a resigned voice, 'It is just the way things are.' I refused to accept that such situations of abuse were 'just the way things are' and confidently vowed that I would never find myself in a situation like that. Yet, here I was, suffering the same humiliation as my father.

Michele made my life a little easier to bear. One of the most adorable things that she did was to insert little handwritten messages with my lunch, which she lovingly prepared. She was gentle and caring while I was falling apart.

On 27 April 1994, the front page of *The Star* read 'Vote, the beloved country'.* It was the first time in South Africa's history that each person had equal status as a citizen. It was the first time in South Africa's history that non-whites could vote.** I was among the millions that voted for the first time. I joined friends standing in queues for hours along the streets of Houghton, my closest voting station.

It was an incredible experience, there was such euphoria and belief

---

* A reference to Alan Paton's famous book *Cry, the Beloved Country*.

** Under British colonial rule in the Cape, suffrage was determined by property ownership, which effectively excluded most non-whites.

amongst those heading for the polls. For the past few years I had been experiencing an immensely strong feeling of not just observing, but being an active part of great events in South Africa's history, and this day was a highlight. I will never take for granted the right of being able to have my say about who governs our society.

In my diary I wrote: 'I am immeasurably grateful for what the ANC has done in South Africa. I admire their commitment to the country and its people and their lifelong dedication to fighting for freedom from apartheid. Today I salute the ANC and those who sacrificed their lives to bring us here.'

The ANC secured a landslide victory in the elections and a few days later, on 10 May, Nelson Mandela was inaugurated as our first democratically elected president. He ended his inaugural address with words that have rung in my mind ever since I first heard them: 'Never, never and never again shall it be that this beautiful land will again experience the oppression of one by another and suffer the indignity of being the skunk of the world.'

I was moved by the strong word 'never' – he gave me confidence that he would personally ensure that the progress was irrevocable. His address was a remarkable summary of our jagged history and his vision and pledge for the future. Mandela's words were powerful and hopeful, '... Out of the experience of an extraordinary human disaster that lasted too long, must be born a society of which all humanity will be proud ... We have, at last, achieved our political emancipation. We pledge ourselves to liberate all our people from the continuing bondage of poverty, deprivation, suffering, gender and other discrimination.' He ended his speech with the words: 'The sun shall never set on so glorious a human achievement!'

I held onto the words of Mandela, they gave me real hope.

It wasn't the onset of democracy that moved me on that day but the removal of the chains of oppression – that my forebears had all come to South Africa in chains and that now for the first time, those chains were completely removed. Even as I was struggling intensely with oppression at work, I felt that my political freedom would pave the way for economic oppression to pass. There is great promise in newness; we were starting afresh on many fronts: a new richly coloured flag, a new profound anthem, a new inspirational leadership and a new hopeful people.

Miracles, miracles ◉

I was struck by what Fyodor Dostoyevsky wrote in *The Brothers Karamazov*: 'For the secret of human existence does not consist in living, merely, but in what one lives for. Without a firm idea of what he is to live for, man will not consent to live and will sooner destroy himself than remain on the earth.' I copied these lines onto a sheet of paper and slipped it into my diary. I had not developed a grand plan for my life but I knew that education would, as it had been to date, be a core part of it, with an MBA in the US, preferably MIT, as the next step.

On 11 April 1994, I compiled a list in my diary of my ambitions and dreams, my version of what I was living for, as Dostoyevsky had written. One thing was sure, I was not merely going to exist. I wanted to live a full and meaningful life. The list contained the following:

1. Publish a book of poetry
2. Rise to a management position in business
3. Rise to MD of an engineering company
4. Obtain MSc, MBA and PhD
5. Do studies in Economics and Politics
6. Play social baseball and soccer
7. See Bruce Springsteen live in concert
8. Become President of South Africa

My dreams ranged from the mundane of playing social sport to the outrageous of becoming president. But the list is quite revealing of what was important to me at 24 and in fact, the list reveals the path that I have travelled. I discovered that there is great power in laying out our dreams. Not the plans to achieve them, these come later, but just those elements of life that would unlock the secret of human existence.

My interest in business was never about self-enrichment. I started one of my MIT application essays with this statement: 'A successful transformation to political democracy is only sustainable if it is accompanied by fundamental business and economic transformation.' I understood then already that to sustain the political transformation in South Africa, the structure of our economy would have to change and I wanted to be a part of that change. While my interest in technology and engineering remained, I felt that a business education would broaden my career horizons. Ideally I would be able to combine my interest in engineering with my new interest in business.

The 7 May 1994 edition of the *Constantiaberg Bulletin* announced the Carroll-Williams engagement. A picture of myself and Michele smiling broadly while rowing a boat was printed along with the announcement. We had been dating for just a few months but, prompted by her father, I needed to reconcile my plans to go to the US with this new relationship. Having Michele travel with me as my wife seemed like the best option so I proposed and she accepted. But it was premature. My parents were furious. Those close to me were perplexed. Nick laughed and in his usual laid-back style said, 'Go for it bro.'

Wedding plans were moving apace with dress designs, venues and dates being discussed. My family did not speak a word of the wedding. Frankly, neither did I. The smiling faces in that newspaper photo belied the frowns and scowls behind the scenes. Trying to remain sane through my work situation and the personal crisis required all of my attention. Furthermore, I was suffering physically and my growing ulcer was a concern. I became impatient and irritable. My behaviour made Michele feel insecure and in her seeking assurance made her appear more demanding, causing me to retreat. I was struggling to keep all the balls in the air. I knew that it wasn't realistic to expect that Michele could live with me in the US. I had to make a choice: abandon my study plans and stay in South Africa in an oppressive work environment to allow our relationship to grow, or drop the relationship ball and pursue my plans to study in the US ... alone. The relationship ball fell. Things started deteriorating between us.

As quickly as our relationship started, it ended. Just three months after proposing marriage, I broke off the engagement. Michele was devastated, her family and friends were angry. I explained in a letter that 'a broken engagement is better than a broken marriage'. This offered no comfort to anyone. My diary entry on 4 June expressed my pain, 'I feel really, really, really sad in my heart. The last few weeks have been terribly painful and confusing with relation to my engagement to Michele. I truly believed that I was ready for marriage ... In recent weeks I have discovered that I'm not committed to marriage and not committed to Michele. I do care for her and I do love her but not as my wife.' The entry ends with the abrupt line, 'We've just broken our engagement.'

I hated seeing the pain that I caused Michele. She didn't deserve this. I felt that in some weird way we were both victims of the circumstances in our country. But I know she saw me as the villain, which I understood. Michele and I had exchanged many letters and poems while we dated. My last poem to her was 'My Sorrow Tonight' which ended with the lines: 'I seek to hold your hand; Though I've failed to hold your heart.' We continued seeing each other occasionally and writing letters until she met someone new and opted to end all communication.

Early in May I received a postcard from MIT acknowledging receipt of my application forms. It was something, a little flame in the colossal darkness so ever present. The daily trips to my post box in Braamfontein became daily pilgrimages of hope. My friend Cate often joined me on these trips. Each day I opened my post box with the anticipation of finding something magical. I would grab at the envelopes in there and with breath held, flip through them quickly to see if there was word from America.

On 24 May I followed this routine, ran up the stairs, opened the post box, pulled out the bunch of envelopes, flipped through them excitedly and stopped at the white envelope with the EOC logo on the top left corner. Standing there, oblivious to the other post box customers surrounding me, I ripped open the envelope. I unfolded the one-page letter inside and read, 'Dear Mr Williams, EOC takes this opportunity to congratulate you on your successful application for a scholarship to study in the United States of America.'

It had happened! The dream had come true! The dream made real! A miracle! I stood there and laughed with joy. I read it again, slowly this time to make sure that I correctly understood what was written. I saw the words 'successful', 'scholarship', 'study', 'United States of America.' It was true.

Tears filled my eyes.

It was the most beautiful words, the sweetest words. I would be rid of the racists in corporate South Africa. Tears just poured uncontrollably as if my eyes too had been anxious, holding back these tears, and now needed release. I flew out of the post office that day and drove through the streets of Johannesburg screaming as loud as I could. It had happened! I was going to study in America! It had been 16 months since I applied – a long and anxious wait. 'I am celebrating tonight,' I swooned in my diary.

The scholarship would cover tuition, books, travel, accommodation, living allowance and health insurance, basically everything that I would need to study in the US for two years. I now absolutely needed to get out of my contract with Boart. I needed to leave for the US in July but I was contracted to work at Boart until the end of the year.

Three days after receiving the EOC letter I met with the HR manager at work, to repeat my request to be allowed to go study in the US. He again reminded me of all the 'steam' that I had caused by contacting the Boart CEO. I let it all out, telling him how frustrated I was and that I was merely biding my time, and that I would definitely be leaving the company at the end of my contract. I again asked him to release me from my contract. 'What is the point of holding me prisoner here? Why won't you offer me decent work?' I asked without expecting a reply.

I had no plan – what was I going to do if Boart did not release me? Would I forgo the scholarship? Would I agree to make some payment to break the contract and then go to the US? I had no idea how much such a payment would be – I never mustered the nerve to ask. Later that day I got a call from the HR manager, who wanted to see me again in his office. I was emotionally drained. I certainly was not up for more character assaults and more painful discussions about my inappropriate actions and my obligations. As I walked to his office I prayed for strength and for good news, ever the optimist. And then the impossible happened. He told me that Boart would release me from my contract. As I sat there I battled to hold back the tears. I wanted to scream with joy and jump up and run around his office. In my mind I did. He said I could leave at the end of May which was only a few days away. 'What a feeling! What a day!' I wrote in my diary.

A month later I received a letter from Paul Falla, the person at head office who had ignored all my faxes, whose Christmas card list I was tasked to prepare and who had belittled me at the meeting with the CEO. 'Needless to say,' he wrote, 'we are extremely disappointed with the outcome of our major investment in your tertiary education and accept that when it came to employment we fell short of your possibly unrealistic expectations.'

They never let up. But he wasn't done: 'We trust that you will take a searching look at yourself to see if your approach to the jobs … contributed to the outcome.' I didn't bother responding, I was rid of the oppression and I needed to focus on more positive things in my life. Despite everything, I *was* grateful to Boart for funding my studies, even as I was aware that I would not have needed a bursary had I grown up in a normal society where my father was able to earn a decent income.

The exasperation of my white bosses, who were playing their

'dutiful role' as my 'guardians' in accordance with apartheid beliefs, is hardly surprising. My situation was akin to that of Percival Brownlee, the black American slave who appears in William Faulkner's short story 'The Bear'. Brownlee exasperated his white masters because of his ambitions to be a preacher rather than spend his days fanning them as they instructed. Eventually his masters free him because he is too much trouble. Similarly I was expected to comply, to suppress my ambitions and instead spend my days 'fanning' their sense of self-righteousness. They might have thought that they were being progressive in employing their first coloured engineer, but the oppressor's pace of transformation is always too slow for the oppressed. Where they thought they were removing the boulder of racial bondage, all they were doing was reminding me that the boulder was ever-present and that they were pushing on the opposite side of the boulder from where I was pushing.

It was time to consider my next move. I hadn't heard from MIT yet so delayed responding to the EOC offer.

A week later I heard from MIT. It was at the end of another 'pilgrimage of hope' to my post box with Cate. There was no excitement, no expectation; it was a trip more out of habit than for any particular reason. I dragged myself up the two flights of steps that led to the post boxes and followed the daily routine. As I opened my post box I saw an envelope with the MIT logo on it. My hands shook as I opened it. The envelope contained a few booklets and a two-page letter. I drew the letter closer to read it: 'Dear Mr Williams, Congratulations! On behalf of the MIT Sloan School of Management, I am delighted to inform you that you have been accepted as a member of the Sloan Master's class entering in August 1994.'

I just stood there, staring at the letter. In disbelief.

'What does it say?' Cate asked impatiently.

'Cate, I am in, I am going to MIT!' I managed to reply as I choked up. We threw our arms around each other in celebration.

I was overwhelmed. I could not believe the miracles that had taken place over the preceding few weeks. Being awarded the EOC

TOP LEFT: Me at 18 months, after my first haircut. Lansdowne, 1972

TOP RIGHT: First day of school. Amanda and me in our St Ignatius Primary School uniforms. Lansdowne, 1976

BOTTOM LEFT: Family picture at home. That's me, at the far right, pulling a funny face. Lansdowne, 1977

BOTTOM RIGHT: My first spectacles at the age of nine. Mitchells Plain, 1979

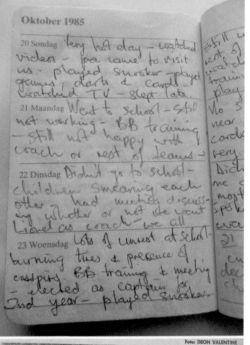

TOP LEFT: Athol, Nick, Roscoe (big to small) – my mother liked dressing us in matching outfits. What's up with those spectacles? Mitchells Plain, 1983

TOP RIGHT: My first diary. The bottom entry reads: 'Lots of unrest at school, burning tyres and presence of casspirs.' Mitchells Plain, 1985

BOTTOM LEFT: At my matric ball. Standing with my sports coach, Chippie Solomon, currently manager of the Western Province Stormers rugby club. Mitchells Plain, 1987

BOTTOM RIGHT: My only baseball action shot. The caption reads: 'Athol Williams of Woodlands is run out on first base by John Hanekom during yesterday's final against Dallas Yankees in Strandfontein.' Cape Town, 1987

TOP LEFT: Family photo at Amanda's house. Cape Town, 1989

TOP RIGHT: Me at 305 Braamfontein Centre, where the security police entered. I was held and beaten against the wall on my right. Johannesburg, 1988

BOTTOM LEFT: Graduating from Wits with a BSc in Mechanical Engineering. Johannesburg, 1992

BOTTOM RIGHT: My Wits T-shirt over a pillow at MIT, finally a bed to sleep on, after the homeless period. Boston, 1994

TOP LEFT: Me and John Mlynek in front of the MIT Dome on our way to a company presentation. Boston, 1995

TOP LEFT: With Prof Bob Cohen at my MBA graduation from the MIT Sloan School of Management. Boston, 1996

BOTTOM LEFT: My picture in the Bain & Company recruitment brochure. Boston 1996

BOTTOM RIGHT: Me with my BMW 850i, number plate: 'BULL.' Cape Town, 2002

TOP LEFT: Reception area of Taurus Associates' office. Woodmead, 2006

MIDDLE LEFT: Taryn and me on our wedding day. Hermanus, 2009

TOP RIGHT: Taryn and me at the entrance to our house. Johannesburg, 2010

BOTTOM: My custom-built dream library. Johannesburg, 2011

TOP LEFT: At the launch of my second book of poetry, *Talking to a Tree*. Cape Town, 2011

TOP MIDDLE: In my study at Harvard; notice the white sheets on the walls. Boston, 2012

TOP RIGHT: Addressing the Mason Fellows at Harvard and sharing a poem. Boston, 2013

BOTTOM: Graduating from Harvard with an MPA. Boston, 2013

TOP LEFT: Taryn and me on a boat cruise along the Hudson River with the Statue of Liberty in the background. New York, 2013

TOP RIGHT: My solo silent protest outside Capitol Hill. Washington DC, 2013

BOTTOM LEFT: Writing the poem 'The Shape of Man' at the WB Yeats memorial. Dublin, 2014

BOTTOM RIGHT: At the bollard erected in my name by the City of Cape Town. Mitchells Plain, 2014

TOP LEFT: Northumberland House was home while studying at LSE. London, 2014

TOP MIDDLE: Taryn and me at a Read to Rise event. Cape Town, 2015

TOP RIGHT: Nick and me in his driveway on that magical day when we celebrated my offer to study at Oxford. I am wearing the famous old Oxford jacket. Cape Town, 2015

BOTTOM: Family picture – Kim (Aaron's wife), Aaron, Mum, me, Taryn, Junita (Nick's wife), Nick, Natalie (Roscoe's wife), Roscoe (with his daughter, Kirsten in his arm). In front: Hannah and Daniel (Nick's children), and Cassidy (Roscoe's other daughter.) Cape Town, 2013

scholarship, being released by Boart and now this. Oh my goodness I was going to MIT. It didn't seem real. This was actually going to happen, I was really going to be free.

A strong sensation welled up inside me, a sense that I was about to embark on a great journey. Everything about MIT seemed out of this world and almost unbelievable.

Ms Desai, my high school teacher was right when she wrote, 'Athol has set high goals for himself. Nothing will deter him from achieving these goals. He has tremendous drive and knows his potential.' I wanted to pursue excellence rather than accept mediocrity. I dreamed of freedom and I dreamed of breaking down barriers and doing the impossible. Wits was an important step along this path. MIT would be next.

Two roads diverged, I took the one with a boulder ◎

How was I going to raise $75,000?

It is so easy to speak platitudes like 'impossible is nothing' as is so often spoken in commercials or on social media. I had talked about 'doing the impossible' and 'betting on myself'. Now I needed to walk this talk. I needed to push an impossible boulder. I had to find $75,000 to pay for my tuition and living costs for the two years of the MBA at MIT Sloan. This excluded travel costs. It equated to R300,000 (exchange rate at the time), more than 10 times my after-tax annual salary. I would have to save for 30 years to have that much spare cash. All I had was cash and assets worth R5,000. My family did not have much more.

To add to my dilemma, I had just nine weeks to find the money.

I sent a fax to Prof. Johnson at MIT to enquire about possible sources of funding, in particular whether there were scholarships available from the university. On 6 June I received a reply indicating that MIT would not be able to provide money for my studies.

The obvious place to turn to now would be the EOC who had already offered me a scholarship to study in the US. The complication was that the EOC selected the American university that I could attend. My scholarship was awarded to attend Louisiana State University (LSU). The solution seemed simple to me; ask EOC to transfer my scholarship from LSU to MIT.

The EOC was chaired by Archbishop Desmond Tutu and the executive director was a Catholic priest, Father Buti Tlhagale who now serves as the Catholic archbishop of Johannesburg. These were the men standing between me and MIT. Surely they would be supportive. I arranged to meet Fr Tlhagale at the EOC offices in central Johannesburg. The meeting did not go well. He expressed annoyance at my request and tried to convince me to accept the offer to LSU. 'Be grateful for this opportunity,' he said. I was tired of being told to be grateful.

Neil Fraser offered me a space at his office that I could use to begin my desperate effort to seek funding. All communication was done by fax and phone, in those days before email and the internet. I found a telephone directory and started calling companies.

This was not an easy time for me, yet it was also particularly difficult for my father, to see his son begging the way I was. He repeatedly apologised for the fact that he could not provide the funds. It broke my heart to hear him apologise. I knew all too well that the amounts required were well beyond what he or most parents could afford.

The poor know that ego can trip you up, and so we have to accept that we will beg. I had to beg for money to study in the US. There was nothing else I could do; I couldn't go work harder or borrow from my family or dip into a trust fund. The absurdity was that in order for me to break free from the hold of white capitalists I had to beg from them. That is the fate of the beggar; he has to beg from the very people who construct or perpetuate a society that turns him into a beggar.

'Good morning, I've been admitted to the MIT Sloan School in Boston, USA to read an MBA degree and was wondering if your organisation would be willing to contribute to my funding requirements?'

'How much do you need?'

'R300,000 ...'

Click, the call was terminated.

Companies explained that with this amount they could send ten students to local universities. I understood, but was disappointed that no one saw value in also sending an occasional student to one of the top universities in the world.

A few days into my search I heard from Prof. Johnson that MIT may be willing to waive tuition fees if I could raise living and incidental expenses. 'This is not an official promise,' he wrote, 'but rather my estimation of how the case is developing.' It was the most promising news I had heard. In the meantime, he assured me that he would ask the Sloan School to hold my place. I was so moved that there were people in the US, like Prof. Johnson, working to help crack this problem.

I learned that to get a travel visa to the US all I needed was funding for the first year of my studies. So if MIT would waive tuition fees, all I needed to raise immediately was $15,600, MIT's estimate of non-tuition expenses, or R57,500. Still way beyond my means, but within the realms of possibility. I got back on the phone. Long days followed – each day I checked for faxes and made a batch of phone calls from Neil's offices. I shuddered to think how I would have done any of this had I still been working.

I was invited to attend an orientation for the EOC programme on 9 June. I thought I would use the opportunity to speak to other EOC officials directly. I cornered an American official and enquired about the possibility of transferring the scholarship.

'Oh, I've heard about you,' she barked. There I was again being an unreasonable troublemaker. In an aggressive and off-hand way she told me that it would be impossible. Upon my insistence, she suggested that I speak to Fr Tlhagale, a door that I had already knocked on unsuccessfully.

At eight weeks to my date of departure I still had nothing, not even a plane ticket.

I went to see Tudor's father at JCI with my well-crafted plea for financial support. Ken Maxwell explained that they were not prepared to set a precedent to fund studies for non-employees. But he did offer that JCI would pay for my return plane ticket to the US. He placed a condition on the offer which was that I would agree to talk to JCI about possible employment on my return. It was the most tangible support that I had received to date and I would have agreed to any condition at that stage – hand over my firstborn son or offer as many organs as they wanted. I happily agreed to his condition. It was only a small step forward, but a step, nonetheless.

In the midst of all the chaos and uncertainty I went to Cape Town to see my family. It was a sort of farewell trip even though I wasn't really sure how things would work out. The Mitchells Plain newspaper, the *Plainsman*, ran a story about my acceptance to MIT. I was amazed a week later to see that the article took up the entire front page of the paper; the headline had huge bold capital letters which read, 'Westridge Man for USA Study'. The article caused a great buzz in the neighbourhood and for weeks afterward my parents received phone calls from people who saw it.

I returned to Johannesburg with seven weeks remaining until departure. Getting MIT to agree to waive tuition was unprecedented and it was all thanks to Prof. Johnson's efforts. Neil wrote to Prof. Johnson, 'From my side my gratitude to yourself for your tremendous assistance – it is greatly appreciated and I know that Athol is an excellent choice and will live up to the high standards of MIT.' I respected Neil enormously and appreciated his confidence in me. Prof. Johnson replied, 'Actually, it is you who is to be thanked by all concerned. I certainly look forward to meeting Athol. I hope we live up to his expectations.' I know I had unreasonably high expectations most of the time, but doubted that MIT would not live up to any of them.

Again Prof. Johnson reminded us that the offer from MIT was conditional on me raising the non-tuition expenses. This significant detail had not escaped me. Realistically, it seemed that EOC was my only hope. My task was clear – I needed to get EOC to change their minds.

I called the EOC offices to inform them of MIT's conditional offer to waive tuition fees. I again pleaded with them to just cover my living expenses for the two years of the MBA. I followed it up with a fax just to make sure. I waited patiently. And prayed intensely.

But again EOC declined my request.

With just six weeks to my intended date of departure the fax from the executive director explained that both the EOC and IIE, the American funders of the EOC scholarships, 'have reviewed your request to be placed at MIT instead of LSU. I regret to inform you that this change of placement is not possible.' I was floored. Absolutely wiped out. Furious beyond comprehension. I wasn't asking for a change of placement just that a small part of the scholarship be reassigned. This just seemed so ridiculous. I just could not catch a break. I had six weeks to go, what now?

Tlhagale's fax continued: 'Any change at this stage has serious implications for the programme. We will therefore assume that you will go to LSU.'

Wrong assumption! It was about rules; the rules could not be broken, I concluded. I was devastated. In my diary on 23 June I wrote, 'Received shocking news that EOC are not prepared to fund my studies at MIT. They've given me an ultimatum – go to LSU or nothing.' I understood clearly what was at stake.

This jeopardised the MIT offer of funding, since it was conditional on EOC's support. It was a good thing that I had quit drinking by then because I would probably have drunk a bottle of whisky daily. After picking myself up off the floor from devastation, I wrote to Prof. Johnson informing him of the setback but maintained a positive attitude, 'I am presently pursuing other avenues,' I wrote. I had not yet applied for housing at MIT; what was the point, I had bigger issues to deal with.

I knew I would bounce back. I shared the bleak news with Neil and my father. They both reacted positively and began actively pursuing funding avenues. We decided that there was no point in contacting companies given my earlier experience so we decided to focus on government and development institutions.

I visited the United States Information Service (USIS) looking for information on financial support. I visited the Wits library and bursary office to see if there might be some organisation that I had not contacted. All these efforts came to nothing.

I wrote to the director of International Education Funding at UNESCO. But got no reply. Neil wrote to the Minister of Education in Gauteng. He got no reply. My father wrote to President Nelson Mandela and to Trevor Manuel who was Minister of Trade and Industry but got no replies or acknowledgements. I think the President had more pressing issues overseeing our fledgling democracy and averting civil war than attending to my financial needs to study. My father wrote to the Premier of the Western Cape, our home province. He received a reply indicating that the matter had been referred to the Minister of Education and Cultural Affairs. The Office of the Minister of Education and Cultural Affairs acknowledged my father's letter, but he didn't send any response to the request. My father was so angry about the situation that he vented his anger in a letter that was published in the *YOU* magazine in 1994. I was grateful for this massive show of support by my father.

I called EOC again. They had already rejected my requests twice but I was desperate so I was forced to develop a thick skin. I went to see Fr Tlhagale who was probably sick of seeing my face and had to draw on all his priesthood training to stop him from tossing me out of the building. I pleaded with him to at least present my case to the decision-makers again. I spoke of the tremendous opportunity before me. I described my vision of what I could do with this education upon my return. What a loss for me and the country I argued, if this opportunity was forgone because of money. He agreed to reconsider my request. I worried that I had pushed him too far.

Five weeks to go

I was running out of time. In order to apply for a student visa to travel to the US, I needed a form from MIT called an I-20. MIT would only issue the I-20 once I could prove that I had all the required funds. I needed to courier original documents to MIT and they would courier the original I-20 to me. So realistically I had about three weeks to secure the funding taking into account the time for documents to travel between South Africa and the US. I had a singular focus, I would not accept defeat. Neil's office became my virtual home. I often missed meals and went days without a change of clothing.

A few more faxes, phone calls and meetings between myself and the EOC followed.

I hit a low. What was I doing? What was all this back and forth about? We were not debating my ability to perform well at and benefit from attending university, we were not debating my dedication to the studies or my commitment to return to South Africa. This was about money. That was all we were talking about, whether I could get the money to go study.

The truth is, if I was some rich kid who had the money I would not be having these discussions. If my father could just sell a few shares from his investment portfolio, then I wouldn't be enduring this humiliation. I was tired of begging and pleading and stating my case; all I wanted to do was get on with my studies. I was incensed that I was trapped again because of money.

I resorted to calling companies again, but my lack of enthusiasm ensured that I didn't get through the first layer of bureaucracy. We were well into the first week of July by now.

Four weeks to go

I was drained; I had nothing inside, except the growing ulcer. A diary entry read, 'I feel like I'm beginning to crack.'

Soon I felt that all the cracking had already happened and that I was beginning to melt and corrode from the inside. Was I crazy? Had I completely lost the plot? Most people would give their right arm for the opportunity to go study in America with a full scholarship. Would I regret all this? My energy to keep up the fight was almost fully drained.

Three weeks to go

Without funding from EOC or some other source, MIT would not waive the tuition and the whole effort would collapse. Neil implored Prof. Johnson to contact IIE in Washington again. A fax arrived from Boston. Prof. Johnson's assistant had contacted IIE and been told that the decision to transfer my scholarship 'did not belong to one person'. We were told that the difficulty was 'embedded in procedural and policy issues' surrounding the awards they make and that they had spent a great amount of time discussing my particular case. Again it was clear that the issue was not the availability of money but rather a bureaucratic one – rules needed to be followed.

How do we know when we must give up? Was this a case where it would be impossible to get the boulder over the hill? I refused to entertain this as an option, I refused to accept defeat.

EOC were pushing me for a final answer as their deadline approached – their departure date was two weeks away. I had tried their patience enough and felt that I needed to respect their decisions and respect their need for an answer. I needed to make a massive call. Do I go to LSU with complete peace of mind knowing that I had a fully-funded scholarship with everything taken care of, but give up on my pursuit of excellence? Or, do I reject the LSU offer in the belief that I could still somehow, as unlikely as it seemed, find the funding to go to MIT to pursue my dream?

If I turned down LSU and did not get the funding for MIT then I would end up with nothing. If I went to LSU I would always be plagued with the question of whether I had given up on MIT too soon.

I had to listen. I decided that I needed to learn to listen not with my ears but with a deeper part of myself.

The wisdom that came to me was that these are exactly the fights that need to be fought to achieve freedom. The fights where we risk everything. The fights that seem impossible to win. I came to know that I needed to be free in my heart first before the chains could be removed. The invisible forces of oppression are built into the societal processes that were designed to hold people like me back. I needed to resist them. I needed to prove now, when it counted most, that I was willing to believe in a miracle and bet on myself. I had nothing against LSU but for my purposes, LSU just would not do.

I was just one miracle away from MIT! I could not give up my fight. I would not!

Two weeks to go

With just two weeks to go, I took a stand. I still had no funds for MIT but I decided that it was important that I be true to myself – true to my desire to be the best and want the best. I was not going to settle for second best no matter what the reasons, especially because of money. I made a phone call to my father in Cape Town.

'Are you sure this is what you want to do?' he asked, after I told him of my decision. My stomach churned. It seemed completely irrational.

'I have a strong feeling that I must keep believing and pursuing the impossible,' I told my father, expecting him to ridicule me, but instead he replied:

'Trust that feeling.'

'I don't know why but I know that I must go to MIT,' I said.

'Then that's what you should do,' my father replied.

So without knowing how I was going to make the MIT option work, I formally turned down the EOC scholarship. I turned down the opportunity to leave my miserable, oppressive environment. I turned down the opportunity to go study in America on a full scholarship.

It was the end of a long and tragic drama, a drama for which I was partly to blame. I had known that with the EOC scholarship they would choose my university. EOC acted in good faith and had to abide by the rules of the programme and their sponsors. They had gone through a selection process, selected me and now I was backing out. As much as I disliked it, I understood their position. In my final correspondence with Fr Tlhagale, I explained that it would be counter-productive for me to embark on a study programme to which I was not committed. I thanked him for his 'patience and understanding in dealing with my appeal'.

One enormous door had closed. I saw no other doors. It was time to dig my way out again, to dig my own door.

I had less than two weeks.

One more day of miracles ⊚

I had to fight my doubts and begin generating positive energy. In my diary I wrote: 'Note from Athol to Athol. Remember these difficult and trying times when you're studying at MIT. When you don't feel like studying, remember the determination that it took to get you there ...'

I still didn't know how I was going to get to MIT but I decided that I was going. *I just decided.* I mustered all the self-belief and positive energy that I could and decided that I would find a way. I felt that though I was standing in front of an enormous, immovable boulder I would find the strength to push it out of the way.

I went as far as making arrangements for a farewell party and arranging farewell dinners with close friends. It was going to be tricky saying goodbye when I wasn't really sure that I was going.

And then I had an idea – my bank. This was my last option other than selling drugs or my body, for which I was certain I wouldn't get much! I had banked with Standard Bank since I was a child. As I was preparing to graduate as an engineer they offered me all sorts of financial products and advice to ensure that I got off to a good start financially and of course to ensure that I remained a customer. It was time to pay them a visit.

I still needed R57,500. At the bank I met a sympathetic person by the name of Lisle Biggar. She could see the desperation in my eyes. I explained my situation and explained my time constraint. She assured me that everything would work out much like a mother reassures a child after falling and cutting himself. I felt that I mattered to her. I really believed that she would do everything that she could to make this happen.

Lisle proposed that the R57,500 be made up of a R30,000 overdraft (which was approved immediately), a R22,500 student loan and my R5,000 cash. The interest charges would be astronomical: 15.25% per annum on the overdraft and 10% per annum on the student loan. My application faced a major hurdle – I had no assets to serve as surety for the loan. The hurdle was made all the more problematic by the fact that I was leaving the country. *Would the bank really extend an unsecured loan for me to go study overseas?* Lisle agreed to process the loan application in the meantime while I figured out how I would get surety.

The bank also wanted proof that MIT would waive tuition fees. All I had was a fax, nothing formal. And besides, the MIT fax made it clear that their offer was conditional upon me securing funding for living expenses. The bank would fund my living expenses on condition that MIT waived tuition. Each wanted the other's confirmation. It was circular. My head spun.

Ten days to go

On 27 July, I received a fax from Standard Bank marked 'URGENT'. The fax read, 'We herewith confirm that we have approved a student loan for R22,500 in your favour.' I cried. I just sobbed, and had to constantly wipe the tears from my eyes so that I could focus on the words written on the fax. I could not believe it. With the overdraft already approved I now had the money to go. I immediately sent a fax through to the Sloan School. 'This is just to inform you that I have managed to raise the required $15,600. A letter from my bank will be faxed to you tomorrow.'

But the bank did not fax anything to MIT the following day. Instead I found myself writing to the university, 'Life is never as simple as we'd like it to be!' The bank would not finalise anything without surety.

Where was I going to find surety? The only person that I could think of was Neil Fraser. But Neil had already done so much for me, I just couldn't ask him to take the financial risk of standing surety. But I had absolutely no choice. As I had done so many times, I put my ego in my pocket and decided to ask. Neil agreed.

This sparked a whole new series of tasks because now the bank needed Neil's personal details and proof of his financial status and so forth. Argh! And they wanted more information from MIT. Everything was sent to them and the loan was approved. Now I could celebrate, but there wasn't time.

Eight days to go

The bank didn't approve of the fax that Sloan sent, they wanted original documentation, so the documents had to be sent from the US by courier. Who knew when they would arrive? Now I was at the mercy of an international courier company. I was so stressed that I could barely breathe.

Seven days to go

On 29 July, the bank issued me with documents showing that they had extended my personal overdraft of R30,000 which again was secured by way of surety by Neil. This man really trusted me! I didn't even bother reading the loan agreements – repayments and costs were something that I would worry about later.

The bank insisted that I take out life insurance to the value of the loan and overdraft, so more costs were added to cover the cost of the loan in the untimely but likely event of my death from stress. With just a week to spare I had all the money I needed to go to MIT. This would cover first-year living expenses. Second year could wait for later. I dared not ask MIT about their waiver of tuition for fear of the answer that I strongly suspected I would receive.

With all the jagged pieces of the funding puzzle fitting together (albeit loosely), the next step was to get the I-20 form from MIT. I waited anxiously.

Five days to go

I went to the travel agent to book my flight to Boston. I couldn't pay yet but I asked them to hold the booking for me. Still no I-20 form.

Four days to go

Still no I-20 form.

Three days to go

I still could not apply for my travel visa because I did not have the

I-20 form from MIT. Really, would this be the undoing of all that I have made happen to date?

I packed my belongings which was to be stored in Johannesburg and packed for the trip to Boston. I packed a few items as gifts for those in the US who had played a part in getting me there.

There were many goodbyes to be said. My days were filled with phone calls, coffee visits, meals with friends, and a farewell party. One of the phone calls was to Sloan to enquire about the I-20 form. I was told that it had already been sent to me via courier. A call to the courier confirmed that the package was on its way – expected arrival was within 24 hours. Did I have 24 hours?

Two days to go

It was two days before departure date. At 3pm on 4 August, the I-20 form finally arrived. With the I-20 was a note from the admissions office at Sloan, 'Thankfully we have gotten to this happy point. We look forward to your arrival.' A welcome positive note but I was not so sure that we had fully reached a 'happy point' yet.

My departure day was a Saturday, so I only had the following day, Friday 5 August to apply for and be issued with a travel visa. I still didn't have a plane ticket and I didn't have traveller's cheques. I had no idea how long these would take.

There was absolutely no room for error – if there was any problem with the I-20 form, my proof of finances or any other aspect of the application, it would be over.

One more day of miracles – that was all I needed.

One day to go

On 5 August I rose at 6am. I did not sleep well – a combination of excitement and anxiety. My head felt hazy but as soon as I began running through the plan for the day my brain awoke as if by shock. This was it; it was the last 100m of a long race, the final stretch.

When I arrived at the US embassy the doors were still locked. I stood outside the building clutching an envelope containing all the documents that I needed with my eyes trained on the entrance door. I waited there for 40 minutes before the doors opened. I was the first person in line. Dressed in the finest clothes that I owned, I stood in front of the glass window waiting expectantly. Still uncertainty raged, still stress crept and still the ulcer grew. I had no idea what to expect – what questions would they ask, what information would they need? There were still so many loose ends and so much room for this to go wrong. I had never been this anxious before.

I whispered a prayer when a woman finally stepped into her cubicle behind the thick glass and called me forward. I handed her the pile of documents. There were no questions, queries or requests for more information. I was told to take a seat. After an anxious wait, I was called to another window and was handed my passport. I flipped through the passport not knowing what to look for. I suddenly realised that I had no idea what a visa looked like and wasn't sure if I'd been granted one. I was taking no chances, so I called to the woman behind the glass and whispered embarrassingly, 'Do I have a visa?'

Realising my embarrassment she was kind enough to whisper back and showed me that on page 9 of my passport an F1 (student) non-immigrant visa valid for one year had been stamped. I was too excited and too nervous to query the 'one year' validity (given that my studies would last two years) – who knew what could go wrong if they tried to make any changes now. I had a travel visa!

Within an hour, I left the embassy armed with a visa-bearing passport and an uncontrollable smile on my face. Now that I had the visa, JCI would issue the cheque for the plane ticket. I called the JCI offices and was told that the woman who was to issue the ticket was away on leave. I just laughed.

This was far too funny. It felt like God was showing off and just wanted to have tight complicated situations created so that He could show how easily He got me out of them. Compared to what had transpired over the previous weeks this was just a wrinkle.

I raced across town to the Standard Bank branch in Braamfontein to collect my traveller's cheques. The banker showed me that the required documents had just arrived from Sloan, stamped with the

Standard Bank 'RECEIVED' rubber stamp, dated 5 August 1994. Just in time! Some things *were* going my way. But then the banker told me that according to foreign exchange controls in South Africa, there was a limit to how much I could take out of the country.

Even though I had access to R57,500 I was only allowed to take R18,000 immediately. I stood leaning forward, with my hands on the bank counter, with my head dropped, my eyes closed. Such strong emotions welled up in me. I had to fight back tears. I was so tired. But I straightened up, took a deep breath and I told him that I would accept whatever I was allowed to take, which came to $4,940, far short of the $15,600 that I needed. He asked for my passport which I handed to him with confidence and directed him to my travel visa. *Read it and weep*, I thought to myself. He then asked for my plane ticket.

'My plane ticket! Why do you need my plane ticket?'

Before he could answer I told him that I didn't have my plane ticket yet. I felt faint. I couldn't remember if I had eaten anything yet that day. My head felt like it was about to cave in. He insisted that I needed my plane ticket. I didn't have any strength to argue so left the bank. It was noon.

I trekked across to the other end of Johannesburg to the travel agent's office. Given the time squeeze, the travel agent kindly issued my plane ticket without payment. My friend Cate worked at the travel agency so they were willing to bend the rules slightly.

In the meantime my friend, Tudor, had taken over trying to get the cheque for my plane ticket issued by JCI. While I was still at the travel agent's desk, he called her to give me the message that the cheque was ready for collection. I grabbed the plane ticket and raced through traffic back across to bank. I was barely able to breathe. With the plane ticket in hand I dashed into the bank to collect the traveller's cheques. My passport was stamped, '5 August 1994, $4,940 traveller's cheques' on the 'Foreign Travel Allowance' page. The stamp included my plane ticket number providing evidence that the banker guy was not just being a jerk for insisting that I present my plane ticket.

In an emotionally charged moment, Lisle Biggar, the incredible banker who had helped me so much, came to wish me well. Right there in the bank this tiny lady reached up to me and gave me the warmest hug. It was a magical moment that moved me to tears. I had no idea how many rules she had to bend to get my loans approved but I knew that she had gone well beyond expectations to help me. My 'thank you' seemed woefully inadequate – I just hoped that she could tell how deeply I meant it.

Next stop was to collect the cheque which Tudor's father, Ken Maxwell, signed and handed to me, wishing me well. The cheque was dated 5 August 1994. The last leg of this long journey was back to the travel agent to drop off the cheque to pay for my ticket.

Everyone at the travel agency cheered as I left. They had some sense of what I had been through. Not for the first time that day I was moved to tears.

By 3pm on 5 August, just over 24 hours before my flight, I finally had all that I needed – passport with travel visa, traveller's cheques and ticket. I didn't have a place to live in Boston nor did I have enough money to survive there, let alone money to pay tuition fees. But I was going!

Praise God.

I called my family in Cape Town to say goodbye and made a few calls to friends.

There were zero days to go.

'Take me to MIT' ◉

I sat in seat 30G on-board US-Africa* flight E8 006 staring blankly out into the night sky. We had taken off from Johannesburg at 7:45pm a few hours earlier, on Saturday, 6 August 1994. Tudor, Cate and a few other friends were at the airport. What a feeling. In my diary I wrote:

> I'm 30,000 feet above sea level headed for Washington DC. This is it. This is what I've waited for, this is what I've been fighting for and struggling for. This is what I've been dreaming of. I'm heading for the MIT Sloan School of Management to do an MBA.

Just three months earlier I was dressed in greasy overalls on my knees working in a factory. Now I was heading to study at one of the top universities in the world.

I thought back to my time at Boart and my experiences of growing up under apartheid, and how small it sometimes made me feel. Not small as in being a child and wanting to be an adult, but small as in being something *less* – less of a man, less of me, less than the greatness that I felt within me. That is what oppression does, it tries to shrink you into what your oppressors want you to be. But I refused to accept their plan for my life. I refused to let their hatred shrink my dreams. My dreams would not be made small. And so I learned to push stones. And I grew strong until I could push rocks. And still I grew until I was a giant who could push boulders.

Sitting on that plane high above the pain and struggle of South

---

* This airline no longer operates.

Africa, tears streamed down my cheeks. I knew now how it felt to be free. I knew what it was to be me, a giant. I slept peacefully for the first time in weeks as we jetted to the US. After a stop in Washington DC, I took the connecting flight to Boston.

I hadn't really thought about what I would do when I landed in Boston. I awoke to this fact as I left Boston's Logan International Airport in search of a taxi. I had nowhere to live. I didn't know anyone to call. I only had a few dollars in cash and traveller's cheques but no credit card. Before leaving home I wrote in my diary that I would probably 'squat on campus or Prof. Johnson's until accommodation is found'.

There was no way I was going to call Prof. Johnson to ask if I could sleep on his couch, the man had done enough for me. I resolved to find some communal space on campus where I could sleep and store my stuff until I found a place to stay.

A great warmth overcame me as I stepped out into the Boston air for the first time. *Wow, I am really here.* I clenched my fist and gave a small fist pump in the air.

'Take me to MIT please,' I shouted at the cab driver. 'Where at MIT da ya wanna go?' he drawled back rather impatiently with a thick accent that I could barely understand.

Little did I know that MIT was a mini-city – one couldn't 'go to MIT', you went to a particular street or a particular building. I flipped through the papers and booklets that I had with me and asked him to take me to Ashdown House, a graduate student residence. I had read that they offered accommodation to students who arrived on campus early.

The cab cruised out of the airport and onto the streets of Boston. The outskirts of the city looked old and poorly maintained – brown buildings with faded signs, cracked bumpy roads and unattractive bridges. The roads were busy – drivers seemed discourteous and hurried. Horns blared as cars screeched to within fractions of an inch of each other. Smoke from the cab driver's cigarette filled the cab and from behind the smoke clouds I could hear him whistling along with the blaring tunes on the radio. I slid around on the synthetic leather seats as he weaved in and out of traffic.

I was surrounded by chaos but I was smiling. I sat with my eyes wide open – I stared at everything with amazement and excitement, reading the names on buildings and billboards just as I had done as a child while taking the bus with my mother.

We drove over the Harvard Bridge crossing the Charles River from Boston to Cambridge, the home of two of the world's greatest universities – Harvard and MIT. The river was vast and meandered in both directions. And then MIT rose from out of the ground – majestic columns propping up magnificent stone buildings. Among the square buildings the Killian Court building stood proudly with its majestic dome. I could feel the excitement well up inside me. No more dreams of MIT or plans to go to MIT or preparation for MIT, I was *at* MIT! I got out of the cab and held my hands aloft, I am here. It was the most incredible feeling, my heart pounded like it too wanted to hold its hands aloft. I've made it, I am here! I repeated softly.

I hauled my suitcase out of the trunk of the cab. The suitcase contained everything that I had come to America with – some clothes, most of them inadequate for Boston winters, and a few books. I stood on Massachusetts Avenue (locally known as 'Mass Av') with my suitcase at my side and I watched the cab drive off. The wide avenue, with two lanes of traffic going in either direction, roared with traffic. The wide sidewalks bustled with people – all going somewhere. Everything looked different to me – the people, the buildings, the cars, even the mid-afternoon sun shone differently.

I headed for Ashdown House. The entrance to the building was lined with pillars and portraits. The building was dark and felt cold; the entrance looked more like a government building than a university residence. My *Practical Planning Guide for New Graduate Students* said that MIT's goal is to guarantee campus housing to all first-year graduate students who apply. I had not applied. The guide continued to state in bold letters: 'Do not plan on arriving at MIT without having made advanced arrangements for accommodation.'

Well, it was a bit late for this warning.

I approached the reception desk behind which sat a young guy with dishevelled hair and a well-pimpled face.

Me: Good afternoon.

Guy behind desk: (looks up from his book, just stares at me)

Me: I was wondering if you could help me.

Him: What?

Me: (Giving up on the niceties) I need a room. I've just arrived from South Africa and need a room.

Him: (Still reading his book) You a student?

Me: (Proud to make my first announcement of my new status) Yes, I'm an MBA student at the Sloan School.

Him: First year or second year?

Me: First.

Him: Did you receive confirmation that you've got a room here?

Me: No.

Him: Then you can't stay here.

Me: But I just need a place to stay until term starts.

Him: We have no space.

Not exactly the warm welcome that I was expecting. I referred him to the guide I had received mentioning that the house offered summer accommodation. After consultation with members of the residence executive, the verdict remained unchanged – I was told that unless I had confirmation of a placement I could not stay. I was told that there was no temporary accommodation available. I could not deal with this. At my request, the sullen desk warden agreed that I could leave my suitcase in the foyer for a short while.

I left the building, frustrated and with absolutely no idea where I would sleep that night. I had no plan. I decided to take a short walk and then to return to make calls to find temporary accommodation – I could deal with permanent accommodation later.

I walked and walked and walked. I walked for three-and-a-half hours. I walked along the Charles River, walked all over the MIT campus even visiting the Sloan School and eventually found my way to Harvard Square. It was a glorious walk, like a meditation, a celebratory meditation.

I was not impressed with the Sloan building. It looked tired and unloved. I took the elevator up to the sixth floor – the top floor. The elevators were slow and whiny and looked like the elevators I had seen in apartment blocks in Hillbrow back home. Suddenly Prof. Johnson's words came to me; he had written in a fax to Neil, 'I hope we (MIT) live up to his (my) expectations.' Well, the building certainly didn't live up to my expectations. I later came to learn that it was a point of great pride among ardent MIT students and faculty that the infrastructure was rather rudimentary. Those associated with MIT were meant to be more concerned with the quality of education, research and teaching that took place within the buildings than the quality of the buildings themselves.

Harvard Square vibrated with activity. It was the perfect place for someone like me (alone and directionless) to roam. There were buskers at the train stations and on street corners (this is where the singer Tracy Chapman was 'discovered'), cafés, restaurants and coffee shops that sold all manners of goodies. Bookstores and convenience stores were all still doing their trade. There were people everywhere which together with the music and bright neon lights gave the place a carnival-like feeling. It was easy to lose oneself there. I was shocked to realise that I had been away from Ashdown for over three hours.

I still needed to find a place to stay, and there I was roaming the streets of Boston. I needed to get back to Ashdown first to get my suitcase. I managed to find someone friendly enough to explain to me how the buses worked and I took a bus back to Ashdown House, arriving after sunset.

When I entered the cold and dark foyer again, I could not find my suitcase. I enquired of the desk warden, a young woman now. She had no idea that I was there earlier and certainly knew nothing of my suitcase. She groaned as she searched behind the wooden counter. She found a Post-It note stuck to the counter. I saw her read the note. She seemed to re-read it a few times; I waited for her to tell me that my bag had been confiscated by the FBI or that some thug had run off with it. She looked up at me, flipped through sheet in a file that sat on the counter, looked back at the note.

What now? I thought to myself, my heart heavy, my body aching. Eventually the lethargic desk warden looked up: 'Your bag is in room 614, here's a key. It looks like you can sleep there tonight.'

'What!' I shrieked.

I was amazed and utterly overjoyed. I couldn't believe it. She didn't know any more – the note just said that my bag was in room 614. I had heard all that I needed to. I grabbed the key, and after getting directions, I started towards the room.

How did this happen? I thought again. It seemed so unbelievable. *Angels are definitely looking after me*, I smiled to myself. I was no longer counting miracles but this latest one was a real life saver. Up in the room I found two beds – simple mattress on a steel base – I didn't care. Because I had no bedding, I covered a pillow with a T-shirt that read 'Wits' across the chest and laid out my jerseys and jackets across the bed to serve as blankets.

Finally, I was able to get some sleep.

I awoke the next morning to a breath-taking view over the Charles River and Boston's famous brownstone buildings in the background. My morning prayer was for finances, accommodation, good health and mental alertness for my studies. I packed up my belongings and headed back down to reception – I returned the room key and left my suitcase behind the counter. I attended a session on campus for students looking for roommates in the hope that I may find someone with a cheap room for me. No luck.

I returned to Ashdown House hoping that I could sleep in the same room or another room of a student who had not yet arrived. Unfortunately, my luck had run out. I took my suitcase and walked over to Stratton Student Centre which housed dining venues, shops, computer rooms, banks, a supermarket, toilets and Stratton Lounge.

The lounge had couches, chairs and small round tables.

Forlorn, I sat on a couch there for hours, unsure what I would do to find a place to live and unsure how I would pay for it. I fell asleep on the couch. At some point during the night I felt something hard poke me in the side. I looked up at the campus policeman who was shining a flashlight in my face. He told me that I couldn't sleep there so I took my suitcase and went on my way. I didn't sleep again that night. In the morning, I signed up with the athletics club so that I could access the showers and a locker where I could leave my belongings.

It finally struck me … I was homeless.

It seemed absurd to me. I was a student at the top business school in America yet I had nowhere to live. Again I felt foolish. I roamed campus aimlessly. That night I again went to the Stratton Lounge. To escape detection by the campus policeman I pushed a couch up against a wall on the far side of the lounge with the back of the couch facing the entrance. This is where I slept for the next six nights. This is how I had to avoid being caught by campus policemen. This is how Stratton Lounge became home.

I had no doubt that I would find a way through this grim patch. This was an unexpected boulder but I didn't mind having to push this one and I knew that I would prevail. Having nowhere to live was a minor issue in comparison to the excitement I felt at being there. But I'd be lying if I didn't admit to feeling sad and deeply lonely. I was in this vast country all alone.

Everyone was a stranger. My future was so uncertain with regard to funding my studies, let alone whether I'd cope with the studies. And then there was the practical issue of avoiding detection by MIT's campus police. I had no idea what the campus police would have done if they caught me again. Could I be expelled from MIT even before starting my degree officially? Would I be arrested for trespassing or vagrancy? It was nerve-wracking.

I had no idea how long I would have to live like this. Sooner or later I would have to go to a hotel which would burn through my limited funds rapidly.

In the meantime, each day I would wash in the toilets in the student centre or at the athletics centre. I developed a staple diet of dry bagels and milk or apple juice. I would buy a bag of six bagels at a supermarket – these were heavy and dense, so two would be sufficient as a meal. The milk or juice made it easier to eat the dry bagel. There was no luxury of having any fillings. On occasion I would spoil myself with a slice of pizza on campus, the only warm meal I would have. I spent my days reading in the library and attending orientation sessions. I spent my evenings reading in the student centre and when everyone left the Stratton Lounge, I went to sleep.

I made contact with Prof. Johnson, who had been instrumental in getting me to MIT. Johnson was a professor in the Political Science department and had been an active member of the anti-apartheid movement in Boston. He invited me to his home in Newton. 'You must be someone special to get into MIT,' Professor Johnson's wife said to me once we got talking. She didn't know the half of what it took for me to get that far.

I was too embarrassed to say that I was homeless – so I told them that I was staying with a friend. We discussed my funding situation. We recounted the drama of seeking funding and he explained the complexities of MIT funding and why we didn't get any in the end. He suggested contacting South African executives who were MIT alumni and gave me a list of names.

A few days later there was some good news on the accommodation front. Ashdown House were likely to have a space for me. It was not a permanent place but at least I didn't have to skulk around campus looking for a place to sleep and hide my belongings. I slept in a room for three nights and then had to move again. This time I moved into room 103A, which I shared with an American engineering student. I stayed here for the next two semesters. I still had no bedding and used my clothes as a pillow and blanket as I had done before. I didn't care, at least I had a place to call home.

By the time I arrived at MIT I had already fought enough battles for a few lifetimes. I had fought to be there. And I wanted to be there.

This was not a second choice option as it may have been for some. This was not the outcome of a casual application process. This was the result of the most determined fight – it was my fight for dignity, for freedom and a fight for the chance to realise fully what I knew I was capable of.

Moving away from the oppressive environment at home improved my psychological state. That feeling of endless possibility returned. I felt invincible again, able to take on any challenge, able to push any boulder. The flame inside me was burning brighter than ever.

Walking into joyful reality ⊚

'That was a particularly worrying time for us at home, worrying about you,' my father wrote on 29 August 1994, in reference to my being homeless. I had called my parents once during the week when I was sleeping in Stratton Lounge. Telling my father about my circumstances brought him to tears. I cried too. I felt that I was letting him down. His letter continues, 'I don't have good news about the Department of Education [who he had contacted for funding], they wish you well but budget restrictions ... cannot help ... nevertheless before getting this reply, I already wrote to President Mandela – no reply as yet – I'm still trying.' I know it broke my father's heart that he was not able to pay for my studies. I never expected him to pay. I was grateful for his continued efforts to find funding.

Word of my financial and accommodation difficulties spread among my friends back home. I welcomed their encouraging letters. Neil, Tudor and Cate were trying to find ways of getting money from my loan account over to me. Cate continued going to my post box and forwarded my mail including the *Financial Mail*, the source that I used for my self-taught business education. In reference to my leaving for MIT, Tudor wrote: 'I was quite bewildered when the whole event took place.' 'I know my friend,' I thought, 'imagine how I felt.'

I attended preparatory Accounting and Mathematics lectures which ran for four hours each day for a week and I attended sessions on Excel, the computer systems and use of email (something completely new to me in 1994) and library orientation. I started meeting my MBA classmates, who were a fascinating bunch. We were from 53 countries, a quarter of the class already had advanced degrees and the most common undergraduate degrees were from MIT, Stanford, University of California Berkeley, Harvard, Princeton, University of Pennsylvania and Cornel. I was the youngest. My study group comprised five Americans, a Japanese, a Korean, a Mexican and an Indian.

MIT ran a Host for International Students Program (HISP) where local Boston families hosted international students. The programme aimed to create friendships and cultural exchange and to provide some linkage to locals for international students. I signed up for the programme and was matched with the Cohen family who lived in the suburb of Jamaica Plain. Bob was a highly respected engineering professor at MIT, Jane was a school teacher and their children Genevieve and Eliot were fourteen and seven respectively.

I thoroughly enjoyed my time with them. They were warm, friendly and took great interest in my welfare. Jane was kind enough to give me bed linen so I could finally stop using my clothing for this purpose. They were a down-to-earth family who showed keen interest in South Africa and were keen to give me as much of an American experience as they could. We played basketball in their driveway, went to a baseball game and they invited me for Thanksgiving dinner after which I joined the tradition of watching a football game on TV and then playing football outside. The Cohens would turn out to be a wonderful source of friendship during my time at MIT and after. Still today no visit to Boston is complete without seeing them.

During my first semester I took courses in Strategy, Economics, Accounting, Communications, Organisational Processes and Data Modelling. My early show of leadership led to me being elected one of sixteen senators representing our first-year MBA class in the Sloan student governing body – not that I could afford the extra time that these duties would consume.

Life at Sloan was intense. I rarely slept before midnight. I calculated that I needed to study until midnight every night during the week and for 10 hours per day over the weekends just to keep up. A diary entry reads, 'I haven't been able to sleep well. I wake up at least three or four times during the night.' There was plenty on my mind. Not least the growing pile of bills.

In August I received a bill for $10,300 for the fall semester tuition and hospital insurance. In September another bill arrived showing that I now owed over $12,000 which included the cost of my accommodation at Ashdown and a late payment penalty. It was tough enough dealing with the volume of studies. My financial situation added greatly to my anxiety. I had come with just $4,950 and had already used some of it for food and winter clothing – I was not prepared for snow and temperatures that would drop to -20 degrees Celsius. A chunk of my money had to be spent on stationery, text books and course packs – for each course, students had to buy the case studies and notes that the professors used.

I approached the Director of Student Affairs at Sloan with an enquiry about scholarships, but just as Prof. Johnson had informed me months earlier, I was told that there were none because all students came to the business school fully funded. I explored part-time jobs on campus and in the area but couldn't find anything suitable. I wasn't even sure if my student visa allowed me to work, but I was not too worried about bureaucratic compliance issues at this stage.

Towards the end of September, I introduced myself to Dr Isaac Colbert at a function, and told him my story. He was the Associate Dean of Graduate Students. I met him in his office the next day and shared more details on what I had told him the night before. He suggested that I go see the Dean of Graduate Students, Dr Frank Perkins. By this stage I had already spoken to so many people that I was quite happy to be passed from one person to the next. Rather than feel despondent I felt more hopeful every time I had an additional meeting. On 29 September I met Dr Perkins. I looked a pitiful sight – I had not slept well for weeks, had not been eating well and my left arm was in a sling – I had sustained an injury to my shoulder during a late-night friendly soccer game.

Dr Perkins was a friendly man who listened intently as I recounted my long battle to get to MIT, the drama with the EOC, the faxes from

Prof. Johnson and that I was basically looking at possible expulsion from the university if I couldn't come up with the money. He seemed sympathetic to my situation. I left his office believing that I might just get funding.

That evening I wrote in my diary: 'I think I will get money to cover all my expenses for two years. Will be praying.' This meeting would turn out to be the turning point in my fortunes. After a few phone calls with his office and one more meeting with Dr Perkins, he informed me that he had created a special scholarship for me that would cover tuition, accommodation and offer me a living allowance. I laughed on the phone as he told me this. I apologised for laughing but I was just so overwhelmed. After the phone call I sat down on the floor of my bedroom and cried and thanked God.

Another enormous boulder out of the way. I could now focus on my studies. I felt vindicated for keeping true to my dream and my determination to walk this path of excellence rather than take the unsuited easy path. I called my parents in South Africa to share the good news.

In early October with mid-term exams looming, I received a letter from Dr Perkins's office, signed by him confirming that he had created the MIT/South Africa scholarship just for me. Soon thereafter I got an account statement from MIT's bursar office showing that my tuition fees had been paid but the scholarship had not yet fully paid my accommodation bills nor paid my living allowance. I continued to receive statements from the MIT housing office stating: 'Your account is still past due. Please bring it up-to-date immediately.' They seemed to stop just short of saying '… or else …' There was still an outstanding amount of over $1,500 and even though my cash was running low I couldn't bear the anxiety of these account statements arriving with these reminders of my account arrears. Dr Perkins had said that he would sort this out, but I couldn't wait. I paid the outstanding balance, now reducing my cash to desperate levels. I still couldn't bring additional money into the country.

Mid-term exams had started and I had project papers due. And I was swamped with company recruiting presentations – a necessary evil in anticipation of job interviews for the summer of the following year. I attended lunch-time and evening presentations with leading strategy consulting firms (Bain, McKinsey and Boston Consulting Group), with investment banks (Lehman Brothers, Salomon Brothers and Citibank), the World Bank and multinational corporations including Exxon, Hewlett-Packard, Motorola and Ford who all came to campus looking to entice us to interview with them. I had to learn fast about how to present myself to American recruiters and how to perform in interviews.

It is embarrassing to admit that my attendance at many company presentations was driven not by interest in their companies but the food that they served. I had basically run out of cash and couldn't even afford my staple diet of dry bagels and milk. There were many company presentations which I attended just to grab a sandwich. I would often stuff a few extra sandwiches in my bag as well, hoping no one would catch me.

Even though I had assurances from Dr Perkins about the scholarship, I was nervous that something had gone wrong and that I would get no additional cash for living expenses. I had no cash by now. I felt desperate.

Weeks went by without money to pay for food.

Finally in November I received a call from MIT's payroll office asking me to collect a cheque. I received a stipend of $5,400, which left me with $4,644 after tax. It had been three months since I arrived and now finally, I could relax and eat, and stop scavenging for sandwiches.

Dr Perkins struck a 'deal' with me – he only committed to funding one semester at a time but at the end of each semester if my results were satisfactory (we never defined this), he would find funding for the following semester. What a powerful incentive this was. This is how I got through all four semesters of the degree: each semester I would deliver good results and each semester Dr Perkins would arrange the funding. I didn't have to draw on the loans from my bank again.

In March 2000, while working in London, I wrote to Dr Perkins who by then had retired from MIT:

> In the fall of 1994 I arrived in the US, alone, apprehensive and without any money. I had no place to live, and I didn't know anyone – in fact, the only certainty I had was that I had a place on the MBA program at MIT. After weeks and weeks of anxiety and stress which affected my health and studies, I finally got to talk to someone who would listen, you. I hope that you remember creating the MIT/South Africa scholarship which enabled me to pay for my studies. I certainly remember the warmth with which you discussed my situation and assured me that you would see what could be done. That was the most promising assurance I had received. I also remember the emails from your secretary, Amy, assuring me every semester that the scholarship would be renewed. I want to sincerely thank you for your efforts in securing the funds … That single act has opened doors beyond what I could have imagined and truly had a profound impact on my life.

After describing the great heights to which my career had risen to that point and thanking him again I wrote: 'My plan is to return to South Africa to not just contribute to its economic development but to the development of the belief that people have in themselves.'

I did indeed return to South Africa years later to contribute to its economic development. I have recently begun to fulfil the second part of this promise through my poetry, children's books, community development work and social justice advocacy.

Two weeks later Dr Perkins replied: 'What a wonderfully pleasant surprise to receive your email. I well remember our conversations during your early days at MIT, and appreciate your kind words regarding our interactions. Please know, however, that it is thanks enough to know that your career has advanced so successfully.'

I was pleased that he remembered me and glad to have had the opportunity to thank him.

My last exam was just a few days before Christmas on 22 December.

When I got my results a few weeks later it showed that I had passed.

It had been a tumultuous year. As I lay in bed watching snowflakes float past my window, I was aware of what I had achieved over the preceding months. Here I was now with a place to stay, cash in the bank and the promise of future funding. I had passed my first semester despite the obstacles and my poor preparation and being among the least experienced in the class. I was not thriving yet, but I had survived.

As the momentous year, 1994, drew to a close and I had some time for reflection, my thoughts turned to South Africa, and the meaning of freedom. While South Africa may have achieved political freedom, following the election earlier in the year resulting in Nelson Mandela becoming our first black president, we certainly were a long way from economic freedom and a long way from the freedom of the pain of our past.

On 14 December, the *Thistle*, an MIT student publication, published my poem, 'Our Time to Taste' which was written in 1991 and was later published in my first book of poetry, *Heap of Stones*. The poem expressed an optimism and a call to South Africans to look to the future as freedom beckoned. The poem also spoke to me personally: it was my time to taste some fruit of what I had planted. It was my time to bring to life the meaning of the freedom for which I had been striving. The worst parts of my struggle seemed to be over. There was still much to do, but I could look with optimism and excitement to a life of fulfilment ahead.

Stuff dreams are made of ◎

In January 1995, I attended a Sloan leadership retreat in Cape Cod. It turned out to be one of my richest MBA experiences. I got some good feedback from group members: 'I am quite impressed with your keen sense of perception, and your ability to grasp the big picture.' 'I find your energy contagious.' 'You are willing to take risks which helps move our group forward.' There was feedback that pointed to areas needing work as well: 'I sometimes feel uncomfortable because you seem impatient.'

It is incredible how we reveal ourselves when we interact with others. I knew my impatience was an issue going into the retreat and yet it still revealed itself. On the flip side I was pleased that my energy, curiosity and appetite for risk shone through.

My appetite for risk and all things unconventional was a source of amusement for my classmate John Mlynek, with whom I had become good friends. John was a banker from California who had worked in New York and the Czech Republic, his country of birth. With all my anxiety of finding funding and a place to live behind me, I could enjoy life a bit and begin to make friends. He thought it was ridiculous that I was a poet writing for 'hippie magazines' and I teased him for being a square. I would drive him crazy by moving things around on his desk – he always had everything lined up straight and aligned. We studied together and spent many hours discussing the ladies in our lives. Unlike me, he ended up marrying Maria, the lady he couldn't stop talking about. One of my favourite photographs of my time at MIT is one of John and me standing in our suits with MIT's Great Dome in the background, an iconic picture of two young men who had overcome much to be there and who were now dreaming of greatness.

The highlight of my second semester was taking Finance Theory with Prof. Stewart Myers, the person who literally wrote the book on the study of Finance and whose textbook was used at all top business schools around the world. The course laid the foundation for my approach to strategy as an economic exercise rather than anything else. It created a desire to explore greater depth in the theory and application of finance and capital markets. A desire that I would fulfil a few years later at the London Business School.

I had by this stage settled on pursuing a summer job in strategy consulting and focused my job search in this area. The summer job, a ten-week period between the first and second year of the MBA, was a big deal because it gave students an opportunity to impress potential permanent employers. It was an intense and competitive exercise in which students would express their interest in companies and the companies would select who they wanted to interview. I had attended interviews with a number of consulting firms and was only invited back to a second round of interviews with one firm, Bain & Company. It was ironic that the less prestigious firms turned me down yet the preeminent Bain wanted to continue the interview process. Interviews at consulting firms consisted mainly of 'case interviews' in which the interviewer presented a business situation and problem that the interviewee had to solve. Given that this was the nature of the job as a consultant, firms found this on-the-spot problem-solving test to be the best way to assess potential consultants.

My diary entry on 6 February is to the point: 'Second round interviews at Bain & Co – a nightmare'

Yet, to my surprise, two days later I heard from Bain that I was invited to their final round of interviews. I wrote: 'The odds are still tough but I'm going to give it my best shot.'

Just the thought of possibly working at Bain made my head spin with excitement. The firm was one of the most prestigious strategy firms in the world. This would be no ordinary job, it would catapult my business career. Success in these interviews would literally change the course of my life. I stood on the precipice of a moment that would put me on a path to economic freedom and completion of my personal freedom struggle.

For the final round, I had three interviews starting at 2pm. I arrived at Bain's office at Two Copley Square at 1:58pm! I was rushed and nervous, my face pouring with sweat and my shirt soaked. I had cut myself shaving (in two places) and my mouth was dry as a stone. I was my own worst enemy sometimes.

All three interviews were with senior partners in the firm. The first went reasonably well; a casual chat with the legendary Chris Zook, author of numerous leading strategy books. However, the second interview was a disaster. I was stumped by the case interview and fumbled my way through. It felt like my Fluids exam back in second year at Wits. I sat there confused and sweating while my interviewer looked totally bored. I swear she looked at her watch a few times.

I broke the tension by asking if I could get a glass of water – probably the most cogent thing I said throughout the interview. We were both relieved when our time was up. The third and final interview went well – I enjoyed speaking to this partner and managed to handle the case interview quite well. I was thoroughly prepared and was able to demonstrate my knowledge of the firm and express my enthusiasm to join them. I left there unsure – would two out of three good performances be enough?

At 9:30pm that night I got a call from Phyllis Yale, the partner who conducted the disastrous interview. *Of course she would be the one to call*, I thought, *so that she could tell me just how dreadfully I had screwed up*. I gasped when she told me that Bain was excited to offer me a job in their Boston office. I was blown away. I stuttered some response and got off the phone before saying anything stupid that might cause her to retract the offer. 'Praise the Lord!' I shouted.

It had happened, it had actually happened. I was one of three students chosen from Sloan and among 25 MBA students chosen from the top business schools in America. I had made it. There could be no greater vindication – where backward white South African companies saw me as a nuisance, this top global firm had selected me from thousands of highly qualified applicants. I laughed and yelled with joy with tears streaming down my cheeks. I had made it!

My salary for the ten-week period was double what I had been earning at Boart for a full year! If I annualised my Bain salary, it would be *ten times* what I had been earning the year before, and I was only half-way though my programme. Bain sent a cheque as an advance and I immediately went out to buy my first laptop which I desperately needed for my studies.

For ten weeks of the summer of 1995 I worked at Bain as a summer associate and had the most incredible time. Bain advises the CEOs and decision-makers at the top companies worldwide from its 53 offices in 34 countries. The firm is renowned for its analytical and fact-based approach to solving business problems. It pioneered the now-common idea of focusing consulting services on results in client organisations rather than merely delivering reports. The firm only hired top academic achievers from a handful of universities including MIT, Harvard and Stanford. Bain placed enormous value on teamwork and so placed a premium on consultants' fit with the firm's distinctive collaborative working culture. It was the perfect place for me.

I worked with a team of brilliant people and travelled extensively across the country including visits to the states of New Hampshire, Maine, Georgia, Tennessee, Alabama and Florida while working on a project for a Fortune 100 consumer products client. The firm exuded professionalism. They had a way of making employees feel valued and provided ample support to ensure that you delivered your best. No wonder the firm has been consistently ranked as the best place to work. Bain also exuded opulence, everything was of the best. We stayed at the best hotels including the Ritz Carlton and Mount Washington Hotel (the location of the Bretton Woods monetary conference that took place after World War II, establishing the World Bank and the International Monetary Fund) and got to enjoy most of

Boston's finest restaurants. Consultant training took place in exotic locations like Monte Carlo and Puerto Rico.

Money was not a constraint. One incident stands out for me. It was a white-water rafting trip.

The upside of doing a great job during the summer was that some summer associates would be offered full-time consultant positions – I wanted to be sure to be among the group that got these offers so committed myself fully to my work. I attended work socials selectively. I went to Red Sox baseball games (how could I miss these) and the occasional party but I certainly was not going to waste two days on a white-water rafting trip.

As everyone else piled into the luxury buses for the trip to Maine, I continued working at my desk. I hadn't even packed for the trip. I soon discovered just how seriously Bain took its fun and teambuilding activities. A partner saw me working at my desk and raised the alarm. Pretty soon I had members of the recruiting department and partners surrounding my desk insisting that I go on the trip.

'But the buses have already left,' I protested, 'and I have not packed any clothes.' Surely this would ensure that I remained behind. But alas, not. A chauffeur was hired to drive me to the airport and make a stop en-route at a department store where I bought clothing and toiletries, all expensed to the firm. At the airport a plane waited to fly me to Maine and once there, a car drove the 90 minutes to where I would meet up with the group. All of this effort and expense just to ensure that I did not miss this adventure.

At the end of the summer I was presented with a letter which read, 'Congratulations! We are pleased to offer you a full-time position as a consultant in the Boston office of Bain & Company.' I had the coveted offer to join the firm full-time. It was such an overpowering feeling of accomplishment. Never in my wildest dreams did I imagine working for such a prestigious firm in the US, earning a six-figure salary in dollars. That feeling that I was fulfilling my destiny returned, along with a new stronger sense that my destiny would far exceed any of my expectations.

Added to the delight of the full-time offer, I was selected from among the summer associates to be profiled in Bain's recruiting and marketing materials. As a result, my face, along with the caption, 'People distinguish the way we work' and a brief biography, appeared on all of Bain's recruiting materials for the following two years, as well as on the firm's website and other business publications. Never before had I felt in such demand and so valued.

And to think where I was only a short while earlier ... at Boart, working in a portable hut being insulted with menial tasks. I had believed in myself. Something strong within me had urged me not to accept the constraints of racist corporate South Africa, and not to believe them when they tried to belittle me. I felt vindicated.

Back at university, Sloan offered a number of thematic concentrations or tracks. I chose the track in Strategic Management and Consulting, which prepared students for careers in strategy consulting, corporate strategy and front-line management. I relished the focus that the track brought. One benefit of the track was an exclusive seminar where leading strategy experts came to speak to our class and we got the chance to interact with them after their lecture.

One of these speakers was Donald Trump. Trump's lecture had nothing to do with strategy but was vaguely interesting in which he argued that business success is closely tied to personal success. After the lecture, I was among the few students selected to have a drink with the larger-than-life character. We stood in a semi-circle in a private lounge on campus making small talk when I noticed something peculiar about Mr Trump ... no it wasn't his hairstyle.

It was his shoes. His shoes were scuffed on the toes as if these were old well-worn shoes. Why would this billionaire be wearing old shoes? Or was he just a slob who had not polished them for weeks, but surely he had attendants to do this for him. His shoes were not as badly scuffed as mine and Nick's in that photo taken of us in our backyard in Lansdowne when we were kids, but they reminded me of that photo. I enjoyed noticing this little wrinkle in his otherwise picture-perfect presentation of himself.

Another significant celebrity encounter happened in Lowell, an hour outside of Boston, where I saw Bruce Springsteen live in concert for the first time. It felt like a pilgrimage for me to travel on my own to see the man whose music had meant so much to me as I was growing up. His songs gave voice to my teenage passions and he kept me company during my lonely years of private ambition.

It was Springsteen's acoustic tour so it was just him on stage with his guitar in an auditorium that seated fewer than three thousand people. The concert was incredible and I stood applauding long after he left the stage and long after others had left. Another of my wildest dreams had come true and one that I could tick off my 1994 dream list. That night I wrote in my diary:

> ... its not Springsteen himself that made this a significant occasion, it was the coming to life of a dream that did. For eleven years his music has been a companion, an inspiration and a joy. But also for eleven years I have dreamed of seeing him in concert. When this dream was first conceived it was as unrealistic as me being Superman, and this is what makes this occasion so magnificent – the occurrence of an event that seemed a distant fantasy. Fuel on the fire of dreams! Power to dreamers!

Another item on my list of dreams of April 1994 was to play social baseball. I tried joining the MIT baseball team but the team was only open to undergraduates. The closest I could come to fulfilling this ambition for now was to join the Sloan softball team. I was eventually selected to captain the team. It was not baseball but I was happy to be back on the diamond. I played short-stop and had a good season with the bat. Each team member had a nickname printed on the back of their playing shirt. My team chose mine as 'Prez', short for 'President'.

At Sloan my passion for the education of others and education institutions came to the fore. I volunteered with two NGOs, Junior Achievement and World Affairs Council, to visit classrooms to teach Economics and share my personal experiences of growing up in South

Africa. For both my strategy projects, I chose education institutions as my subjects rather than businesses as was the norm. In first year I worked on a strategy for the Harvard Graduate School of Education receiving the comment from my professor 'You picked a challenging and unusual topic for your paper, and I greatly enjoyed reading it.' In second year I chose Cambridgeport, an elementary school in Cambridge. These experiences planted early seeds for the more significant role that I would play in education later in my career.

The *Thistle* printed another of my articles in 1996 across two pages titled, 'From Apartheid Bus to New South Africa'. It was my reflection of living under apartheid. I included six poems. The article started with:

> All I offer readers are the written expressions of one who lived in confusion and pain under the dark veil of apartheid in South Africa. ... No one gives more testimony to the reality and harshness of apartheid than those who have strived to rise above the ankle-high ceiling, those who tried to act contrary to the script written by society and those who dared to dream.

These lines so concisely capture how I saw life under apartheid – 'dark veil' and 'ankle-high ceiling', and show that at 25 I was awake to the way that I was living; my decisions and steps were not blind actions but a conscious life of striving to 'rise above', 'to act contrary to the script' and a life that 'dared to dream'.

I graduated with an MBA on 7 June 1996, the first black South African to earn this prestigious degree.* American Vice-President Al Gore was the graduation speaker. When I applied to Sloan in 1994 it was ranked the No 2 business school in America, behind Stanford and ahead of Harvard. By the time I graduated it was ranked No 1.

I am still proud of having graduated with a master's degree from the

---

* There may have been one or two before me who completed master's degrees but not the MBA.

top university in the world and the top business school in America, as MIT and Sloan have been ranked recently. *Can dreams come true? Of course they can!* If I had succumbed to the manipulation at Boart to be grateful and become a 'mixer' I would not have the opportunities now open to me. If I had taken the easy route offered by EOC I would not have had the amazing experiences and opportunities that lay ahead. I had taken the tougher riskier path, the one littered with numerous boulders and dips and rises, even hills, and I have been blessed by this decision.

I always believed that I was greater than the obstacles placed before me. I had proven this at Wits and now at MIT. My experience strengthened my belief that despite the disadvantages into which anyone is born, we can rise above these circumstances and find success. I had witnessed many miracles along my journey – impossible and inexplicable events. But this should not be surprising. By dreaming big and working relentlessly to fulfil these dreams, I believe we invite miracles into our lives.

Head or heart? ◎

Three days after graduation I started as a strategy consultant at Bain & Company. Bain's Boston office, its head office, was located in two office towers within Copley Place, a precinct of Boston which included a high-end shopping mall and luxury hotel. The mall housed luxury brand boutiques Louis Vuitton, Gucci, Bally and Tiffany & Co and many more. It was an impressive working environment with great work and relaxing spaces, great library facilities and boardrooms that had wood panelling and leather chairs.

My first projects involved developing a market-entry strategy for a luxury retail company and a strategy for a public-utility company needing to deal with the advent of deregulation of the power industry in the US. The retail company project turned me into an expert on ladies' luxury brands which served me well at fancy cocktail parties. The expectation was to work long hours, rarely leaving the office before 8pm, and to travel extensively which I didn't mind.

I loved the work and the pay more than compensated for the demanding work environment. I received a massive sign-on bonus which allowed me immediately to settle my debts with Standard Bank back home, and the salary was more than I could spend. I had moved into an apartment in Central Square, an unfashionable part of Boston, so rent was cheap. I saved most of what I earned. Bain certainly made its consultants work for their money – in my first year I worked over the Christmas period and was back in the office again the day after New Year.

In addition to appearing in Bain's recruiting brochure, MIT Sloan included a picture of me in their recruiting brochure for two successive years along with a long quote by me extolling the Sloan MBA. I was clearly on a roll.

After a year in Bain's Boston office, I put in a request to be transferred to the London office. This caught my colleagues by surprise. I was performing well and had not given any indication of being unhappy, and I wasn't. I loved my job and I enjoyed living in Boston. The reason for my transfer request: a woman named Grace Love.

I had met Grace seven years earlier in Johannesburg and saw her regularly owing to numerous mutual friends. She was South African but was now living in England. I had sent her a letter while still at MIT. She replied warmly and so began a cordial exchange of letters and postcards. We then started talking on the phone and so a special friendship blossomed. During a university break I flew to London to visit her. We spent an exciting and fun-filled week together travelling around England. By the end of the week it was clear that we had fallen in love.

During the intervening period we had tried everything that we could to be together. I spent the third semester of my MBA at the London Business School (LBS) in England just so that we could be in the same city. I was accepted onto an International Exchange Program between MIT and LBS, which meant that I could take courses at LBS and get credit for them at MIT. We shared a tiny room in a house in Willesden Green, but I didn't care – it was blissful being with her. During my final semester at MIT, Grace came over to Boston for a few months but she could not get work authorisation and so returned to England. We wanted to be together. I was in Boston and she was in London. No small obstacle. Bain had an office in London, so I thought that transferring there was the best option.

My transfer request was declined and so, yet again, I was faced with a tough choice. Stay in Boston to further my career, for which I had worked so hard and sacrificed so much, or quit Bain, choose love and go to London.

Bain had been good to me and had given me the career break that

I'd been yearning for. In my head it was clear, I should stay. But my heart questioned this. What mattered more, career or love? Would I regret not following my heart? I could get another job I reasoned but this was the first time that I had felt this way about a woman. And I had always relied more on intuition than logic in making my decisions – my heart said I should go. I just could not bear the thought of resigning from Bain. And besides, what work would I do in London?

Around the same time, I received an email from the MIT Sloan careers office saying that they had been contacted by an executive search firm who described a role that was a great fit with my profile. The job had been advertised in *The Economist* but when a suitable candidate could not be found, the employer turned to an executive search firm. The one drawback, the career advisor pointed out in the email, was that the job was based in London. *London!* I saw this as a sign.

The employer was the world's largest mining and minerals company Rio Tinto that had its corporate headquarters in London. I agreed to attend an initial interview at the New York offices of the executive search firm, Korn/Ferry International, who were handling the process.

The whole interviewing experience was surreal. A luxury car fetched me at home, drove me to the airport for the flight to New York. There, a limousine was waiting and drove me to a skyscraper in Manhattan. I was greeted warmly and made to feel like a star baseball player. The role was explained to me – it was for an executive in the business evaluation department of Rio Tinto – the person would review potential corporate investments around the world and make recommendations to the board. The interview lasted for an hour and then I was driven back to the airport. When I arrived home, there was a message on my answering machine telling me that they wanted me to fly to London. I took a few days off work and flew to London – pretty much the same treatment – car from home to airport, business class flight to London where a luxury sedan drove me from Heathrow to a hotel in Piccadilly, a few streets away from Rio Tinto's offices in

St James Square. The next morning I had four interviews – two with members of the board of directors, one with the head of the business evaluation department, and the last interview was with someone who worked in the department. As I left the office to walk back to the hotel after a gruelling morning, the department head called me back into the office and right there in the foyer of the building, told me that they wanted me to join them. I was speechless.

It was an incredible job which would allow me to delve deeply into corporate decision-making and value creation, and do so across the globe. And of course, I would be in London with Grace.

Suddenly my head and heart were aligned. I returned to Boston to resign from Bain. I chose love over career, definitely a first, although my career would actually be getting a boost. Bain's reaction was to make a counter offer and agree to a six-month trial transfer to London, subsequent to which it could be permanent move if mutually agreeable. But this counter offer came too late as I had already accepted the Rio Tinto offer. So, in July 1997 I packed up the few belongings that I had, mainly clothes, books and CDs and left for London. I had already been to London ten times for a mix of business, study and personal visits but would never have imagined I'd relocate there.

I was sad to leave Boston and sad to leave Bain, which held a special place in my life's journey. Even in my departure they were wonderful, giving me an open offer to return. I was moving on but I had a strong feeling that I was not done with Bain.

In London I moved into apartment 472 in Chelsea Cloisters on Sloane Avenue, South Kensington. It was a furnished and serviced apartment, paid for by Rio Tinto, where I stayed for two months before moving to 13 Rankin Close in Colindale, North London. It was in my Chelsea Cloisters apartment that I sat glued to the television as news emerged of Princess Diana's death. I walked over to Buckingham Palace and experienced the great outpouring of grief by her followers. I was there to see, first-hand, the thousands upon thousands of bouquets of flowers left at the palace gates.

I started work in my new role at the beginning of August. The culture was formal and conservative. Men wore their jackets to lunch which was served in the building, and the executive floor had a butler in a long-tail tuxedo who served tea on a silver tray. Luxury and opulence dripped everywhere. Head office had a painting collection that was so valuable that it required regular valuations by art experts. I was showered with company perks including a company car – a brand new BMW 3-series. This would be the first of four brand new BMWs that I would drive over the years – two 3-series, a 5-series and a 6-series.

When I travelled for business, I'd be collected at home or the office in a chauffeur-driven 7-series BMW. My flights were always booked in business class or first class. I developed a taste for single-malt whisky, cognac and fine cigars, and would visit specialist shops to find these in England or on my travels. I had two humidors at home which were fully stocked with Cuban cigars and I only drank out of crystal glasses. I bought my suits, shirts and silk ties at the finest stores in London and New York. My cufflinks were all gold and some had precious stones. All of this at the age of 27. It was a life completely foreign to how I had been raised. I knew it wouldn't last forever so I enjoyed it while I could.

I loved my job. I was called into action whenever a CEO of one of Rio Tinto's businesses around the world proposed a major investment. This could be a major capital injection into an existing business, an acquisition, establishing a new business or a disposal. Most of these investments ran into hundreds of millions of dollars. To conduct my review of proposed investments, I would visit the location of the proposing business which created numerous opportunities for me to travel to Indonesia, Australia, the US, India and Zimbabwe on separate projects.

My work entailed gaining insight into the economies and politics of these countries to assess opportunities and risks, and translating strategic and operational insights into financial outputs, which required complex financial modelling. The work taught me to think about long-term economic value and long-term investments, since the nature of mining was that it required major investment upfront to develop a mine and all the infrastructure around it, and then earn returns on this investment over the 20–30-year life of the mine. I quickly realised that I would be able to excel at this job if I could couple my strong strategy training (gained at MIT and Bain) with high quality finance training, and so, in September 1997, I enrolled at LBS to study towards a master's degree in Finance, my second master's degree. Rio Tinto agreed to pay.

LBS has been ranked the top business school in Europe for many years and ranked in the top 10 globally. Its Finance degree is particularly strong, ranking number one globally. The degree explored finance theory in great depth and then expanded into areas of capital markets and corporate finance, the latter being my concentration. I shared lectures with top investment and banking professionals in London and even a few who travelled weekly from Amsterdam and Paris for lectures.

I attended lectures in the evening twice a week for two years while holding down an intense job that often had me travelling internationally. Many of my assignments were faxed to professors from the hotels in foreign countries or the business class lounges at airports. Even though work and studies were intense, I was thriving and having fun.

There was less fun on the personal front, however. Even before I had arrived in London, Grace moved to the north of England to study and then stayed there to work. So we never got to live in the same city. I was doing our relationship no favours with my frequent travel, long hours and my studies. Most weekends one of us would drive the four-hour trip between London and Wigan, where Grace lived. It was physically taxing, and it placed our relationship under enormous strain but despite the occasional argument and break-up, we managed to hold it together. After all, we had been struggling for years to be together and had every incentive to make our relationship work.

My time in London thankfully wasn't all work and no play. I managed to enjoy much of what London had to offer by way of entertainment, culture and sport. I got to see my favourite Bruce Springsteen again in concert, twice, this time with the E Street Band. I also attended live performances by Eric Clapton, Alanis Morissette, Rod Stewart, Mike Oldfield, Bananarama, Boy George, Belinda Carlisle and the Lighthouse Family. I saw a number of plays and attended a London Symphony Orchestra performance but I always preferred the ballet and Swan Lake at Royal Opera House was my highlight.

The best part of being in London, though, was the opportunity to see my favourite English football team, Arsenal. I have seen Arsenal play close to 20 times, including some memorable matches like the one against Barcelona at Wembley Stadium in the Champions League and my first match at Highbury on 23 September 1995 at which the great Dennis Bergkamp scored his first two goals for Arsenal in a match against Southampton. I have seen many of the Arsenal greats play including Thierry Henry and Tony Adams, and even attended the unveiling of the Dennis Bergkamp statue at the Emirates Stadium many years later in 2014.

Against this backdrop, my trips to some of the poorer parts of the world opened my eyes to the bleak realities of the squalid conditions in which millions lived. These trips contributed significantly to the changes in my outlook that were brewing. My visits to India, remote parts of Indonesia and Zimbabwe were disturbing. Not just because the poverty was so obvious but because suddenly I had become a 'have' in a world of 'have nots'. Such visits sparked for me important questions about the role I would play in society.

What was this strong sense of destiny that I felt? Was it guiding me along a path of luxury and indulgence, or along a different path?

Hints of a new path ◉

In early 1998 I was given responsibility for the review of a massively complex coal mining project in India. As negotiations with the Indian government progressed the financial evaluation of Rio Tinto's planned investment had to be revised. As part of this revision I spent a week in India and then a few days in Australia with some of our technical experts. It was an intense time with massive pressures. My work was guiding the negotiations in India while simultaneously providing inputs to board decisions in London. I was on the phone or in meetings constantly dealing with real-time changes and giving updates on the evaluation of the investment which ran into the hundreds of millions of US dollars.*

While travelling I called my mother as I regularly did. She told me that my father was very ill. He had been of poor health for all the years that I could remember, going as far back as the time he went into a coma when I was seven years old. I knew from his letters that his health had deteriorated and that he had stopped working. I started sending money to my parents to sustain the family and cover medical expenses. I knew my father wasn't getting the best medical treatment and so was keen to set this straight. This was one of the many things that angered me about structural inequality: that some people were confined to horrendously inadequate healthcare because of their economic status.

When I got back to London, I called my mother again. My father

---

* Even though Rio Tinto was headquartered in the UK we conducted all our international business in US dollars rather than British pounds.

still wasn't well and she suggested that perhaps I should visit since this would improve his spirits. I was keen to visit but with the review of the Indian project at a critical stage there was just no way that I could leave.

A few weeks later, towards the end of February, I found a gap to go to Cape Town for a few days. While travelling I outlined a plan to deal with my father's healthcare which included hiring a private nurse and prepaying for visits to a private hospital. I hadn't seen my family for seven months, so I was looking forward to the visit. As I walked towards them at Cape Town airport my mother rushed forward and threw her arms around me. She started crying and I tried comforting her telling her that I was home and that I would take care of everything. And then my mother said, 'Daddy is dead. Your father died.'

My legs buckled and I fell to the floor. I have vague recollections of people holding me up and trying to pacify me as I screamed and cried. *How did this happen? How could my father be dead?* My mother hugged me tightly and we both just stood there at the airport crying.

My father had died while I was on my way home.

My mother told me how excited he was that I was coming home and kept asking when I would arrive. Through the night before he fell asleep he asked if I had arrived yet. 'I kept telling him you were on your way,' my mother told me between her cries.

I was destroyed. This was not just a new boulder in my path but a boulder rammed into my chest. The man who had supported me, kept encouraging me to get an education, to rise above what life had thrown at me, had died. And he had died waiting for me. I looked at my life, at the struggles, at how hard I was working to be a success and it came down to this moment. My relationship with family. I just couldn't reconcile the two, because I felt selfish. While I was away doing miraculous things, furthering my career, my father was asking for me. He had asked for me and at the time of his greatest need, and I was not there. I felt sick and was disgusted with myself. I felt a pain that I'd never felt before. I just cried.

The next few days passed in a haze. Visits to the undertakers, funeral arrangements, the funeral and a steady stream of people in and out of our house. I don't remember anything about the funeral other than my mother leaning over my father's coffin crying. I refused to see anyone. Something inside me had broken.

My anger returned – at God, at my mother for not telling me how urgent the situation was, at hospitals and doctors who treated my father with disrespect because he was poor. For example, I was told how hospital staff left my father on a stretcher outside the hospital, in the afternoon sun, while waiting for an ambulance to take him home. But most of all I was angry at myself. And that is the worst kind of anger.

My father was only 53 years old. His health had deteriorated rapidly while I was overseas. My family recounted the sacrifices they had made to care for him. My sister, Amanda moved back into my parents' home to help my mother around the clock. My brothers and our neighbours had been involved while I lived my life far away. The thought of this destroyed me.

My father and I had a tumultuous relationship while I was growing up. Even as he had a profoundly positive impact on me with regard to education, we argued often, about politics, religion, most topics. I often accused him of scarring his children psychologically. My father was angry and frustrated by the constraints and indignity that he suffered all his life as a coloured man. While he celebrated my success, I believe that my achievements sometimes reminded him of what he was denied by apartheid. This led to occasional feelings of resentment. He sometimes responded to my new lifestyle as though it indicated a rejection of my family and my roots. One year at Wits I called home to let my family know that I would spend Christmas with friends in Johannesburg and so would not be home. My father responded sharply: 'So you're choosing your white friends over us, are we not good enough for you anymore?' This cut me deeply. At my Wits graduation celebration he sulked because I thanked others before him, souring the event. At my MIT graduation, he and my mother left the ceremony before I was called on stage to receive my degree. I spent hours after the ceremony searching for them which robbed me of the opportunity to celebrate with my classmates and to have photographs taken.

However, we established a good written relationship, writing over 100 letters, postcards and cards each during the ensuing ten years since I left home. He often addressed me in his letters as 'Kid' and signed off with 'lots of love'. I may not have said it to him but my father was the rock upon which my success was built.

In my last birthday card from my father, in June 1997 while I was home, he wrote: 'Today we want you only to enjoy love and happiness. Let us spoil you – when will we enjoy another birthday together?' – and of course, the answer was that we would never enjoy another birthday together.

In our final exchange of letters my father began expressing himself more openly. 'I must express my pride in your success,' he wrote, 'I thank the Lord that I played a minute part in your quest for greatness' and 'enjoy the fruits of your labour – you deserve every moment of it.'

In retrospect I can see that he knew he was dying. His last few letters were his way of saying goodbye and asking that I care for the family. I was just too blind to see this at the time: '... ensure that Roscoe gets his chance at educating himself ... I don't know how long my health holds – don't ever let your mother ever want of anything – take care of her – these tears that are now flowing from my eyes are tears of humiliation, I have stripped myself of my own dignity having to admit that I have failed.'

It is so blatantly clear now what he was saying but when you've got financial models to create and board papers to write, I guess you don't see this. I can't imagine the pain he felt writing this. I can't imagine any father writing this to a child. He wrote that he may not be able to work again and apologised for failing the family. I replied: 'I really don't think you've failed the family and I seriously doubt whether anyone feels you have. ... If indeed it is true that you'll be unable to work again, then so be it. I can only guess at how difficult this must be for you to deal with and I can understand why it would make you feel like you've let us down.'

My father was known to be melodramatic at times so I didn't pay too much attention to what he wrote but could tell that he was troubled so tried to ease his worry. I continued: 'You should have absolutely no concern about Mum or Roscoe should your health deteriorate. I know this is a difficult thought for you and a difficult request to have made, but you can be 100% assured that they will be wanting of nothing. I love Mum and Roscoe dearly and would never allow (as far as I am able) them to be wanting – this goes for my whole family. I hope that eases your worry Dad.' To this day I continue to honour this promise to my father.

In October, just four months before he passed away, he again focused on the family's finances and made statements indicating that he knew he was approaching the end of his life. Perhaps cognitive dissonance made me not see the obvious. 'I guess I don't have that much time left. At least there will be life insurance money when I go … Athol I want to take this opportunity to sincerely thank you from the bottom of my heart for sending money for your mother, this is comforting knowing at least she will never want of anything … your assurance is gratifying that she will not suffer.'

He wrote about 'now in the end' and then wrote a startling statement: 'I would like to offer you my unreserved apology for messing up your early years – please forgive me.'

It is heart-breaking reading these letters now. I have always been adamant that I would not live with regrets. I always tried to live my life to the full, walking my path of opportunity boldly. But I wish I had taken my father's letters more seriously and engaged with him on what he wrote. Instead I rambled on about my work and travels, believing that these would provide light relief from his woes.

'In your work, in your life, everything is God's plan for you … live in his light and people will see God in your actions. Athol my hands are now aching so I am going to sign off. It has been a great privilege having you as a son.'

These are the last words that my father wrote to me.

I never fully recovered from losing my father. I don't think we're ever the same after losing a loved one. I was tormented by the fact that had I not waited the few weeks to go home I would have had time with my father before he died. An awful burden to carry.

For the first few months back at work I just went through the motions. My performance dipped and my manager was not happy. But I wasn't happy there either.

A rethink of my life, and my struggle to reconcile my work and my conscience had begun. While I enjoyed the intellectual elements of my job, moral concerns began to surface. Mining is a business with massive inherent risks to people and the environment, and I began reading about allegations that my employer was not doing enough to mitigate these risks. Some alleged that we were explicitly and consciously causing harm. It came as a shock to wake up to the realisation that even as I was struggling against personal injustices I may have been complicit in injustices committed against others. Do I not benefit from injustice if I earn a salary at a company that generates its income partly by depriving people somewhere on earth of their human rights? I shuddered at the thought.

A turning point was a project I had to review in Zimbabwe. A coal-mining development was proposed in a rural area of north-west Zimbabwe and Rio Tinto had been granted the mining license. Zimbabwe desperately needed to generate additional electricity, so this coal mine and associated power station were seen as a strategic investment for the country.

During my visit to Zimbabwe to review the project proposal I quickly learned that the local people around the proposed mining site were not happy with the plans. They valued their land which contained ancient burial grounds and saw little value in the proposed infrastructure and services that were promised as compensation. I didn't like what I heard and read. This experience moved me so much that weeks later while sitting in a pub in Dublin, Ireland, I poured out a long, rambling text which include the lines:

Do they know ... that the corruption of their own is plotting their demise; that mouths of the great coloniser salivates with their blood, that the claws of the criminal invader are being sharpened, all in the name of economic progress, all in the name of civilisation? But economic progress for who? Progress towards which civilisation? ... Do school buildings and clinics and roads mean civilisation? By giving a man a job and a telephone and a TV, have you made him civilised? 'No!' I scream. He *is* civilised, he *has* his civilisation. Does he not live with a social order? Do his people not have a moral code, a pattern of life of their own? What evil consumes the ignorant [or greedy] to presuppose that the introduction of these soul destroyers makes a man civilised? What violence! What utter bloody violence.

I came to learn that the people who suffer the cost of 'development' are often not the ones who benefit from it – all the electricity produced in this area would be transmitted to the cities and nothing in this area would be electrified.

My report on the coal project expressed support for the investment but also expressed concerns about the impact on the indigenous people. Someone deleted my concerns from the report that was submitted to the board. When I raised hell about the fact that my report was tampered with I was told that my comments were 'inappropriate' and 'unprofessional'.

I began questioning executives about allegations of wrongdoing on the company's part and in every investment I reviewed I began raising issues of indigenous people's rights. Colleagues urged me to practice restraint. Unsurprisingly my relationships at work began souring. Again I was being 'not a mixer'.

Towards the middle of 1999 I was contacted by the company's attorneys informing me of a problem with my UK work permit. I understood what they were telling me indirectly. I could not work in this place any longer, and so after two years at the company I resigned. I had enjoyed the professional aspects of the job and the money, perks and status were fantastic, but something deep inside me told me that this was not where I should be. I wasn't sure what my next move would be, but I knew I was doing the right thing by leaving.

What were my options, what work would I do? I recalled Bain's offer that I could return at any time. I contacted the Boston office and soon I had an offer to return – 'On behalf of the Partner group, I am delighted to be able to offer you the opportunity to rejoin Bain', my offer letter read. I was excited to be returning to strategy consulting, to Bain and to Boston. Grace got an offer to transfer to the US with her company. We vowed to live together this time.

On a trip to the Netherlands, sitting among millions of tulips in Leiden, I asked Grace to marry me. Her first words were, 'It's about time.' And so we were engaged to be married.

Grace moved to the US while I waited for my work authorisation for the US to be processed. While I waited, I spent a few months working in Bain's London office doing some fascinating work explicating Bain's approach to corporate strategy. The company rented a serviced apartment for me in Marylebone on Chiltern Street – the 18th place that I called home, excluding of course the couches in the student centre at MIT. I was excited to be back at Bain and felt like I was coming home. In January 2000 I was finally able to join Grace in the US.

I had enjoyed my time in the UK; it was enriching in many ways. I recalled with fondness the visit I got from my mother and then later from Nick and his girlfriend Junita. Nick, Junita and I travelled to Paris, where Nick proposed to Junita atop the Eiffel Tower. I was tasked with taking a photo of the moment but couldn't get the camera to work; good thing I didn't do this for a living. We also had a marvellous time travelling to Rome and Venice, my British Airways frequent flyer miles coming to good use. Nick and I went to Highbury to see Arsenal play against Newcastle – an unbelievably special experience since we had been Arsenal fans since youth, and now there we sat, in that great stadium watching our favourite team play, albeit from seats in the last row virtually in the roof. Again I got to see Dennis Bergkamp score. We drove across England and of course I insisted that we visit Oxford.

I loved the city and the magnificence of the university buildings. I guess the dreamy spires were appropriate for those like me, who looked upon them with dreams in their eyes. I had often spoken and written about my dream of studying at Oxford so being there was something special.

Only once we arrived in Oxford did I realise that I had forgotten to book accommodation. After driving around for hours unsuccessfully looking for a room at a hotel or bed and breakfast, the three of us ended up sleeping in my car which was parked in the carpark of a petrol station. How we avoided being questioned on suspicion of being criminals on the run I still do not know. Imagine, three brown-skinned foreigners sleeping in a new BMW parked in a carpark. A more significant, and less suspicious, event also took place while we were in Oxford. Nick had slipped into a shop and bought me an Oxford University jacket as motivation to pursue my dream of studying there. This jacket would come to have powerful symbolic meaning for many years. As we stood along Broad Street in Oxford I made a vow that I would only wear the jacket once I was a student at Oxford. And I was determined that I would indeed wear that jacket one day.

Back to America, home? ◎

When I arrived in the US in January 2000, Grace and I rented an apartment on Winn Street in Woburn, a town 18km northwest of Boston. After a short while we settled in the quiet town of Winchester, in a two bedroom, semi-detached house at 271 Cross Street. We both bought small used cars, I drove a black Dodge Neon which was advertised on TV as being ideal for college students, and Grace bought a green Mazda MX3. This was a huge regression from the new BMW that I drove in London. I would sometimes drive to the office but this could take over an hour and parking in Boston was expensive, so only did this on the odd occasion. Most days I drove to a T-station (Boston's underground train system) on the perimeter of the city and took the T to the office.

At work I was flung straight back into the thick of things and I loved it. I worked on the most unusual project – advising a client that had won a US government tender to clean up the site where the nuclear waste from Project Manhattan was buried – this was the project name for the manufacture of the atom bombs that were dropped on Hiroshima and Nagasaki during the Second World War. How does one price a contract to do something that had never been done before? Of course 'clean up' didn't mean getting a bunch of guys with mops and rags, the nuclear waste needed highly specialised processing to make it inert.

This was one of the projects that Bain's marketing team were referring to when they again chose to use me in their campaigns. This time the tag line was 'hedge your bets' and text detailing some of the work that I had done. Beneath a picture of my face the advert read:

> Athol Williams, consultant at Bain. Helped three multi-billion dollar clients evaluate 'bet-the-company' investments. Hedged the bets by analysing the complex sets of risks involved and collaborating on plans to mitigate them. The companies are now actively pursuing these big ticket investments ...

It was great seeing my picture in the business media and at universities again. Work was high speed and super intense. Most days I was on the road travelling to Washington DC for the nuclear clean-up project, travelling to Toronto, Dayton or Chicago for a paper company, to San Francisco and Portland for a technology company or to New York City for an education publisher. Our office was abuzz with activity. These were the days of the dot com boom and we were helping new and established companies develop strategies to benefit from the boom which included many new stock market listings. Bain was renowned for taking equity stakes in client businesses in lieu of fees and senior consultants like myself were awarded a portfolio of non-tradable shares in Bain's equity positions.

Then, in March 2000, the dot com bubble burst. I had personally invested heavily in the equity markets with a focus on technology stocks. I lived a frugal life, driving a cheap car and living quite modestly so that I could save most of my income to provide a capital base for my future plans. In one day, the value of my entire portfolio fell 30%. From peak to the bottom of the crash, the NASDAQ dropped by 78%. My Bain equity portfolio was written down to zero.

The wealth that I had accumulated was mostly wiped out. I was devastated. After four years of working and saving, I now had nothing to show for it. I swore then that if ever I had money again I would enjoy it and do something meaningful with it rather than blindly invest for some unknown future which may never come.

In early 2001 work got even more intense. I wouldn't have thought this was possible. I was moved to a specialist division within Bain, the Private Equity Group. This group advised many of the world's largest private equity firms on their buyout transactions, whether evaluating potential acquisition targets, conducting valuations or developing post-acquisition strategies.

These projects were much shorter, only a few weeks versus the usual consulting engagement of a few months. This meant that we had to have a clear plan from day one and execute it flawlessly. The work was brutal. I led teams to develop strategies for buyouts of a clothing manufacturer, micro-processing business, a chain of eye surgery outlets, a scale manufacturer, a company that owned a vast network of cell phone towers and a diverse range of other businesses. I helped clients review their portfolios and internally I was involved in developing proposals for new projects.

I hardly slept. On one occasion I was so exhausted I fell asleep at my desk ... with my eyes open. Thankfully a colleague saw me and helped me find a place to lie down. I was working seven days straight including holidays. When you're advising a client on a live transaction you must be available 24/7. Even when I was home I was on my laptop or on the phone to my team, my partner or the client.

I eventually started spending most of my time in our New York office which had just opened. Most of our private equity clients were based in New York so it made sense for me to be there. I flew into New York on Monday mornings and left Friday evenings, living in a hotel all week. Our office was right on Times Square, which was exciting, but the throngs of people and chaos of cabs and other cars in the streets made the walk to work rather intense. It was fast-paced and high intensity. This suited me, I loved the high stakes and the drive to find solutions quickly. I was learning so much about strategy and value creation, and was happy to be doing work that I enjoyed and as it turned out, I was good at it. After six months I was promoted.

But it wasn't all good news. My success at work came at the expense of my relationship with Grace. Other than serving on the board of the MIT Club of Boston I did little else but work. Grace and I didn't see much of each other and when we did I was distracted or just too tired to engage. She rightly demanded attention but this only made me withdraw more. We stopped talking about wedding plans. Eventually we stopped talking altogether.

It was clear that our relationship was in serious trouble. We had both made many sacrifices over six years in our efforts to be together but it was clear now, to me at least, that it was over. Grace refused to give up and wanted us to seek counselling. I now admire her commitment to our relationship but then I didn't see the point in trying. It was my second broken engagement. A few years earlier I had chosen love over my career by moving to London, but in the long run, I had again chosen my career over my relationship and hurt someone in the process. My career success came at a high price.

As I celebrated my 31st birthday in June I needed to make a big decision. I needed to decide if I was going to settle in the US, making it home, or if I was going to return to South Africa. Going to America was important to realise my freedom. Looking ahead, the country offered me great career prospects and I would be able to live a prosperous life there. But I felt a strong pull towards South Africa. It was where I belonged. South Africa had undergone profound changes after the fall of apartheid and I wanted to contribute to its growth and development. I had always wanted my life to have meaning and that meaning would come from being near my family and being where I could have the greatest positive impact. It was clear, after being away for seven years it was time to return to South Africa. I wasn't quite ready yet for public service but I knew that being home would take me a step closer.

I contacted a few recruitment firms and soon I had an interview for the role of head of strategy for South Africa's largest life insurer, Old Mutual. A few days before flying over to Cape Town for the interviews I attended a mind-blowing concert at Madison Square Garden in New York. I had only been to the Garden once before to see Madonna in concert. This was a celebration of Michael Jackson's

30th anniversary as a solo artist. All evening the who's who of the music and movie world made appearances on stage – Lionel Richie, Whitney Houston, Destiny's Child, Shaggy, Britney Spears, Lil Kim, Samuel L. Jackson, Chris Tucker, Elizabeth Taylor, Marlon Brando, on and on. Just amazing! Each singer performed a Michael Jackson song as a tribute to him. And then it was his turn. He performed all his hits and I joined everyone else losing their mind when he performed 'Billy Jean', including the famous hat and glove routine and the moonwalk. The highlight was seeing Michael reunited with his brothers on stage to form the Jackson 5 for the first time in many years. A breath-taking night.

The following day I had the thrill of attending the women's final of the USA Open at Flushing Meadow to see Venus vs. Serena Williams. I didn't really care who won, it was just fantastic to be there and to see these two gladiators battle it out. The few days were the most fun I'd had in New York City for a long time, perhaps only topped by seeing the Boston Red Sox play the New York Yankees at Yankee stadium.

I returned to Boston and shortly after 6am the next morning I took off onboard Delta Airlines flight DL631 from Boston's Logan airport for the two hour and fifty-minute flight to Atlanta on my way to Cape Town for my job interviews. While we were in flight a plane hit the North Tower of the Twin Towers in New York.

It was September 11, 2001.

American Airlines Flight 11 took off at 7:59am from Boston Logan Airport, the same airport where I had boarded, heading for Los Angeles. At 8:46am, less than half an hour before my plane was to land in Atlanta, this plane struck the North Tower.

When I landed in Atlanta I had no idea that anything had happened in New York, the city I had visited just the day before. But as I walked through the airport I could sense that something horrific had happened. People were rushing back and forth; crowds were forming around televisions. People looked to be in a state of shock. I rushed to the nearest television and there I saw the tower with smoke bellowing out of it. The text scrolling across the screen indicated that a plane had hit the building.

At first I thought it was a light aircraft that got its flight path wrong. But the commentary and the chatter around the television indicated that it was a commercial passenger plane. While we stood there we saw live footage of the second plane hit the South Tower and eventually both towers collapse. A woman grabbed my arm crying. People embraced in tears. Others, like me, just stood, bewildered, stunned. There was a heavy gloom in the air.

Announcements were made for us to board our flight to Cape Town. Still in shock we followed all the usual boarding procedures – going through security, standing in line waiting to board and showing our boarding passes to the attendant as we got onto the plane. Before many of us could take our seats there was another announcement. We were told to disembark. When I got back to the main terminal building it was in a state of chaos. Announcements were made that all flights across the US had been grounded.

After a brief session of self-pity and a micro hissy-fit directed at the airline staff, I clicked into 'do mode'. I hopped in a cab and found a hotel where I was to stay for the night. I would end up being there for three nights. Only once I was settled in the hotel room did I turn on my cell phone. I found voicemail messages from anxious and crying friends and family wanting to know if I was okay; they knew that I was flying from Boston that morning and upon hearing that the planes that hit the towers had left from Boston, were understandably upset. I called them all to let them know that I was okay.

It was an anxious, uncertain three days. I sat watching the news all day, reading the newspapers and calling the airline to see when we would fly again. Each day I was told that they didn't know. When we eventually did take off again, fighter jets flew alongside our plane, my first thought was, 'I hope these are friendly jets.'

I still have my boarding pass from that flight and the *Atlanta Journal* newspaper which was printed the next day. Without being too dramatic, I realised that I was on the close outskirts of this tragedy, the fact that I was in New York the day before the attacks, how both planes left from the same airport where I boarded my flight, so it could easily have been my plane that was hijacked. I was a little freaked out by the thought that the hijackers walked around the same airport where I had just been earlier that morning. I was glad to be safe.

I was offered the Old Mutual job and so in November 2001 I said farewell to my dear Grace, to Bain (again) and to the US. The time in the US had been instrumental to my rapid growth and contributed to the freedom that I had dreamed of and achieved. But now it was time to return home and I would start this new adventure where I grew up – in Mitchells Plain.

Path of opportunity ⊚

'Coming home' was the headline of article in the *Plainsman*, the Mitchells Plain community newspaper. The article covered the 25th-year celebrations of my old high school Westridge High and featured 12 former students who had been deemed to have excelled in our respective fields. In our ranks we had national sportspersons, journalists, an attorney, a chartered accountant and myself. It was a coming home for the 12 of us, to our old high school, but for me being in Mitchells Plain was a deeper coming home because I briefly called it home again. It was 2002; I had left Mitchells Plain 14 years earlier, and now I was back.

A few years earlier the *Cape Argus* ran a story with the headline, 'Athol's come a long way from Westridge High'. 'Top US investment consultant has Cape dream' read the article's subtitle; after a recap of my career since leaving high school it describes my dream of returning home one day to start an advisory business. Now here I was, home.

I had travelled the world, visiting many of the most exotic places on earth. I had lived and worked in some of the great capitals of the world. And now I returned to the very house in Mitchells Plain where I grew up. It was there that my revolutionary plan had been developed and executed, that plan to liberate myself through education. It was there that I was faced with the choice of the bomb or the pen, and I had chosen the pen.

There was an ironic peace to being home; ironic because it was the chaos of life in Mitchells Plain that made me so desperate to leave all those years ago. I wanted my new life in South Africa to be symbolic, and starting where I grew up offered that. Fourteen years after leaving,

I now slept in the same bed in the same room where I had grown up.

Additionally, being home gave me a chance to reconnect with my mother and to develop a relationship with Roscoe my youngest brother, who was only six years old when I left home. It gave me time to reconnect with Amanda, her son Aaron who I had hardly seen, and of course it gave me the opportunity to spend time with my best friend and brother, Nick.

The great thing about being near the people you care for is that you can just do simple things, pop in for a cup of coffee or do the mundane like go with them to the mall, but still feel that you are connecting. It was a respite to spend quality time with my family in contrast to what I had been doing for the last 14 years; trying to cram in time with them when I came to South Africa for frenzied week-long breaks. Now we could watch Arsenal games on television, throw baseball on a field, or go for an unhurried drink or a walk.

I arrived home with two shifts in attitude, both of which would be later overturned. Firstly, after the heartache of the relationship break-up with Grace, I vowed never to enter into a serious romantic relationship again. So I would meet women and have a good time but make it clear that it would never develop into anything permanent. And after being burned by the stock market crash that wiped out most of my savings, I promised myself that I would enjoy some of the fruits of my labour. The first thing I did was to buy my dream car.

In 1990, BMW released the majestic 8-series. The top of the range was the 850i, a 2-door monster which had a 5-litre, V12 engine, one of the largest of any car. It was the most beautiful car that I had ever seen and as far back as my days as a student at Wits, I kept a scale model of the car on my desk. As with my other dreams, I kept my sights on my dream car. I had already driven a 3-series in London but this was the ultimate BMW.

Fortunately, it was a short search as I found a black model for sale in impeccable condition. Without hesitation I bought the car and ordered personalised license plates which read BULL, a return to my nickname. I had always loved driving and now driving was an even greater pleasure. The car had all the luxuries and gadgets that one could want, and had astonishing performance – it was not uncommon for me to have to slow down while driving on the highway because I would reach speeds of close to 200km/h without knowing.

There were no boulders in sight. I had a sense of freedom driving on the open road and a sense of achievement, being able to drive the car of my dreams. Heads turned wherever I drove and wherever I parked, without fail, a crowd would gather around the car. But the absurdity of the car wasn't lost on me. I was living in the low-income township of Mitchells Plain driving a car that was worth more than my mother's house. The car was so large it could barely fit onto the front of her property.

I have had a few moments of epiphany over the years. One such moment happened while driving my treasured BMW 850i. I was leaving Mitchells Plain, driving along Vanguard Drive and stopped at a traffic light. On my left was a vast area of shacks. These tiny makeshift homes were pieced together from scraps of metal, wood and plastic in which families lived. In some areas the government had installed temporary toilets that had to be shared by people living in these areas. People lived without running water, without electricity, in such states of vulnerability and need, and yet there I was sitting comfortably in my luxury BMW.

I felt the hypocrite. *How could I live a life of luxury while people around me languished in poverty?* I reminded myself that I deserved my good life, after all, I had worked for it and had struggled and sacrificed so much to achieve what I had. But I also cared deeply for other people. There was no way that I could live a life of excess when others lived with deprivation.

This was not a theoretical exercise; I knew deep down that my lifestyle would have to change. I resisted and denied this knowledge for a long time but a new flame was lit within me that day, a flame that would grow larger and more powerful with time. A flame that shed light on a new type of boulder that lay in my path and that needed pushing over a hill – the boulder of others' suffering and lack of freedom.

My Old Mutual job was a disaster from the start. The cultural mismatch was stark. I had just been working at Bain with high-energy and dynamic private equity investment firms in New York, the complete opposite to my new environment, a 160-year-old life insurer that had only just converted from a member-owned mutual society to a corporation. I managed to irritate everyone with my drive to action and impatience for change.

It was obvious to me that this was not going to work. I quit after three months. My resignation caused a massive stir given my seniority and the high profile of my appointment. I agreed to stay but my stay was temporary; after a year I resigned again.

I recalled the deal that I had made with Ken Maxwell in 1994 that I would discuss opportunities to work with JCI when I returned from the US, in exchange for them having paid for my plane ticket to Boston. However, Ken had moved on from JCI which was in turmoil – Brett Kebble and his father, Roger, who took over the company, would both later commit suicide. Ken was pleased that I sought to honour our agreement but he had nothing to offer me.

I was keen to either return to strategy consulting or expand on my private equity investment experience. I was wary of joining a large corporation given my Old Mutual experience but then an interesting opportunity emerged at Shanduka – named Millennium Consolidated Investments at the time – the investment company founded by legendary trade unionist and lead ANC negotiator in the 1990s, Cyril Ramaphosa, who would later become South Africa's Deputy President. He was looking to launch a private equity business within his broader organisation and my background was a perfect match.

South Africa had introduced legislation to facilitate economic transformation called Black Economic Empowerment (BEE). Companies were required to introduce black shareholders in order to be considered 'transformed' and the key catalyst would be government's intention to give preference to transformed businesses when issuing commercial contracts. This created a massive pipeline of transactions that needed to be done for white-owned companies to sell equity stakes to black investors.

Ramaphosa's business was perfectly positioned to be a significant beneficiary of the deal flow given his stature as a leading ANC figure. After a series of interviews with Ramaphosa and his colleagues, I had an offer to join them. My offer included a direct share in the value created by the firm which all but guaranteed that I would earn several tens of millions.

But I had some major doubts. I didn't like the premise of the business, that we would buy equity stakes at a discount because we were black. When I asked how we would add value to the companies in our portfolio, the answer was that by virtue of us being black we would be adding value. And they were right – if companies needed black shareholders to get lucrative government contracts or to avoid sanctions for not being transformed, then having us as shareholders and on their boards we would be adding value by avoiding value destruction. Moreover, there was a claim that we would open doors to additional business opportunities but this was never going to be the main source of value. BEE was basically a license-to-operate and a value-preservation play for white-owned companies who would transfer some of this value to black shareholders.

I fully supported the need for economic transformation and fully supported the idea that, owing to blacks suffering decades of discrimination, we needed a programme of preferential opportunity to begin to rectify the economic imbalance. The mechanism through which I wanted to see this was to engineer preferential opportunities for blacks to *create* wealth rather than have wealth transferred from white hands to black hands, as the BEE legislation largely directed.[*] This system led to cronyism and corruption that only enriched an elite few and not the millions of South Africans who needed to improve their economic situations.

---

[*] The legislation has changed substantially since 2002.

The proposed source of my value-add was just not the kind of value I wanted to add. I had worked hard to develop the skill to be able to support a company's management team to grow their business – this is how I wanted to add value, not just by the colour of my skin.

We were still in discussions about whether I would join when I was invited to a dinner at a prominent restaurant in Rosebank, Johannesburg. It turned out to be a dinner where Ramaphosa was to introduce new members of his leadership team to shareholders and board members. The only problem of course was that I had not yet accepted their offer. When I declined the job offer a few days later the folks at Shanduka were livid. I managed to anger the future Deputy President. No surprise I guess, I'd been rubbing people up the wrong way all my life.

I decided not to pursue any further corporate opportunities, choosing instead to start my own strategy advisory business. But I had no capital, no business contacts because I had been out of the country for all of my business career and I had no partners with whom to execute any plan. Would any CEO really hire a 32-year-old strategy advisor to help them with their toughest business decisions? With my experience and approach that uniquely combined strategy and finance, I believed that I could help companies grow and create value as I had done with Bain in the US. But would executives see this? Would they choose to work with me rather than one of the established international or local consulting firms?

It was the end of 2002 and just as I had done in 1994, I compiled a new dream list:
1. Study at Oxford
2. Publish a book of my poetry
3. Win a prize for poetry
4. Inspire one person to follow their dreams
5. Fund university scholarships
6. Have a fulfilling marriage
7. Drive a Lamborghini

8. Travel to Russia and China
9. Fit into a size 32 pair of trousers
10. Plant a tree and nurture it to maturity
11. Meet Bruce Springsteen

Oxford appears to have been a specific goal. Publishing poetry is repeated from the 1994 list. It is interesting that I listed marriage given my vehement anti-relationship stance at the time, but I guess this was a long-term list of dreams. I didn't just want to simply *see* Springsteen in concert which I had already done three times by now (and would eventually see him five times), I wanted to *meet* him. The most distant of these dreams was fitting into size 32 trousers ... I would need to lose significant inches to make this happen! I still had a taste for the exotic and adventurous as indicated by my travel destinations and car choices. The Lamborghini had extra meaning because its insignia is a bull.

What was also interesting about the list was that starting a business did not appear in it. In fact, it was silent on any career ambitions, instead it talked about studying, writing, inspiring, nurturing a tree, travelling, relationship and supporting education for others. This was consistent with a note that I wrote in October 2002 titled: 'My Life, the Remaining Days.' It set out what was important to me and how I would live my life. It concluded:

> I will spend my remaining days giving. And fulfilling my dreams. In the end, my legacy will be uncertain, but I will have no regrets, for my days will be filled with the elements that matter most – the elements of my happiness, the elements of my fulfilment and greatness my way.

Again the call to walk a different path grew louder. What did I mean by 'giving'? It was a note that was short on specifics but long on intention. I resolved that I would not follow the path of least resistance but that I would follow the path of least regret. I would follow the path of greatest meaning. I would trust my intuition and pursue greatness my way. It was a sign of things to come but for now I needed to walk what looked like the next stage of my path of opportunity … taking the leap to start a strategy consulting business.

The *path of opportunity* approach to life became central to my outlook. It says we cannot know exactly where success lies but we can know its general direction. Knowing the general direction, you can then set out on the path with confidence. It is an uncertain path, with bends and dips and rises, and boulders, but at least you will know that you are heading in the right direction and most of all, you are taking action.

Such action gives your life more meaning than just standing still. If you want to be a movie star then perhaps your path of opportunity should lead you to Hollywood. This means that even if you have to work in a grocery store in Hollywood, at least you will know that you are in the right place, moving in the right direction. If you want to succeed in business, going to business school could be your path of opportunity.

If opportunity is in the lab, sitting in your office won't help. If opportunity requires calm and peace, then running around being busy won't help. Put yourself in the way of opportunity. Find the right people, the right organisation, the right place. Go there. Go where it could happen. Start walking the path. It acknowledges that one thing leads to the next. Exercise, practise, study, rehearse, sharpen your pencil. Be ready. Take a shot. But do not stand still. We cannot know for certain whether there is gold in the ground until we dig a hole.

The path of opportunity doesn't guarantee success, but it sends you in a direction and gets you actively pursuing your dream. It is an uncertain path with uncertain terrain. Sometimes you must run and other times you need to stop or walk or crawl. The point is that we need to keep moving. Instead of spending all our time trying to figure out the destination and how to get there, just get started. Get moving.

It is extremely liberating to live by this philosophy because I don't have to know all the answers upfront. Many of us spend so much time agonising about the future but we can never have certainty.

Path of opportunity says – know what you want, have the courage to pick a direction and then take small steps in that direction. You then adjust as you go along. You are far better placed to make informed decisions about your future after you've taken a few steps than from the position where you started.

I could see that joining Old Mutual was unquestionably on my path of opportunity, even though it looked like a terrible move. My time there gave me two powerful assets that would stand me in good stead as I walked the next stage of my path – it showed me that there was a great opportunity for me to build a strategy consulting business, and it gave me a powerful network of executives that would form the foundation of my business. If I had not gone there, neither of these would have been available to me.

It was time for this step. I had no idea how I would do it but I had an irrational certainty that it was the right thing to do. I needed to trust myself. I needed to bet on myself.

And that is exactly what I did!

Betting on myself ◎

I guess I have always bet on myself. Many of my education and career moves to date required risky moves involving high stakes. Through all these decisions and choices, I bet on myself. But to bet on myself with the creation of a business was something new.

I had not run a business before, let alone start one. I don't think my childhood newspaper delivery operation counted, although it did teach me valuable lessons. I was not only looking to start just any business but one that required me, at 32 years old, to convince CEOs of major companies to hire my company as their strategy advisor. I had no brand, no intellectual property (other than what was in my head), and no team.

I had no answers to these tough questions but I knew that I would figure them out. So in 2003 I registered Taurus Associates, a niche strategy consulting firm. I chose the name 'Taurus', Latin for Bull, my nickname, as well as the bullish approach I would take to business. My plan was to build the business around my strategy and finance expertise and, given my industry experience to date, with a particular focus on companies making large capital investments and financial services firms.

I did the proverbial pavement pounding associated with the start of any new business. I arranged meetings with the CEOs of three companies to present proposals. All three were unsuccessful. It quickly became apparent to me that I would struggle to make the business work from Cape Town. My potential client base was in Johannesburg so that was where I needed to be. Again I had to move, and again I had to be apart from my family.

In Johannesburg, I rented a two-bedroom apartment in the upmarket suburb of Morningside, near to the business district, Sandton. I set up my office in the spare bedroom – installed a landline telephone, bought a computer and printer/fax machine, and rented a post box in Sandton. I printed my first set of business cards on a sheet of cardboard and cut them out with a pair of scissors.

While in Johannesburg, I did a consulting project with another small consulting firm to get some cash in and there I met Earl van Zyl, a young engineer, who had also worked at Bain. Earl would later be the first person to join me at Taurus.

As with most businesses, strategy consulting had two broad elements – sales and project delivery. I had experience delivering projects but I had never sold a consulting project before. Even if I did sell a project I didn't have a team to deliver the project.

It was a chicken and egg situation – if I hired a team without any revenue I would be out of business and broke within months, but without a team how could I sell a project since delivery required a team. I tried to attract others to the business asking them to take some risk and offering them equity in the business but I had no real proposition for them. A few months passed and more rejections followed – the rejections were depressing. Perhaps I had been too rash in resigning from Old Mutual? Perhaps I should consider joining an established consulting firm and after a few more years branch out on my own? My cash was running low and I began running out of executives to call; my confidence started waning and self-doubt reigned supreme. But I refused to give up.

Around the middle of 2003, the CEO of one of Old Mutual's largest divisions invited me to submit a proposal outlining how I could help his executive team develop a business case for a massive technology investment they were planning. This fit squarely into my area of expertise. Two other firms, both well-established, were invited to submit proposals as well.

A call came through a few days after submitting my proposal – Taurus Associates had been awarded a three-month contract! Six months after starting Taurus and I had the break I needed. Just like that, Taurus had its first client. Taurus was in business. I was moved to tears. It was really happening; I was the managing director of a start-up strategy consulting firm. Most consulting firms are started when a few senior partners leave their existing firm together to set up a new firm. They usually take a few clients with them. I had done it completely the hard way by starting on my own without any clients.

Within a few days Earl quit his job and joined me. A few weeks later, my brother Nick joined us to run our administrative operations and later deliver consulting projects. At work, I often turned in my chair to look at Nick and smile – I got to spend every day with my best friend. We were now embarking on this new venture together.

It reminded me of our childhood days of playing and exploring together. It was a huge leap of faith for both Earl and Nick to join me because I was running on passion and really had no firm plan about how this business would succeed. Having responsibility for the careers and incomes of two people added pressure to an already pressurised situation as we set out to deal with a complex project for our client.

I worked day and night, seven days a week to cover all that was needed and to solve my client's business challenge. We managed to develop a business strategy that was signed off by the executive team and the board. We then developed the business case for the technology investment that ensured execution of the strategy and one that delivered the best return. The project was a massive success and soon word spread across the other Old Mutual businesses and the market that Taurus was a firm that was worth hiring.

Soon Taurus was thriving. Client work poured in – we counted among our clients many blue-chip organisations, companies listed on the Johannesburg Stock Exchange, domestic divisions of multinational corporations and state-owned enterprises. We were hired by government departments as well, including the Department of Communication where we were part of the process to establish the second landline telecom company in South Africa. We advised a number of investment firms on portfolio strategy and international capital raising.

By 2005 Taurus was growing rapidly. We had moved out of my townhouse and into offices on Wellington Road in Parktown but even this space was now too small. In a business like ours, professional image was critical to attract clients and employees. And one of the most effective ways of portraying professionalism was with an office. This was not just where staff worked but where we had client meetings and corporate events, so we set out to rent higher quality office space closer to Sandton.

To my surprise, no landlord would lease us A-grade office space. For their best offices, landlords preferred blue-chip companies with strong balance sheets. We did not fit the requirements. Unwilling to compromise on the quality of our offices, I was left with only one option – if no one was going to lease us high quality offices then we would buy them!

I again found myself in one of those familiar situations where instinct pointed me in the direction of taking a substantial risk. This time I would be taking on the debt to buy offices for our business that had no guaranteed income. All logic suggested that I follow a more prudent route to continue leasing but I was not interested in playing it safe. Without a rapid improvement in our corporate image and location, the business would stutter. Taking on massive debt would place the business and myself under enormous pressure but I didn't have time to doubt the success of Taurus and so I threw all my energy behind the idea of buying offices and putting the business on a path that I believed would give us a fighting chance.

I found a new development in Woodmead which was close to Sandton and close to the highway offering easy access to the Johannesburg CBD, Pretoria and the airport. The building was still to be built and the developer was struggling to attract interest because the site was adjacent to a municipal rubbish dump. Literally! Buy a building that hadn't yet been built on a dodgy site that no one else wants to occupy? Of course it seemed ridiculous, but I had a good feeling about the place. Besides, the situation allowed me to negotiate a discount on the price.

I decided once again to bet on myself and so in March 2006 I signed the purchase agreement to acquire an office building in Woodlands Drive Office Park. It was an impressive elevated location which offered views over the centre of Sandton and the Johannesburg CBD. At 530m^2 it was more than we needed, but would offer us tremendous growth capacity.

After an extensive application process, a bank agreed to a commercial loan to which I added all the savings that I could scrape together. I had some cash saved in South Africa and meagre investments in the US and UK which I liquidated. My entire financial future was tied to Taurus's success. I entered a completely unhedged position – if Taurus underperformed, not only would I lose money from the business but I would face the risk of losing my investment in the office. Investment common sense said it was a terrible idea, but for me it created an extra incentive to ensure that Taurus succeeded.

In November 2006 we moved into our new offices which we had furnished and equipped to the highest standard including an impressive boardroom, a library, a full kitchen, a shower and even 'chill out' rooms where staff could relax or take a nap. Our reception area had a huge aluminium sign on the wall with our company logo and name.

It was an extraordinary feeling to walk into the office each day: to think that this was something that I had created, that I had created jobs for the many people who we employed and that we were contributing to the South African economy.

Our star was rising so high that we were attracting top-performing students from universities and attracting people away from established firms. We were winning projects against the established international strategy firms.

We had a strong media presence with publications such as *Business Day* regularly publishing articles that I'd written and regularly calling me for comment on events in the economy. I was a regular on a business radio show, 'Leadership Platform', where I discussed business strategy with company CEOs. I was asked to write a review of the legendary businessman Raymond Ackerman's book *Hearing Grasshoppers Jump* which was published in *Business Day*. Business publications such as *Management Today*, *Business Briefs* and *Entrepreneur* featured our business or published articles that I had written. With my business profile growing I was invited to serve on the boards of companies and institutions, and started delivering guest lectures at business schools.

Our company motto was 'Do the impossible' which we regularly had to do to complete our ambitious projects with the limited resources that we had. I knew that if we were to succeed we needed to be bold and behave and appear larger that we really were. I was determined that work should be fun and coined the phrase 'doing serious work in a fun way'. We hired mavericks, people who wanted to shake up the status quo.

We started investing heavily in our team by hiring outside experts to deliver training sessions. I too invested heavily in training for our staff and invested heavily of my own energy in them to sharpen their consulting and business skills. We had company offsite meetings at some of the great resorts in the country and regularly had company dinners at Johannesburg's finest restaurants.

We were spending so much time working in Cape Town that the business decided to buy a house in the coastal town of Hout Bay. We furnished and equipped the house to a high standard and staff and their families could stay there when they were working in Cape Town or they could use the house for leisure.

Taurus offered a rewarding but tough work environment. The standard was extremely high and I expected my teams to meet this high standard constantly. Inevitably some people battled to keep up and found constructive ways of dealing with this or they would leave. I was devastated every time someone left because I was so aware of how much we had invested in them. And it felt like a mini-failure that we hired the wrong person or that our environment was one where they could not thrive.

With the financial success of Taurus I was able to buy some

expensive toys. I already owned the BMW 850i, to which I added a beautiful classic Rolls Royce Silver Shadow for my 34th birthday – it was a 1970 model, the year of my birth. This was followed by a Lamborghini Jalpa, identical to the one Rocky Balboa drives in the movie *Rocky IV*. I could tick this item off my 2002 dream list. While living in the US I salivated over the Mustang, the all-American muscle car, and finally I was able to own one – I bought a convertible Mustang GT Cobra.

This was followed by a new X-type Jaguar and when BMW introduced the new 650i into the country, I just had to have one. I bought the 650i without even seeing it or test-driving it. I was invited by BMW to the launch of the 6-series in South Africa and had registered my interest at that event. When a dealer called me to say that he had a black one coming into the country I said I'd take it. With a fleet of six luxury cars, I had to rent garages around the city and leave one or two at the office.

Membership of the Rolls Royce Club gave me access to an influential network of people. I made my landlord an offer on my apartment in Morningside which he accepted and I renovated the two-storey apartment as my bachelor pad with high-tech entertainment and sound installations and mahogany shelving for a growing collections of fine books. In addition, I bought a house in the upmarket suburb of Bryanston which stood on an acre of land, and bought two further plots of land where I had intentions of building houses – a two-acre stand in Chartwell, outside of Johannesburg along the Klein Jukskei River and a four-and-half acre piece of land near the lion park in Farmall.

The bet on myself was paying off.

For a short while I strayed from my determination to live a modest life. Indulging in material possessions was partly necessary for my business of being an advisor to corporations but they also served a need within me to satisfy fantasies of luxury after a life of deprivation. Cars were one easy way to showcase my success, to show that my years of studying and hard work had been worthwhile. These reasons all seem shallow now but they were important motivators. My material indulgence would continue for a few more years but soon that time would come when I would adopt the modest lifestyle that I knew was right for me. This would free me to dedicate my financial resources and my energies to do the work of serving others.

As Taurus's profile grew we began attracting the attention of competitors. Some invited me to meetings to find out who we were and how it was that we were taking business away from them. Others offered collaboration deals, some of which we accepted. In 2006 I got an offer from a UK-based consulting firm to acquire Taurus. It was a massive compliment that after only three years we were seen to be an attractive acquisition target. The UK firm already had a small presence in South Africa and saw the acquisition of Taurus as a substantial boost to their presence in the country.

I saw such vast growth potential for the business and was having way too much fun to give it up no matter what they were offering, so I walked away from that offer even though it would have given me a huge cash boost.

Besides, something exciting was brewing that could redefine our business.

Too many boulders
at once ◉

Sometimes we have to push to the end of our abilities, the end of physical limits to the point where we either explode into greatness or collapse. That was the way I was operating. I operated at one speed – sprint. I was in my early 30s running a successful advisory firm with CEOs and senior government officials as my clients. I had taken great personal risk in building the business, buying an office building and had invested myself fully into it.

While the business was thriving, its demands began to take a toll on my health. I began having dizzy spells. I was on the road all the time, I was hardly sleeping, did no exercise and was eating unhealthily – the standard formula it seems that modern business success demands. Thankfully, I had stopped smoking and was not much of a drinker. I was diagnosed with high blood pressure requiring me to take medication and given stern instructions by my doctor to slow down. It would have been easier to convince a goldfish to leap out of its bowl than convince me to slow down.

The very nature of a consulting business is an insecure one. There are no annuity revenues and to keep earning you've got to keep selling and delivering projects. With Taurus's growth the salary bill was astronomical. At any point we could be massively successful with a flow of lucrative assignments or run out of cash. It was a terrifying position.

This was one of the key reasons for wanting to launch an investment business. The fees earned from investments would give us a stable income and besides, an investment business offered the opportunity to gain significant upside. This was always my intention, to start with a consulting business and then to use it as a platform to build an investment business just as Bain had done in the US. The model was quite simple. Taurus Capital, which I had already registered, would raise capital from institutional investors and buy equity stakes in mid-sized unlisted businesses. We would use the expertise of the consulting firm to improve the performance of the companies we buy in order to grow their earnings from which we would derive our return through cash dividends, or we would sell the companies at higher prices than we had paid.

My colleagues were excited by the prospect of the investment business but some were concerned that we were already too thinly stretched. I too felt stretched but this move into investments would put Taurus on a whole new growth path. It might have been too soon in our development but I decided to push ahead anyway.

We put together a business plan and a proposal for investors. The key was to get an anchor investor. For weeks and months, I invested my time in improving our story, re-running our numbers and reworking our presentation. I spoke to whoever would listen. I flew up and down the country and spoke to international investors. I shopped our proposal around and while there was enthusiasm for our concept there were no takers. Then, as had often happened in my life when I showed full commitment to a task, I got a break.

At a whisky-tasting event in Constantia with clients I was introduced to Gareth Ackerman, the billionaire chairman of national retailer, Pick n Pay. We spoke well into the night about investment opportunities in South Africa, and were the last people to leave the venue. This encounter led to numerous discussions with Ackerman, at his office on their family estate in Constantia or at a private club. We explored a range of potential investment ideas and settled on a plan to establish a $50 million private equity fund for investment in the mid-sized market in South Africa.

As our discussions entered an advanced stage, Ackerman

introduced me to his associates who ran his investment companies. Once we had settled on a model to pursue, I started meeting more with his associates than with him. Talks moved quickly and in no time I was meeting potential investors in South Africa and the UK where I got to present my approach and business model. Such was the enthusiasm that it seemed we would be able to raise more than the target of $50 million. I could not believe it, there were actually investors excited about my vision and were willing to put their money behind it. In my jacket pocket I carried a Montblanc pen that I had bought especially for the signing of the agreements to launch Taurus Capital. Sitting in the investor meetings in London I played with the pen in my jacket pocket expectantly, feeling that its inaugural use was imminent.

But I would not get to use the pen. I left London frustrated and disappointed.

The economics of the proposed deal was extremely attractive for me but the structure would be unattractive for Taurus Associates, the consulting firm. The partners and investors wanted me to run the investment business but separate myself from the consulting firm. By doing this, not only would I be abandoning the team of people that I had recruited but my investment philosophy would also suffer since it relied on privileged access to the consulting firm's skill. I proposed that I be CEO of the investment business and serve on the board of the consulting firm and continue to lend my name and credibility to its work as well as support the team in securing projects. It was a stretch and even I did not know how this would work. This was rejected.

I had to choose. I could either follow my dream of running a substantial investment business with world-class experts and become exceedingly wealthy but abandon the business that I had built. Or, I could honour my commitment to my staff and clients, and pass on this opportunity.

All logic said go with the investment business. This was a once-in-a-lifetime opportunity. My heart said stay with the consulting business. And that is what I did, I followed my heart. Not for the first time I strained relationships with powerful and influential people by not going along with what they wanted, but it was important to me to follow what I believed to be right. I had built strong business relationships with prominent CEOs like Peter Moyo, Thabo Dloti, Ralph Mupita, Seelan Gobalsamy and Ben Kodisang whose businesses counted on the strategy advisory work we offered. They had been great supporters of mine and I was not about to abandon these relationships.

I continued trying to establish Taurus Capital but it all came to nought. After months of trying, I was tired and disillusioned. But at least I had the comfort of Taryn's arms.

Taryn Lock was a Taurus employee, and quite an unlikely candidate to be embroiled in an office romance scandal involving a young analyst and the boss. She had been working at Taurus for two years before we started dating. We had spent plenty of time together for work and occasionally outside of work as well.

It had been five years since my last serious relationship and my declaration that I would remain single for the rest of my life. But as the wise Bruce Springsteen sang in his song 'Hungry Heart', nobody likes to live alone. Because we were the only two unattached people in the firm, we often spent time chatting when teams went out or at company functions. She was smart, sincere and hard-working, a real determined go-getter like me. And she was gorgeous. I had not been looking for a relationship but sometimes joy just finds us. There was no magical moment of falling in love but I do recall noticing her more and more, and beginning to admire her, until I finally had the courage to ask her out on a date.

I brought my A-game ... made reservations at a top restaurant and polished up the Rolls Royce. Being as down to earth as she is, Taryn laughed at the car, thinking it was ridiculous. She thought the car looked like Noah's Ark. *How rude!* Okay, the car was lost on her but at least she'd be impressed with dinner. Wrong again. She thought the place was too stiff. I just couldn't catch a break. For weeks she insisted that we could not date because I was her boss. I jokingly suggested that that could be solved if I fired her. My pursuit continued in earnest and I don't know what it was, but I eventually wore her down. We tried to be discrete at the office but it was the worst-kept secret. I guess when you're in love it shows in your face.

As we approached mid-2007 the office was working at full capacity. We continued to serve clients in financial services which was our core strength, and managed to secure assignments with two oil companies. After the disappointment of the investment business we were getting back to focusing on our main business and again we were flying.

And then a bombshell hit.

Within quick succession, two of my three senior managers informed me that they wanted to leave. I was stunned. They felt that they had better financial prospects elsewhere and that the demands at Taurus were too excessive given their personal circumstances. Despite my best efforts, I could not convince them to stay. Their resignation would have a devastating impact on the business – it would be impossible for me to lead the business and fill the gap that their departure would leave. Hiring in new senior managers was not an option because there were very few experienced people in the market. I could scale down the business and then build it up again over time, developing a new senior team, but that would take years.

I was devastated. I was tired. And it seemed that Taurus was nearing its end.

There was one last option. I had received another offer to sell Taurus, to a large international accounting firm this time. Part of the deal was that I would be locked in for five years. This would have been financially attractive for me but was not something I wanted to do. It was over. I had tried to lift this business off the ground to fly into the stratosphere but in the end it nose-dived.

So after five miraculous years Taurus would shut its doors.* I was

---

* Taurus still continues to operate but in a much more scaled-down version and a more variable cost model where consultants are contracted in on an as-needed basis rather than employing them as permanent employees.

too numb to process this and there was too much to do to wind the business up. I had to inform our clients, cancel contracts and I had the heart-wrenching task of retrenching all the staff. I met with each of them one by one, and had to accept their anger and expressions of disappointment, and comfort them as they shed tears. I gave them each as much of a financial cushion as I could.

I thought back to the sacrifices that I had made to keep the business going, how I sacrificed personally even to the extent of my health failing. I thought back to personal opportunities that I had foregone to keep the business going such as the investment business with Ackerman. I wondered if the sacrifices had been worthwhile.

I managed to find a tenant for the office building which I sold a few years later. The office turned out to be the best investment I'd ever made. I still have the painting that hung in Taurus's boardroom and a few other smaller artefacts to remind me of the brief but exhilarating time.

A business can fail when, as the leader, you fail in 'bringing people along with you'. This was my quote in an *Entrepreneur Magazine* article just a few months earlier. Not for a moment thinking that I may be guilty of this. I always thought that if Taurus failed it would be because we had no clients. Quite the opposite was the case, we had a string of clients.

I never expected that it would fail from the inside. This was a major oversight. It points to the challenge of running a successful business, that all elements need to be successful or at least in balance for the whole to succeed.

I had failed in an area that I knew was a weak point for many businesses. But how could this happen? My first lesson was that knowing about a weakness was a good first step, but the knowledge was useless unless you did something about it. This reminded me of the feedback I received at the leadership retreat when I was at MIT. I knew my impatience was a flaw but clearly I still acted impatiently based on the feedback that I received from my peers. Secondly, it appeared to me that the very elements of my personality that contributed to Taurus's success had led to its downfall – my ambition, risk-taking and strong personality.

With regard to the latter, my MIT classmates warned that 'people may tell you only what you want to hear'. In other words, even if they disagreed or were not aligned, they would say they were just to appease me. I think this happened often but I was blind to it. Blinded by my own ambition, I failed to bring my team along in pursuing my ambitious vision, and that was ultimately the downfall of Taurus.

As I packed up the things from my office tears streamed down my face. Loss is always sad but sometimes loss can be good for us. It is possible that my health would have suffered severely if I continued at the pace that I was going and so perhaps stepping away from this business was a good thing. I was glad for the experience and we had done some remarkable work. Our clients were generous in their praise of our work: 'They have a way of simplifying complexity which then made our decision-making a lot easier,' said one CEO at an event; 'You could tell that they were thinking hard about our problems, they were not just dusting off old frameworks and imposing it on us, they customised their thinking to our organisation and our challenges' said another.

I had much to be thankful for from the Taurus experience – it proved that a successful business can be built when you offer clients a differentiated offering and it renewed my belief in the power of conviction and 'betting on yourself' in pursuing that which you feel drawn to do. I had built a business doing what I enjoyed and one that I believed gave our clients great advice and great value. It was a business that competed successfully with top local and international consulting firms to advise the CEOs of major companies and national government departments. The business allowed me to work with exceptional colleagues and meet incredible people across the business world. While the financial rewards were modest the greatest wealth that I derived from the business was meeting Taryn.

On 26 September 2009, Taryn and I were married outside Hermanus in the Cape. The ceremony took place in the open, overlooking a small lake on a wine farm and the reception was in a nearby restaurant that overlooked picturesque vineyards. My Wits friend Bert Frahm danced the tango with a partner as a gift to us. Many of my dearest friends from high school, baseball and work were there, as well as those who had played significant roles in my life like Tudor (who travelled from Australia), Cate, and Neil and Hazel Fraser.

I had proposed to Taryn less than a year earlier in our favourite place, Hout Bay. We sat on a rock with the waves producing spray that carried rainbows, and the occasional shower over us. I told Taryn that I loved her and offered her the ring while asking her to be my wife. Tears poured down her cheeks as she extended her left hand. I took this as a sign of acceptance of my proposal but I needed confirmation. 'I take it that's a *yes*,' I said with great hope in my voice. 'Yes,' she replied, nodding. We kissed and sat there on the rock for a while, holding each other and enjoying the magnificence of the ocean and each other's company.

Leaning on her Chinese heritage Taryn chose the Chinese symbol for *double happiness* as the symbol for our wedding – it was apt, I was certainly experiencing more happiness than I could have imagined in a relationship. Nick was the master of ceremonies and Roscoe was my best man – both of them delivered beautiful and moving speeches. As a true Bruce Springsteen fan, even my wedding included one of his songs – 'If I should fall behind' played as Taryn and I cut our wedding cake.

Taryn and I were still living in my apartment in Morningside which was becoming too small for us, made all the more so by the thousands of books that I had stacked on the floor in every room. I had always had a large collection of books, split 50-50 between books relating to my studies and those for pleasure or private study. Within the space of a few years, my private collection ballooned to peak at 10,000 books. I became an ardent collector from 2008, visiting rare book stores, subscribing to catalogues and buying at auctions. Most rare books dealers in Johannesburg, New York and London knew me personally and would often contact me when something came their way that they thought would be of interest to me. My interests were focused on

South African history and poetry initially, but expanded to politics, philosophy and literature. I had books dating back to the 1600s and some exquisitely bound sets.

Some of my prized books included editions signed by John Masefield, Robert Frost and Nadine Gordimer, a first edition in English of Machiavelli's *The Prince* and an eighteenth-century copy of *Paradise Lost* by John Milton. I had complete collections of the works of some of my favourite writers such as H.G. Wells, George Bernard Shaw and William Wordsworth.

I loved the smell of old books and felt profoundly moved to hold a 400-year-old-book in my hand and feel connected with our human past. Can you imagine whose hands such a book would have passed through over such a long time? I loved the feel of books, the paper texture, the craftsmanship of the lettering and detail on the leather binding. On 3 April 2010 I wrote with great excitement:

I am surrounded by books. I have surrounded myself with books. Beautiful, beautiful books. Beautiful to touch, to hold, to feel their texture, their shape, their weight in my hands. Beautiful to the eye, in their design, tooling, lettering, gilt-edges, leather, cloth, vellum, dustjackets. Thousands and thousands of books. That contain millions of ideas, thoughts, desires, fears. Stories, facts, poems that inspire. That make the universe seem infinite. That make me feel so small and finite and trivial. But most amazingly, they allow me to touch people, they provide a channel to many thousands of people, dead or alive, of all ages, all nationalities. People who wrote these books. People who owned these books – their fingerprints, their perspiration, their thoughts, their lives still trapped in these pages. The books connect me. They make me part of something larger, something timeless, something magnificent, an exploration, a pursuit of all things, a journey that all men have been on for hundreds of years. My world is richer for it is dimensionless; I have a mind alive, thanks to these books, this library.

I loved the mystery of opening a book to find notes by previous readers and even better when I found a letter, postcard or photograph. I have a box filled with such amazing treasures which include letters written by John Masefield and a letter written to the actor Ralph Fiennes.

Given our space constraints, we decided that it was time to relocate. We found a beautiful house in Bryanston in an estate of eight houses with great space and a stunning garden. We refurbished the entire house, replacing everything and we built an additional room to serve as a study and a further room which served as my library. It was an incredible room, around 80m^2 in size with 3.5m-high ceilings. I had solid wood shelving and cupboards fitted all around the room along with ladders and display cabinets. The floors were covered in reconditioned teak and the walls painted crimson. The room was temperature and humidity controlled and there were strict rules against eating and drinking in the library, except for the occasional whisky or cognac. I spent almost all my time in the library, it was a place of peace and a wonderful place to think and write. It was a room which encouraged ambitious thoughts and these thoughts spurred me on to start pushing some of my largest and most daunting boulders.

One finite life ◉

For the three years following the winding down of Taurus I tried different opportunities. I would have three jobs in the three years. All were substantial senior executive roles but I was searching for clarity and struggling within myself to make some of the tough choices I increasingly knew I had to make. Acting upon our convictions can sometimes take time; there are twists and turns and sometimes we have to go back in order to go forward.

The appointment of a new CEO at Old Mutual, where I had worked in 2002, came with much-needed change in the business. He was a respected businessman inside and outside the company and so when he asked me to join his executive team as Strategy Director in September 2007, I was flattered. To be the strategy director of the country's largest financial service group at the age of 37 was quite an achievement. In many ways I was the perfect person for the job given that over the preceding five years, while at Taurus, I had advised the CEOs of every division. The role came with all the status of a large corporation, access to a chauffeur, huge corner office which had a fully stocked refrigerator, cooked meals that were delivered in my office daily and so on. It reminded me on my days at Rio Tinto in London ten years earlier.

Then I was employed by leading private equity firm RMB Corvest, who I represented on the boards of 12 of their portfolio companies. Lastly I returned yet again to my first love, Bain & Company, as a partner in their South African office and a lead in their African Financial Services practice. I was the first South African partner appointed in their African operations.

Even as I was employed in these powerful and high-paying jobs, it was a testing time. I knew I no longer belonged in the corporate world and that my calling was elsewhere. But the corporate world was the only world I knew. I was good at the work I did. It was not going to be easy to just walk away from it. I knew what I'd be walking away from but had no idea what I was walking toward.

I recalled that as far back as 1996, when I had just started working in the US, I already had doubts about whether corporate life was for me. I had gone into corporate business as an avenue to express my ambition, to earn respect denied for so long and to earn money that would break me out of poverty and dependency. But I carried with me a spiritual and ethical sensibility that protected me from becoming entirely consumed by greed and ensured that concern for human society never waned. The economic inequality that I came to experience disturbed me. While undergoing training in Monte Carlo with Bain I wrote poems that expressed disgust with the opulence I saw. I came to realise that wherever there is luxury, there is deprivation. I saw this quite starkly on a business trip to Puerto Rico in 2000. I was staying at the Ritz Carlton luxury resort on the beach in San Juan and began chatting to some of the resort staff, asking them about life outside of the resort. Unsurprisingly, they described the conditions of deprivation under which they lived. Ignoring all safety warnings I explored the city of San Juan beyond the glitzy beach resorts and was horrified by what I found. On 16 June I wrote:

> There is a path which runs from Isla Verde to old San Juan, not a straight path for it winds from street to field, from beach to alleyway. Not a straight path for it winds from joy to misery, from light to darkness. Not a straight path for it winds from the Ritz to a barbed wire compound, from a Condado condo to a patched bungalow ... from Tiffany's to polluted sidewalk, from refreshing health spa to

trashed playground. A path not to be signposted, not to be mapped, to be walked each day, but to be forgotten.

I had wandered into an area where close to 70% of the population lived below the poverty line, yet not too far away I was having lobster for lunch and drinking fine wine. I felt that massive tension that I had felt in India and that I would later experience in Cape Town – how could I live a life of luxury when there are people who are suffering under such deprivation? I felt a far greater connection with those living in squalor than my business colleagues in our six-star hotel.

I knew that profound personal change was afoot; I just needed to learn to listen deeply and have the courage to act.

In his book *Tuesdays with Morrie*, author Mitch Albiom talks about the time he spent with an elderly man named Morrie. He tells us about one of Morrie's key philosophies; that you first have to learn to die before you can learn to live. I find this to be a profound approach. It tells us to acknowledge the fact that our lives on earth are finite, that we *will* die. Only once we can peacefully reach this point can we begin to live full lives.

I had watched films about people who discovered that they only have six months to live and then proceed to live free, fulfilling lives doing all those things they always wanted to do. Why wait? Why wait until death stares us in the face to begin living? This just didn't make sense to me. There were so many people 'saving for the future' who couldn't tell when this future would arrive and what they would do if it ever did arrive.

And so I decided not to wait until I had only six months to live before I lived a fulfilling life – I wanted to live now. My life was short and I wanted to make it count. I would not live irresponsibly, I would live consciously, not just going through the motions of life but actively choosing to live one way or the other. This message of life's finiteness hit me hard between the eyes towards the end of 2007.

One morning at 4am my phone rang. I thought it may be a work emergency. But at 4am? *Who the hell calls at 4am?* It was my brother,

Nick, who was in Johannesburg on business. *Why the hell was Nick calling me at 4am!*

'Bro,' he said in a flat tone, 'Amanda passed away'.

'What did you just say?' I replied, still shaking the sleep from my head.

'Amanda has died,' I heard my brother say.

'What!' I screamed into the phone, 'What did you say! What did you say! What the *fuck* did you say!' I didn't cry. I just shouted and shouted.

My sister, Amanda, had been to hospital for minor routine surgery but a blood clot had formed while she was recovering. This led to her death. Nick came over to my apartment and we both stood in my kitchen crying our hearts out. I felt an enormous hollow in my chest, a deep, dark hollow. I punched my fists on the kitchen table, still shouting. 'How can this happen, this is not supposed to happen!' I shouted over and over again. I had never known such pain and grief, even worse than when my father passed away. I was bent over with pain, the pain choked my throat and pulled tight on my chest. I could hardly bear my own weight and just slumped over the kitchen table sobbing.

Amanda was just 39 years old. Her passing reinforced the idea that our lives were short and needed to be lived *now*. I had to push aside the boulder of my pain, my anger, my confusion about life and death as the mourning gave way to healing. Losing our sister drew our family closer together. As we picked up the pieces of our lives after the funeral I felt my resolve strengthen. I would make my finite life count.

After a tough few months, in March 2008 I decided to take a break, something I had not done since returning to South Africa seven years earlier. Among the many passions that Nick and I shared, one was Bruce Springsteen's music. While I had seen 'The Boss' live in concert a few times, Nick hadn't. So we decided that we would go see a Springsteen concert in the US. We travelled to New York City where we spent a few busy days seeing all the main attractions. I got to show

Nick where I worked on Times Square and he got to satisfy a desire to have a meal at Sparks Steak House located in Midtown Manhattan, not for its great food or wine selection but for no other reason than it was in front of this restaurant that mafia boss Paul Castellano was gunned down on the order of John Gotti. Nick even dressed as closely to a mafia boss as he could as we went to dinner. We were like two teenagers sitting in the restaurant pretending to be mafia bosses. For all we knew, there could have been real mafia gangsters at the table next to us.

In New York we rented a car and embarked on an 11-hour road trip to Cincinnati, Ohio passing through New Jersey, Pennsylvania, West Virginia and into Ohio. Driving through the chaotic streets of New York City doubled my blood pressure. As we entered Cincinnati I momentarily lost concentration forgetting that cars drive on the opposite side of the road to what we do in South Africa, and drove into oncoming traffic. It was horrific seeing three lanes of cars coming directly at us.

We hoped to catch a glimpse of Springsteen before the concert. We managed to locate his buses parked in a private area of the concert arena but his guards were onto us in a flash. At least we tried. The concert itself was an experience of a lifetime. To be standing alongside my brother singing along with our musical hero while he sang our favourite songs was an experience beyond description. We smiled throughout the three-hour concert, hugging each other on occasion and on others like during 'Born to Run', screamed at the top of our lungs. Definitely one of the highlights of my life!

I returned from the trip invigorated. Springsteen's energy still seemed to vibrate within me and some of his lyrics reverberated in my mind. A few weeks later the poem 'One Finite Life' emerged as a personal manifesto that captured my approach to life and my newfound focus. The poem starts with:

Short this life is, just one I've got,
finite in tenure whether I like it or not.

Death, is embracing fear, replacing dreams with 'I cannot,'
life, is taking a new step, having a shot.

I will do the impossible, I will change the world.
I'll give hope to a despairing nation, I'll give bread to a starving girl.

The core of the poem reads:

I will rise up as sure as the sun,
as sure as the springbok I will run,
as sure as the eagle I will fly
'cos I choose to live until I die.

I have subsequently recited this poem to thousands of people and it served as the inspiration for the song 'One Life' sung by Blaque Nubon and Nonhlanhla Mdluli, and produced by Keith Hutchinson. The poem and philosophy crystallised the way I had already been living but brought it to the fore now for me to make a conscious decision about living this way. The poem made it easy for me to share the philosophy with others. There is an impatience to this life philosophy, it says we should live consciously, discover who we are and live our lives to the full. Time becomes more than a mere abstract commodity, it becomes fractions of our lives. *Wasting time is wasting life.* I did not want to waste my life, I wanted it to matter. The poem still challenges me today to live a life of meaning both in terms of personal excellence and in serving others.

I reached the point of clarity about the purpose of my remaining years – to enhance the freedom of others. To help those like *Sisyphus* who were struggling to get their boulder up and over the hill. Or to inspire those who were so overwhelmed by the task of pushing their boulders that they hadn't even started trying. Mostly, I wanted to inspire those who had come to accept that their boulder was their lot in life, to show them the possibility of freedom.

I understood that the right to vote did not entail freedom. Freedom was more complex than that. The fall of apartheid and the onset of democracy may have given South Africans political freedom but this is just one component of freedom. I learned this many years before reading Nobel laureate, Amartya Sen's book, *Development as Freedom*, that freedom also entailed social and economic freedom. Freedom entails the absence of constraints as well as access to the means to live a meaningful life.

Most South Africans, and most people around the world remain trapped by economic and social chains, and so are not free. We have been led into the trap of believing that democracy equals freedom; it does not. Democracy as a political process and ideology may be a channel to freedom but does not guarantee freedom. Democracy certainly does not equate to prosperity – we can see this in the hundreds of millions of people living in democracies who live in conditions of suffering and deprivation.

By this measure of freedom as political, social and economic freedom I could claim that I was free, or certainly that I was significantly freer than I was in my teens and early twenties. I had the privilege of having resources that allowed me to live anywhere in the world and do just about anything of interest to me. But it is not the fact of our privilege that matters so much as what we do with our privilege.

What does the slave do once he is freed? I asked myself this question over and over. In the poem 'After Freedom' I offered an answer. Of four freed slaves, one rushes home, who could blame him? Another cannot be un-slaved so returns to slavery – an all-too-common occurrence today. A third slave indulges in his new freedom, living it up with his friends, completely absorbed in his own good fortune, as we see so commonly among those who emerge from poverty; an amnesia sets in, they seem to forget the struggles of the compatriots in the old slums or townships and so live lives of indulgence rather than seek to uplift others.

However, there is a fourth former slave, a freed person who understands true freedom, that it is not just the unshackling of the individual that constitutes freedom but the unshackling of humanity.

And so this person returns to where the others are being held captive to fight to free them all. The idea of this poem was so powerfully reinforced by that profound statement by Nelson Mandela: 'For to be free is not merely to cast off your own chains but to live in a way that respects and enhances the freedom of others.' If I was to take Mandela's challenge seriously and walk the talk of my poem, then I would live to enhance the freedom of others.

Whereas my journey until then had been focused on casting off my own chains, pushing my own boulders, my path now entailed striving to enhance the freedom of others, to help them push *their* boulders. I wasn't sure yet what shape this would take but it awakened me to a new purpose. I reduced my mission to the simple line: *By my words and deeds to enable and inspire others to thrive.*

My words, whether spoken or written in my poetry, children's books or other writings would be used to lift others up, not merely to entertain. And all my work would be geared to creating structural change in society so as to enable people to live larger more fulfilling lives. Rather than focus on micro injustices alone, I would focus on society-wide injustices, built into our political and economic systems, and seek to reform these to the benefit of those suffering injustices.

I immediately stepped up my involvement in a number of NGOs and social enterprises, including Family Life Centre, which provided counselling and other services for people enduring personal and family difficulties, where I became chairman. I served on the board of an NGO that sought to rehabilitate prisoners and volunteered on the boards of organisations at Wits including the Centre for Entrepreneurship which trained young graduates in new venture creation.

I was one of the founding directors of a social impact investment firm focused on job creation and I served as chairman of a private equity business that directed a large share of its profits to an education NGO. I produced and presented two radio talk shows – 'State of the Nation', which discussed political, social and economic issues with politicians, business people, civil servants, professors and so on – and 'Words Alive', a show in which I interviewed writers of every genre, whether poetry, biography or fiction. I started investing personal funds into a number of social ventures and causes relating to healthcare, education and job creation, as well as producing two human rights films, one focusing on the horrors of war and the other on the atrocities of human trafficking.*

It seemed appropriate that I end my business career at the firm where I first flourished, at Bain & Company. Bain had given me a massive boost back in 1995 by offering me an internship position while I was still doing my MBA and then offering me full-time employment. It was the first time that I felt valued as a professional. And now Bain appointed me as a partner, it was like earning a gold medal at the Olympics. It was an unspeakable honour for me to count myself among the great global thinkers and strategy advisors who have held partnerships at Bain over many decades.

I spent a year with Bain helping to establish the South African office and spending a few months in London. But then the time finally came to make the big change, to begin to fulfil my personal mission.

I was touched by the messages from colleagues as news spread that I was leaving. I had had a relationship with Bain for 15 years. In an email a colleague wrote: 'I am really sad you are leaving Bain! You are a real inspiration to us all, and I admire your dedication to South African development.' The managing partner wrote, 'Your decision tells a lot about your commitment to the people and the development of this country and I personally admire you for this.' I was leaving for the right reason, to go pursue my mission. I felt that I was leaving on a high. I supported the business as a senior advisor for a while after I left.

Finally, at the age of 40, I took a firm stand. I retired from business. Just at the time in my career when I would be able to earn many millions and have status and power, I walked away. I was walking away from the only work environment I had known, one that I had begun to master, and into a new unknown world. I finally had the

---

* I was the executive producer.

courage to do what I had known needed to be done for a few years.

I knew that if I worked for 20 more years I would have more money and influence to be able to have the social and political impact I wanted to have but I didn't want to wait till I was an old man before having a direct positive impact on the world around me. I wanted to give of myself not just money. I wanted to spend my remaining years in the service of others, to inspire and enable others to push their boulders as I had learned to do.

I was free but I wanted others also to be free. I wanted others to know this feeling of possibility, this feeling of self-belief that I knew. I felt this so strongly within me, so clearly, and I knew this was what I wanted others to feel.

Inspiration would not just stem from my words but also from my actions and the way I lived my life. So I would keep pursuing excellence and walking my path of opportunity. I had been an economic entrepreneur and had begun to be a social entrepreneur but I also wanted to be a *hope* entrepreneur – raising the levels of self-belief and inspiration in a world that seemed to lack it.

The first thing I did was to sell my cars. I had already replaced the BMW 6-series with a new BMW 5-series. I sold them all – the 5-series, BMW 850i, Mustang, Jaguar, Rolls Royce and Lamborghini – and added the proceeds to my war chest for future development ventures. I went from six cars to having none.

I felt unburdened with the sale of the cars. I had finally acted on the conviction that arose that day in Cape Town driving my BMW 850i past people living in shacks. I was rid of the cars and would use the money to uplift those very people whose poverty had challenged me.

In 2011, I launched Taurus School Solutions (TSS), a non-profit education consultancy that used whole school development programmes to improve school performance in poor areas. I hired a team of experienced professionals to design and deliver our programmes while I provided oversight. I would later be awarded the Inyathelo Award in Education from the South African Institute for Advancement for the work that TSS did.

I was flattered by invitations from companies who were keen for me to join them. One example was McKinsey & Company, an arch-rival to Bain. After a long series of discussions they made me a job offer but this just didn't make sense to me so I turned it down. Another interesting approach was from Roelf Meyer who was a cabinet minister in the apartheid government along with F.W. de Klerk. Meyer had been the Government's lead negotiator during the transition from apartheid to democracy. I first met him when he was a guest on my radio show 'State of the Nation'. Meyer was collaborating with Cyril Ramaphosa in a business consulting venture, and offered me the CEO job. My connection with Ramaphosa had gone full circle. Again this was a job that would guarantee significant wealth creation for myself given the networks that I would have access to in business and government through Ramaphosa and Meyer.

How could I possibly walk away from this? But I did. I would have to resist many such offers, most with remuneration packages exceeding R10 million, if I was to remain true to my mission.

2010 was a momentous year for South Africa, with the country's stadia hosting the FIFA Soccer World Cup. Taryn and I went to the opening match between South Africa and Mexico and our screams joined the tens of thousands in the stadium when we scored. I watched a few group-stage matches in Johannesburg and Cape Town and was pleased that I got to see both Lionel Messi and Cristiano Ronaldo, two of the modern greats. I then treated Nick and Roscoe to the final match between Spain and Holland, and watched the Spanish lift the World Cup. It was such an extraordinary experience to be at the games and to feel the heightened energy in our country. And so incredible to share this time with my brothers.

Later I travelled to Spain with Nick and Roscoe to watch El Classico, the soccer match between Spanish giants Real Madrid and Barcelona. The Santiago Bernabéu Stadium in Madrid vibrated with the hyped-up emotions of 100,000 fans as the gladiators on the pitch had it out with each other. Again I got to see Messi and Ronaldo. It was incredible to see how passionate the Spanish supporters were, screaming till they were red in the face. We were delirious.

In addition to soccer, both my brothers also shared my enjoyment of cars. We had lots to enjoy with my range of exotic cars over the years. On one of their visits to Johannesburg, before I had sold the cars, we drove the 175km to Sun City in three cars, Nick in the 850i, Roscoe in the Mustang and I drove the Lamborghini. The three black sports cars driving in tow certainly made many heads turn. We had the time of our lives.

Back home in my quiet library, I was pondering the question: What now? 'The deepest feeling always shows itself in silence,' the poet Marianne Moore wrote in *Silence*. I needed to find silence and listen. I spent days and weeks in that room, emerging only for physical essentials – sleep, eat and bathroom visits. My phone was turned off, I didn't open my laptop to check emails.

I read ferociously – biographies, poetry and modern literature, as well as philosophy, economics and politics. The reading served as a form of meditation, it helped me reflect on what was important to me and what I was going to do with my remaining days. I wrote volumes – poems, short texts and diary entries. My attention was turned squarely on the state of modern society and the need for something different, inspiration perhaps or maybe love?

It was around this time that I reconnected with an old Wits engineering classmate. Steve Tsakiris and I weren't friends back then, only greeting each other in passing. I don't recall if we ever had a proper conversation. We made a brief connection in second year when we both failed Fluid Mechanics dismally – nothing like failure to connect people. The timing was perfect as I was beginning to explore deeply the state of man and society. Steve had been doing deep spiritual work and so served as valuable sounding board during my exploration.

We began spending many hours together, meeting regularly in my library for day-long discussions. We debated topics that included religion, spirituality, science, politics, psychology and social philosophy. The friendship was a real blessing for me, for the first time I had someone with whom I could share my ideas and debate them. Our engagements reinforced the understanding that any effort toward a better society required both inspired individuals and reimagined social structures. This would be the focus of my future work.

'I must write that down' ◎

'I must write that down.'

I spoke these words often during conversations or in my mind during times of contemplation or reading. Any idea or fact of significance needed to be written down. If it was important I would write it down. And so my living spaces would always be littered with loose sheets of paper strewn across desks and tables, or stuck on the wall or pin board, containing lines of text and scribbles that I thought was important. Many of my books have annotations or slips of paper inserted between their pages with scribbled notes. These formed the raw materials, the inputs, to ideas which developed over time. It also started creating the habit and discipline which would help me develop as a writer.

It is always a wonderful surprise after many years to find a book that contains my notes or scribbled ideas. One such book was *Against the Tide* by Douglas A. Irwin, a book on the history of free trade which I had read while working at Bain in Boston. On 21 December 1996, on the front-end page of the book I wrote:

International simplicity (political, economic and social) could be achieved in one of two ways: Firstly, the world could be one economic entity, with one government, one set of laws and one national interest – no concerns about national security, immigration or international trade. Secondly, we could revert to having independent, isolated, self-sufficient nation-states – no trade, no tourism. Due to the current state of the world with communication and transport as developed as it is, the latter option seems ridiculously unlikely. Our options are therefore global unity or international chaos.

I propose an extreme set of options and some radical ideas but I'm glad that I captured these thoughts as a reminder now of how I saw the world at the age of 26. It was such an unlikely set of thoughts given that I had just graduated from business school six months earlier and was working as an advisor to corporations where my focus was maximising profit not rearranging the world order. These early ideas would become more developed later to form important parts of my political philosophy particularly relating to political cosmopolitanism.

My writing habit started at the age of 14 when I began keeping a diary. This exercise of capturing my daily activities, thoughts, feelings or ideas continues today. My diaries offer me a rich record of my experiences and provide a valuable tool to aid my reflection upon my life, to gauge growth, healing and accomplishment.

I also wrote letters extensively starting in 1988 when I first went to university. Living away from home and from friends was a catalyst for letter writing. My father and I exchanged close to a hundred letters each. I wrote to Nick and Amanda fairly regularly and occasionally to Roscoe. As a teenager, I had a pen-pal named Nadine Pillay who lived in Pretoria and then in Natal, with whom I communicated for close to ten years. During the early years of my relationship with Grace, when I was in the US and she was in the UK, we exchanged letters frequently, writing close to fifty letters. While in the US I started exchanging letters regularly with Cate and a Wits friend, Aasifah Omar, who remain among my longest-standing friends. I've maintained written communication over the longest period with Martha McAlpine, a friend who I met in Boston in the 1990s – we have maintained written contact for over 15 years and continue to correspond today.

I love handwritten letters. There is nothing more personal and intimate that the exchange of a letter personally penned. Writing by hand slows me down, especially when I write with a fountain pen, and gives me time to experience special moments with the person to whom I'm writing.

Poetry started as a form of diary-keeping, simply capturing what I may have written in my diary. But it evolved over the 25 years that I have been writing to come to be a vital avenue for spiritual and philosophical expression and discovery, as well as the medium through which I would express my social and political visions and challenges to my readers. While I wrote a few poems between 1987 and 1989, I started writing poetry in earnest from 1990 and have maintained an output of roughly 50 poems per year since then. I've already mentioned that my first published poem was 'New South Africa', published at Wits in 1991. During this same period I had two poems published in the Wits health services publication *Sex*, and during my days as an engineering student I wrote numerous poems for funerals, weddings and other occasions upon the request of friends. Unsurprisingly my classmates thought I was weird for writing poetry and spending my spare time at events in the English department rather than at the Engineering faculty bar.

In 1992 I compiled my first manuscript titled *Writing on Flesh* which I sent to a few publishers but none were interested. It would be 17 years before I would have the courage again to submit a manuscript to publishers.

My professional work from 1996 to 2000 involved extensive travel. I chose to use these experiences as catalysts for poems and started the routine of buying a postcard wherever I travelled, writing a poem on the postcard, mainly about my impressions of the place visited, and then mailing the postcard to my home address. As a result I have poems on postcards from numerous cities across the US, including Chicago, Philadelphia, New York, Las Vegas and many smaller cities, as well as from Canada, Puerto Rico, England, Australia, India, Spain, France, Portugal and Germany, among many others. It was another way to capture valuable feelings and to maintain records of my experiences. For example, one of my most recited poems, 'Taking Notice of Time' was written while on a business trip to Boise, Idaho in 2000.

In total I have written over 1,000 poems, filled more than 20 diaries and exchanged close to 500 letters and postcards.

In 2009, I felt ready to fulfil another item on both my dream lists, to publish a book of poetry. I sent my manuscript for assessment to a South African poetry expert. His feedback was that I should discard most of the manuscript, not even bother reworking the poems. The money spent on the assessment was wasted since I ignored his advice.

In the foreword to *Poems 1938–1945*, Robert Graves writes that '[t]o write poems for other than poets is wasteful'. I disagreed. I wrote for ordinary people, people who would benefit from my poems, not a few robotic poets.

I did what I usually did in such situations; I ignored the 'advice' and created the publishing imprint Theart Press and published *Heap of Stones*, a collection of 40 poems under the pseudonym AE Ballakisten, reflecting my original family name and because I wanted to maintain a separate identity from my business identity. The poems had great meaning for me and many of the poems had come to have meaning for others. I was keen for this book to be my introduction to the literary world and wanted to make a statement about the purpose and content of my poetry.

To this end I included 'Poet's Pledge' in which I vowed that 'My pen might fail in art, but it will write my true word, at all times', and 'A Consecration', which stated that my poetry would praise 'the selfless giver, taking less so others can have more' and 'those defending humanity, challenging man's destructive greed'.

The *Plainsman* reported on 17 February 2010 on the low-key launch of *Heap of Stones* at a coffee shop in Cape Town. The article, titled, 'Poet's journey written between the lines', gave a brief description of my view of the book. It was at this event that I met author Angela Read-Lloyd, who upon reading my book wrote: '... it is such a satisfying thing to read the work of someone who is a real poet, able to work an image into a new existence ... There are many people writing what they call poetry today, and it does not seem to me to be poetry at all. It lacks the understanding of what words can do. When I began to read your book, I thought at once of W. H. Auden, who to my mind is one of the greatest poets of the 20th century.' Angela's enthusiasm for my poetry was a massive boost.

I got encouraging feedback from readers in Johannesburg: '... just had few minutes to read your poetry ... am quiet inside now ... you really have a wonderful gift!' and 'I must say that poem 'Still Standing' has had a profound effect on me, it hits you so hard in the gut, it has stayed with me, so insightful and ... I run out of words.' Reactions to a poem like 'Still Standing' opened my eyes to the profound reality that different people drew something different from each poem. This was a poem of my experience of a violent incident under apartheid, yet a woman with completely different experiences was able to find deep meaning in it. I came to realise that even as the poet, mine was just one interpretation of a poem. A true poem is larger than the poet who is merely the scribe of the spirit.

From Cape Town readers wrote: 'Inspiring words' and 'I think there is so much truth in it that it scares people.' I even got messages from London: 'Deeply moving', 'Intense, honest, passionate ... beautiful!' and 'Fascinating and moving to read your poems', as well as from a reader in Washington DC who encouragingly wrote: 'I believe we are at the start of an exciting literary career.'

The most moving comments came from a man in Johannesburg named Clayton, who I met when he came to do some maintenance work at our house. He wrote: '... your words have really touched the depths of my heart. You have a talent and a destiny to change people's lives through your writing! The hurt and pain, the excitement and belief of which you write! I have read your entire book and I thank you from the bottom of my heart for blessing me with a copy. 'One Finite Life' has inspired me to be all that I can be and I thank you for that! 'Princess's Crown' and 'Saying Goodbye' brought tears to my eyes! ... Thank you for your book ... I am extremely touched and encouraged. Today has been a defining moment in my life!' Ordinary people were touched by my poetry. There could be no greater reward.

On 16 June 2011, the 35th anniversary of the Soweto uprising, I was invited to read a poem at an event in Mitchells Plain hosted by Minister in the Presidency, Trevor Manuel.* At the event, with attendance close to a thousand people, including government and business leaders, I recited my poem 'One Finite Life'. The crowd rose to their feet applauding afterwards and I was thanked with a warm hug by the minister. This was the power of poetry in action.

As one would expect, not all the feedback was positive, after all, it had been recommended that I 'discard' most of the poems. 'Too much rhetoric with no signature voice,' wrote a reader from Cape Town and 'Strong messages but the craft needs work' was the comment from a reader in London. I had no complaints, I would develop my voice and most certainly improve my craft.

I had fulfilled another dream, I had published a book of poetry and the reactions to the book had exceeded any of my expectations. I felt deeply that I had something to say and that I wanted to contribute to the vast library of humankind's documented experience of life. The rejection and discouragement had been small boulders which I pushed aside without fuss.

In 2011, I published my second book, *Talking to a Tree: Poems of a Fragile World* in which I reflected on the conditions leading to human conflict and imagined a world at peace. The poems captured the sadness I felt from reflecting upon the violence and suffering I saw in the world. This book followed my long and intense period of reading and reflecting upon society. In it I expressed my shock at the state of our world and what we as humans were doing to each other. This greatly influenced my academic work in public policy and political philosophy and also subsequent poetry.

I dedicated the book to Nelson Mandela who for me epitomised the character of taming the snake of violence. In my view he was much more than a political leader, he was able to inspire people to rise above their differences and to work harmoniously to create a world better than anyone could imagine. In fact, Nelson Mandela

---

* The same minister to whom my father had written in 1994 pleading for funding for me to go study at MIT.

was the supreme boulder pusher – pushing his own boulders to earn his freedom and showing a nation how to push aside the boulder of political oppression and hatred.

South African author, Fiona Ingram, wrote: '*Talking to a Tree* brilliantly captures the essence of despair that can force humankind to change. Thought-provoking, devastatingly direct, this anthology is one that will shake the reader out of complacency.' I certainly hoped that it would shake us out of our complacency and draw us closer together.

American professor of English, Camille-Yvette Welsch wrote that the collection of poems 'seethes with rage over the violence humanity inflicts upon itself and the natural world'. She picked out the poem 'Flightless Birds': 'The metaphoric resonance of the idea is powerful …'. In comparing my two books Welsch wrote: 'this collection has stronger imagery, a stronger sense of metaphor, and greater cohesion than his first.' As with *Heap of Stones*, this book attracted criticism. Welsch felt that the book needed stronger editing and that the strong messages came 'sometimes at the expense of artistry'.

I was pleased that Welsch saw flickers of hope in the poems and recognised that the book ends on a hopeful note. This was my intention. It captured some of the images I had of a better world or how I imagined we could get there.

An often overlooked poem in the book is the short poem 'Only the Listening', which was a manifestation of the belief that truth is found when we listen deeply. This was an important moment in my poetry and in my development as a person. John Masefield, one of my favourite poets, has described poetry as coming from an 'inner overwhelming power', and I began to recognise the same. I realised that I could not even remember writing many of my poems, that some seemed to have been written while in a trance-like state. On the origins of my poems I wrote in 2013, again in a trance-like state:

… life depends on my voice to be spoken upon this page but these are
not my words. I knock on silence, on the mystery, and when it opens

I hear a music, chants, heralds that en-trance me. I quiver, euphoric convulsions immerse me in thick viscous honey – on my eyelids, between my fingers. I am singing, I am traveling from dark to light in search of breath and then from light to dark in ecstasy to find wisdom. I am singing, and then the music stops. The page is covered in my voice, but not my words. Poetry.

Just as reading served as a form of intellectual meditation, poetry now began to serve as a form of spiritual meditation. As I began taking the messages of the poems more seriously I found myself walking a deeper spiritual path, one that led me to make changes in my life, changes that would manifest themselves in surprising ways.

I began feeling drawn more closely to nature. The poem *'Talking to a Tree'* stemmed from the awakening to the fact that there is life and wisdom in all of nature, trees in particular seemed to hold a special energy to which I was drawn. I was drawn more to silence and becoming guarded about how and with whom I spent my time.

I came to appreciate that I had faculties beyond the physical and cognitive and that I could listen with my whole body. I began experimenting with ideas on sources of wisdom and truth and developed the concept of *peak listening*. Peak listening has roots in 'peak experiences', which according to psychologist Abraham Maslow 'are transient moments of self-actualization'. As I see it, we have peak experiences all the time ... that first sip of wine or mouthful of beer after a long day, that first spoonful of your favourite dessert or cake or the first touch of sexual foreplay. These are moments that take our breath away, that seem to, momentarily, put us in a trance, an elevated state of ecstasy, moments of self-actualisation, in Maslow's words. These peak experiences are intensely pleasurable and perfectly natural.

Peak listening is the practice of listening for messages of wisdom during these peak experiences. While hedonism is the seeking of pleasure for its own sake, peak listening pursues bodily pleasure, not for its own indulgence, but to open up paths to the unconscious, to our spirits, so that we can listen, so that we can begin to know our own truth. This practice has similarity with chanting, meditating and prayer that elevates us to a state of being where we are able to connect with our spiritual realm.

Whereas I saw myself symbolically as a bull in the past, now the bull grew wings, able to soar, to rise up, to be an inspirational figure with courage and self-belief but also with a spiritual beauty. A new breed of spiritual poems began to emerge even as I continued writing poems with my characteristic socio-political themes.

These socio-political themes filled my third book of poems, *Bumper Cars* published in 2015. I had grown sufficiently in stature that a UK-based publisher, The Onslaught Press, published this book. I felt my poetry star rising. The book drew incredible reviews from accomplished writers and artists. Irish poet, Gabriel Rosenstock, author/translator of 180 books wrote: 'An energy pervades this book, a raw, shocking energy. In an age when intellectual robots are in danger of taking over the world of poetry, here's something hauntingly different, something savage and visceral and human, a cry we cannot ignore. There's no danger of not knowing what's going on in these poems, poems such as *where to start*, a straight-talking, hard-hitting, political poem of the first order.' Naturally, I was flattered by this exuberant review.

In my own copy of the book I inscribed some of the ideas I hoped to convey: 'The free will always bump into each other, this is the very nature of freedom, but the free do not harm each other, rather they collide like bumper cars and bounce off each other, in love, and carry on with their beautiful lives.' A central theme of the book is – how we see each other determines the nature of the society we create. When I signed copies, I mostly inscribed the words: 'less order, more freedom.'

A short while after the book was published, I was announced as the winner of the Sol Plaatje European Union Poetry Award for 2015, for the poem 'Streetclass Diseases' which was included in the book. I was elated. The main judge was acclaimed poet Mongane Wally

Serote which gave the award extra meaning. After a long poetry writing career dominated by rejection, it was rewarding to receive this recognition. The media attention was wonderful with vast online media coverage, newspaper articles and a television interview. I could tick another item on my 2002 dream list – I was an 'award-winning' poet.

Whereas I had to fight for recognition as a poet before now I was invited to read at events. My work started to be quoted more broadly and published in literary journals and anthologies. I even had a poem, 'Athol Williams', written in my honour by South African poet, Abigail George.

My writing career required that the occasional boulder be pushed aside, especially when rejections came, which was often. But importantly, my writing offered me a place to reflect, a place to which I could escape and a platform for expression. Writing offered me a space where I could create imagined worlds and where I could explore my humanity. It energised me and energised my dreams which ultimately drew me further along my path of opportunity.

As I looked ahead it was clear that writing and thought leadership would continue to be key channels for me to have an impact on the world around me. I determined that if I wanted to make a contribution to thought leadership in public policy and political thinking, an advanced degree in this area would be useful, and so I began contemplating returning to university to reskill in preparation for my new challenges. There were new boulders to tackle, particularly boulders of social and economic injustice. I also felt that a period of study would serve as a sabbatical, a time of reflection after many years of running at full pace.

Interestingly, the two remaining gaps on my 1994 dream list related to studying – I wrote that I wanted to study Politics and that I wanted to earn a PhD. My 2002 dream list mentioned Oxford. Perhaps all three dreams could be fulfilled at once … a PhD in Politics at Oxford?

I had been taking courses at UNISA on a part-time basis for three years by this time, having completed 15 courses in History, Politics,

Philosophy and Development. These subjects fascinated me – they were so different to what I had studied in the past. They overlapped with my private reading enriching this endeavour immeasurably and now laid the perfect foundation for more advanced study.

Education is obviously a fundamental enabler for life in our modern society but it was not this fact alone that would drive me to spend more than 15 years studying to ultimately earn six degrees. I was doing what I loved. When I set out my dreams it was never about cars, houses and money, it was mainly about attending university, to learn, to grow my understanding about the world around me. It was a continuation of me sitting at home as a child flipping through my father's encyclopaedias, in awe of the wonders in the world. And if I was going to attend university why not attend the best in the world.

I had a copy of a 1993 Oxford graduate brochure that I had kept all the years. Many were the hours that I flipped through the pages admiring the spired buildings and imagining how my thinking would expand if I was to study there. Similarly, I had a brochure from the Harvard Kennedy School of Government that I had received in 1996.

Oxford didn't offer a degree that suited my immediate interests other than a Creative Writing degree in poetry, which would run for two years on a part-time basis. I had never wanted to study poetry, preferring my poetry to be an intuitive rather than academic exercise. With my desire to go to Oxford I thought I would apply nonetheless. At Harvard I applied to the Kennedy School for a one-year Masters programme in Public Administration which was designed for midcareer professionals. Taryn often asked me which I would choose if I was accepted to both degrees. Harvard had the ideal programme but I doubted that I could ever turn down Oxford. I had the strong conviction that Oxford was my destiny and of course I had the Oxford jacket that Nick had given me in 1998, so of course I *had* to study there.

I made it through the initial stages of the applications and both universities invited me for an interview. Harvard interviewed me in Cape Town while I opted to go to Oxford for their interview. The

Harvard interview went brilliantly. In complete contrast the Oxford interview was awful. The interviewers were aggressive and make me feel like a literary Neanderthal, an imposter.

I was angry. I marched out of the interview and even though I had planned to spend a few hours in Oxford before leaving, I returned to the airport immediately. Unsurprisingly, when I arrived back home I received an email rejecting my application. *But what about the strong feeling I had inside that I should go to Oxford? How could I get this wrong?*

My disappointment subsided with time. I was excited to be offered a place at Harvard. I applied, without success, for every scholarship that I could find. This reminded me somewhat of those intense days running around looking for funding to go to MIT. Thankfully I had saved some money for just such an eventuality. So Taryn took a sabbatical from work, we locked up our house and headed for Harvard.

Finding myself at Harvard ◉

We arrived in Boston on the day of my 42nd birthday. My circumstances were vastly better than when I first arrived there to study in 1994. Now I had a place to stay, money to pay my way and I had the companionship of my wife. Colleagues and friends had high expectations: 'Come back with wisdom and knowledge that helps you lead us to a gentler, kinder, more humane place,' wrote a business colleague; 'May you return with vigour to reshape the social landscape,' wrote a schoolteacher friend. Taryn wrote a note in my diary the day before we left, 'I know that after Harvard you will be wiser and even more determined to make a difference in the world. I believe in you.' These are the most powerful words to say to anyone: *I believe in you*. The support and high expectations spurred me on.

It was overwhelming to think that I was actually a master's degree student at Harvard University, one of the most prestigious universities in the world. Harvard consistently topped university ranking tables and produced graduates who went on to achieve great success and assume influential positions of leadership around the world. I had been to the university before for meetings and conferences and admired its beauty but now as a student, the place was so much more majestic and awe-inspiring.

The beautiful red-brick buildings with ornate decorations around door entrances surrounded by manicured green gardens gave the university an air of grandeur. The colossal buildings fronted with columns and enormous flights of stairs appeared symbolic of the vast scale of learning that was available to me. At the centre of the university was Harvard Yard, a vast grassy quad with criss-cross

232

walking paths and ancient trees surrounded by majestic buildings. This is where the John Harvard statue is located. I walked past the statue on most days on my way to my favourite reading and study place, the Lamont Library. This library contained the Woodberry Poetry Room where I spent many hours reading from the extensive poetry collection.

Harvard swirled with an energetic buzz, a sense of possibility. Students were dreaming up new inventions, contemplating redesigning computer systems or political institutions, or finding ways to push the envelope of human endeavour. There was a can-do attitude, that if you could think it then there was a way to make it happen. This was my kind of place. It was like Disney World for dreamers and for nerds. I was both!

It was the space to think that I valued most about being there. It is rare to find the time and right environment to think deeply about issues that are important to us. The time of contemplation was more productive owing to the access I had world-class professors who could offer guidance or serve as sounding boards. I had the privilege of studying social capital with the founder of the concept, Robert Putnam. I got to think about global governance with John Ruggie, a world leader on the subject. I explored the interconnectedness between politics and economics with James Robinson, one of the world's leading political economists.

The absolute highlight for me was to take a course and befriend the philosopher Roberto Mangabeira Unger. Prof. Unger holds the legendary status of being the youngest tenured professor at Harvard; he was just 26 years old when he received tenure.* He didn't just offer me a rigorous framework for thinking about progressive politics, his real value to me was to open my mind to the possibilities that exist in political, social and economic arrangements, highlighting that we should not consider ourselves confined to the arrangements that

---

* Tenure is a concept prevalent in American universities whereby a professor is appointed for life; naturally these are prized appointments reserved only for faculty of the highest calibre.

we have inherited, that the prospects for human greatness are often realised when we break from our institutional traps. He inspired me, truly lifted me up. I had the honour of having regular conversations with this great thinker and was encouraged that he saw merit in many of my philosophical ideas. He supported my work so much so that he was willing to write letters of support for my later academic endeavours.

One of the fruits of my time of reflection was the clarity that emerged that political philosophy was my area of academic interest. Political philosophy seeks to ground solutions to social and political problems in moral and political theory. My interest in promoting social justice and the role that economic institutions ought to play, would be perfectly served by deeper exploration of political philosophy. Harvard presented rich opportunities to explore these ideas and interact with some of the world's leading political philosophers. Among these was Noam Chomsky who I also got to meet – he was visiting from MIT.

By a surreal series of events, my new area of interest almost resulted in me being appointed as a professor at Harvard in early 2013. Two of my professors from MIT Sloan now held posts at Harvard Business School (HBS). I had kept in touch with Rebecca Henderson through the occasional email but hadn't seen Paul Healy since 1996. I went to see him in his office and told him about plans to explore this new area of justice and economic institutions and the possibility of doing a PhD. 'Why come here to study,' Healy replied, 'have you considered coming here as a professor?'

Obviously I had not considered this; the thought hadn't even crossed my mind. He explained that HBS occasionally hired faculty who have expertise that the university needs but who aren't necessarily interested in tenured positions. With my background and interest, he thought HBS would be keen to have me. There were certainly worse places to develop an academic career than at Harvard. Healy was Head of Faculty Development so understood the needs of the university. He set up interviews with five HBS professors including Henderson.

Over the next few days I met with each, having robust discussions about my background and my proposed approach to the new role. These all went well. I was most excited about the discussion with my old Strategy professor Henderson. After our meeting she wrote an email: 'It was a great pleasure to see you ... It would be great to have you as a colleague.' Henderson was one of only 14 university professors, the highest ranked professors across the whole of Harvard not just the business school. What an incredible email to receive from someone of her stature. The thought of being her colleague was overwhelming.

After the set of interviews, I was invited to have lunch with Healy at the business school faculty club fully expecting to get a dream offer of employment. Taryn and I were giddy that morning, imagining how our lives would be transformed in just a few hours – I would come back as a Harvard professor or certainly well advanced in the recruitment process to getting there. At the lunch Healy talked about how HBS was 'reconsidering the role' and how the fact that I did not have a PhD was a challenge. I was dumbfounded, I just stared at him in disbelief.

All indications from all my interviews were positive, including the email from Henderson. But it wasn't to be. Something had gone massively wrong.

It was raining lightly as I left the business school and walked across the bridge that spans the Charles River. I was numb. When I got home, Taryn and I just sat in silence, so stumped we were. When the dust settled I was able to acknowledge that it was a great honour just to have been invited to explore the opportunity. Harvard was living up to its promise of being a place of opportunity.

I began receiving invitations to share my views on development and prospects for peace. I was invited to speak at the Harvard Law School conference on African development and the Harvard Education Seminar Series. MIT Sloan invited me to share my life story and personal philosophies with their students. Harvard i-Lab (the innovation centre) hosted an event called the Unreasonability

Initiative where speakers were invited to share their radical ideas about how the world could be improved. I shared my emerging ideas of a borderless world where societies were comprised of people with common interests not nationality. A great learning experience for me and a privilege to get to share thoughts that swum around in my head.

I was mostly asocial, preferring to be at our apartment reading and thinking. In my study at our Peabody Terrace apartment I had white plastic sheets on all the walls which I used as writing boards. Each wall was designated a topic or issue that I wanted to think through or solve and so the walls were covered with writing in different colours, with lines, arrows, decision trees and scribbles in all directions. Anyone who walked into the room usually looked at me as though I had lost my mind. I read and wrote non-stop. It was an incredible time of inspiration and I felt that I had come into my own, like I knew what I was about and had found my groove.

Nonetheless, Taryn and I did get to do some fun things in Boston like going to watch the Boston Red Sox play the New York Yankees at Fenway Park, watch the Harvard-Yale annual football match and we got to see Bruce Springsteen perform live at Fenway Park, my first open-air concert – just mind-blowing to be partying with 'The Boss' for three hours.

When time allowed I visited schools in the Boston area to read to children and deliver an educational or motivational talk. These were always uplifting experiences. A classmate ran a programme called ReadBoston so I went along with her a few times. Knowing that basic literacy would be one of my key activities in future I tried to learn as much as I could. I even took a course on organising social movements taught by Prof. Marshall Ganz who had worked on Martin Luther King's campaigns as well as Barak Obama's grassroots social movement which led him to the presidency in 2008. I was learning from the best and was loving it.

Being in Boston gave me the opportunity to reconnect with Bob and Jane Cohen, who had shown such great friendship when I first arrived in 1994, and I got to visit Prof. Willard Johnson who had played a pivotal role in getting me to MIT all those years ago.

Boston is unquestionably my favourite American city, I enjoy its size; it feels like you can wrap your arms around the city. It has everything you need, though not at the scale of New York City. I loved the walks along the meandering Charles River. Each afternoon I would walk from campus along the river back home to our apartment. Taryn and I had our favourite bench along the Charles where we would spend hours chatting, sometimes having lunch or dinner there.

When I needed a break from my books and scribbles on my study walls, I would go down to sit on 'our' bench. My other favourite bench was on campus in the JFK Park. It was a peaceful place to sit and dream or just watch people. That is of course while the weather permitted it.

As the snow began to fall, being outside was suicidal with temperatures dropping well below freezing point. We got to endure a few snow storms, experiencing snow of up to 1m deep and we survived a rare hurricane to hit Boston, Hurricane Sandy. Taryn and I were petrified as news broadcasts warned of the danger of the coming hurricane. We were advised to stay away from windows so we moved our sofa into the kitchen, which had no windows, and sat there for most of the night until the hurricane passed. We were fortunate, not much damage was done in our area.

The storm was so severe that the university was closed for the first time in 35 years. Bizarrely, Harvard was closed twice recently, the second time when the entire city of Boston was in lockdown after the bombing at the Boston Marathon.

It was sheer laziness on the morning of 15 April 2013 that kept me from joining the crowd at the finish line of the Boston Marathon. A few classmates were running the marathon as charity fundraisers and so a group of us discussed the idea of waiting at the finish line to cheer as they finished. My laziness saved me from injury or possibly from death. I slept in that morning and did not feel like trekking all the way downtown to stand in the heat, so I stayed home.

Just before 3pm two bombs were detonated that killed three people and injured 264 others – many people lost limbs. It was a horrific scene. Fortunately, none of my classmates were hurt. The resultant search for the bombers led to a complete shutdown of the city. No one was allowed to leave their homes. The police announced that people on the streets ran the risk of being shot. We were freaked out and stayed indoors. I was able to follow the news online and Harvard sent us regular email updates, all of them ending with: 'Please stay inside and be safe.'

All day and night we heard sirens of ambulances and police cars screaming up and down the streets. The bombers were seen at a petrol station just around the corner from where we lived which brought the drama close to home. The drama was brought even closer to home when it was reported that the alleged bombers, the Tsarnaev brothers, lived just 12 streets away from us and this is where they planned the attack and made the bombs. I felt fearful that night, that this attack would cause international violence to escalate. I felt a deep feeling that now more than ever, humanity needed to learn to love. These strong feelings flowed into my poem, 'We Rise' which ends with the lines:

In the cold darkness, love,
love smiles its warmness,
its hopeful light, love,
our gentlest healer,
our greatest need,
our best response.

The fallen will rise,
with love,
we all will rise.

Eventually the brothers were tracked down. One was killed by police and the other was tried for murder and terrorism, being found guilty and sentenced to death in a US federal court.

Before leaving the US in 2013, Taryn and I took a short break to visit Washington DC for a bit of sightseeing. While there I staged a silent protest. I had been appalled by the US government's treatment of people held in Guantanamo Bay. Detention without trial was one of the mechanisms the apartheid government had used to terrorise those who opposed its tyranny so I was particularly sensitive to this injustice. The US government was holding prisoners without trial for the mere suspicion of being involved in the 9/11 attacks. I had no view on the guilt or innocence of those being held, but what I did want was for those being held to be charged or released.

The whole disgusting facility, known colloquially as Gitmo, should be closed. I created a large banner with the words 'Close Gitmo' on the one side, and 'Poet 4 Peace' on the other. I climbed the steps leading up to Capitol Hill and held up my banner. I didn't say a word, I just stood there holding the banner aloft. It was a show of solidarity with those being deprived of their freedom for more than ten years and a statement in support of human rights. A security agent dressed in black approached me saying that I couldn't stand there. I then walked further down the steps and then stood there. Again he walked towards me telling me to move away. Again I walked a bit and again he approached. Eventually, I was all the way back down in the street. It started raining, but still I just stood there holding my banner. Cars and buses drove by and people pointed and took pictures.

I then walked over to the White House and did the same. Here a set of policemen walked towards me and stopped a few metres away. I had no idea what they would do. I felt a little fear well up. They just stood staring at me. There was a large crowd in front of the White House so I squeezed in among the crowd, held the banner up to the building and then turned and held the banner up to the crowd. I then calmly folded the banner, put it in my backpack and walked away, feeling the eyes of the policemen on my back.

We often don't know the impact of our small actions but I think it is important for us to act on our convictions. Whenever I read about a prisoner being released from Gitmo I celebrate. But I am holding my big celebration for the day that the prison is permanently closed.

A few months earlier Nick, Junita and their two little ones, Hannah and Daniel had come over to the US. Taryn and I flew to Los Angeles to meet them. As had become so common after a flight, I spent the first few days there in bed with the flu. It was in a Los Angeles restaurant that I ate animal flesh for the last time. My conviction had been growing that I should stop eating animal products and ever since that dinner meal in December 2012, I have stuck to this conviction.

Nick and his family returned to South Africa while Taryn and I continued on to San Francisco where I got to see my old MIT friend John and his wife Maria, as well as their beautiful children. My time with John and Nick, and their families reminded me of the different paths our lives can follow. They both commended me for my successes yet I looked at them as the success stories, having raised children, grown loving families and following successful careers. I still had a lot of catching up to do.

My time at Harvard was an unbelievable year, one in which I grew tremendously and felt that I had gained immense insight into public service and addressing social ills as well as learning about myself. At an awards ceremony I was honoured with a Lucius N. Littauer* Award and designated a Littauer Fellow in recognition of my 'academic excellence and significant contribution to the Harvard Kennedy School community'. I was deeply touched by this award. I was invited to join the Scholars and Practitioners Network for an initiative at the Kennedy School relating to business and society.

On one of the rare occasions when I was feeling sociable, I joined a few classmates on a drive out to Walden Pond, made famous by writer and philosopher Henry David Thoreau who lived there for two years. My time at Harvard was drawing to an end, another dream fulfilled. As I walked the shore of the vast pond, dipping my toes into the icy water, I recalled Thoreau's words, 'I have learned, that if one advances confidently in the direction of his dreams, and endeavours

---

* Littauer was one of the founders of the Harvard Kennedy School.

to live the life he has imagined, he will meet with a success unexpected in common hours.'

This certainly was another step along my path of opportunity, in the direction of my dreams. I had been striving to live my life as I had imagined it in my youth and I had certainly experienced successes that exceeded anything that I had dreamed. It was a timely message which was repeated on graduation day.

On 30 May 2013 I graduated from Harvard with my third master's degree. A coloured man from an apartheid ghetto-township was 'Harvard-educated'. I smiled to myself. It was true, nothing is impossible! Our graduation speaker was Oprah Winfrey. Something struck me from her speech. 'What became clear to me,' she said, 'was that I was here on Earth to *use* television and not be used by it; to use television to illuminate the transcendent power of our better angels.' She got to the point in her career, she explained, where she could use the powerful medium of television to do good. This idea excited and challenged me because it got me thinking about what medium and platforms I would use or create to do the good that I planned.

I needed to think about what I could leverage to push boulders, to push more cleverly. There was still lots to learn but I took heart that I was leaving Harvard with some clarity and direction.

Poetry emerged as a powerful force during my year at Harvard. I felt massively inspired and it seemed that my 200 classmates were drawn to the inspirational force-field that poetry created. We were an unlikely group to show any enthusiasm for poetry. Our class was made up of senior military officers, police detectives, presidential candidates, diplomats, journalists, those running NGOs or development institutions and businesspeople. Not exactly a group ordinarily associated with poetry.

Early in the year I wrote two poems that I shared regularly on campus. 'These Few' described my hopefulness that just a few inspired and skilled people could change the world. A copy of this poem has a permanent place on the office wall of the Director of my programme at Harvard. The second, 'These Words' talked about the power of words to connect and transform us. Whereas in the past I might have been the class clown, now I was firmly the class poet, a more desirable accolade.

I was invited to recite poems at university functions, award ceremonies, a religious festival, at dinners and birthday parties. I had the privilege of discussing my poetry with Josh Bell, a professor of poetry in the English department. I wrote the poem 'Euler's Daughter' as a dedication to my Mathematics professor, Judy Holdener. She was passionate about Mathematics and rekindled my love for the subject. After many years of struggling with Mathematics, I finally returned to earning 100% for tests. The poem was selected and read at the Joint Mathematics Meetings of the American Mathematical Society in California in January 2013. Taryn teased me that I was my teacher's pet because I had written her a poem.

'For 20 years I have been looking for soul at Harvard and tonight I've seen it,' these were the words spoken by the enigmatic Prof. Marshall Ganz at the conclusion of a beautiful and powerful event that had people in tears.

I was convinced that poetry had the power to transcend boundaries and connect people. With my classmates representing people from all walks of life and from across the globe I had the perfect audience to prove this. What was more, many of us would ordinarily be in conflict with each other – capitalist against community worker, competing militaries, contesting politicians and so forth, and we were from countries that were often in conflict. Could poetry really transcend all these boundaries?

I conceived of a project whereby I invited my classmates to write a poem about their vision of a better world. That was the only requirement. They could write one line or a hundred, in any form or structure that they chose. Most said that they had never written a poem before but I encouraged them to just find a few minutes of silence, to dig deep within themselves, contemplate their vision of a better world and write it down. It was astonishing what was produced.

An Israeli wrote about global friendship, an Indian about hearing each other, a Jamaican about hope, an American about possibility, a Syrian about change, a man from Benin about dreams, a woman from China about togetherness, a Turk about living life in the present. A classmate produced a series of striking paintings. Collectively the poems expressed a deep yearning for global understanding among all peoples, that we might hear and see each other, that we might seek harmony built on our belief in our common humanity.

The poems were filled with dreams of a better world and the actions, especially urgent actions that needed to be taken to realise this dreamed world. There was a recurrent theme, that there can be no change in the world unless we, individually and collectively, change. I compiled the poems and published a book which I titled, *Our World, Better Together*. Harvard included this book in its library collection along with my book *Talking to a Tree* and a DVD I had produced of poem-videos from my two poetry books.

The final step was to have a book launch event. I invited those who had written a poem to read and a group of classmates arranged to perform a set of songs. We were expecting a small turnout but on the night the venue was packed. We had to bring in extra chairs and even then there wasn't enough space, forcing some to sit on the floor or stand against the walls. I shared with the audience the role I saw poetry playing in the world:

> I believe that poetry offers us a language to connect with each other in ways that ordinary language cannot. I believe that poetry-writing is a powerful act since it offers us a space to dream, to express our visions and hopes in an uncensored way. Poetry therefore can, and should, have a role to play ahead of policy and ahead of politics so that we dream first, crystallise our visions for humanity first, and then begin to design policies to fulfil that vision.

One by one the authors of the poems stepped forward and read their poems. It was one of the most powerful and moving experiences for most of us in attendance. It was like the whole of humanity had sent representatives from their corner of the world to present their vision. And when we looked at these messages we realised that we all have the same vision, that our lives will be better when we come together. People in the audience were in tears, embracing each other, others sat with their eyes closed, many wore broad smiles.

It was at this point that Prof. Marshall Ganz spoke those incredible words during his closing speech: 'For 20 years I have been looking for soul at Harvard and tonight I've seen it.' I was honoured to have orchestrated the writing of the poems and this remarkable event and to have demonstrated that when we see our reflection in others, and see their humanity, we can overcome any obstacle facing modern society.

Old man in his old Oxford jacket ◉

I called it *dematerialising*: we were getting rid of material things. The process had started soon after I left the business world in 2010 with the selling of my cars. This was the next step. Taryn and I awoke to the fact that we did not need a 500m² house and so decided to sell it. We signed the agreements while still in Boston. We counted that we had 32 seating places in the house ... for *two* people. It was ridiculous, especially in a country where millions did not even have one chair to sit on. There is an absurdity to living with excess when many live in desperate need. What was left to do was to give away or sell the things that filled our enormous house. Even my beloved library books had to go ... nothing is sacred when you're determined to unburden yourself of material possessions.

With our few remaining possessions we relocated to Cape Town. I was home again. In a stroke of bizarre good fortune, we rented an apartment in the same street where Nick lived in Thornton. It was fantastic, like the old days. We popped over to each other's homes regularly to have a quick coffee and a catch up. It was brilliant.

Taryn and I adjusted to our new living conditions – our entire new home was the size of our bedroom in Johannesburg. It was sufficient for our needs, although I did miss my library.

It was now time to set in motion my plans for the future. First was a rethink of my involvement in addressing the desperate state of education in our country. Taurus School Solutions had stalled and I wanted to focus more directly on the burning issue of youth literacy.

South African ten-year-olds performed the worst in literacy across Africa and ranked second last in the world. When we looked closely at what was happening in our poorer communities we discovered two startling facts – children do not have books at home or in their communities, and schools do not have libraries.

How could literacy possibly improve if children did not have access to the books they need for their development? So Taryn and I set out to address these issues, and in 2013 we founded Read to Rise, an NGO which would ensure that children got to own new reading books and that they had access to all the required age-appropriate reading books that they needed, right in their classrooms. We created the mini-library, a brightly coloured bookshelf that contained fifty reading books that we placed in classrooms. Now children had access to the books they needed at school. And we issued each child with their own copy of a new reading book that they could take home, read and share with others.

My personal mission of wanting to enable and inspire others to thrive was built into the name and philosophy of our organisation – 'Read' was the enabler, and 'Rise' reflected my desire to see children inspired. Our vision is that we will become a nation of inspired readers. I believe that an inspired person can overcome the challenges that life throws at them. An inspired person will have the determination to find the solutions even when the odds are stacked against them and the solutions are not obvious. This is how *I* managed to escape the traps that were set for me by apartheid and I wanted our young people to be able to do the same.

To deliver this message of inspiration I started writing a series of children's book which were both educational and inspirational. In no time I had two books published, *Oaky and the Sun* and *Oaky the Happy Tree* which Taryn illustrated magnificently. We designed an interactive classroom programme around the books which included posters, props and songs. To date, we have distributed over 30,000 of these books!

I never imagined that I'd be writing children's books. I was trained to do many things in engineering, business and public administration, but not to write stories for young children. But Nick pointed out that my story-telling had started when I was ten and he was seven. As part of our nightly routine, I would conjure up stories as we lay in our beds with the lights out. My favourite creation recounted the adventures of the kitchen utensils, particularly the cheese grater and the rolling pin, along with the egg-lifter and the frying pan. Nick loved these stories.

Taryn quit her corporate job to oversee our programmes and soon Roscoe joined us as well. Nick served on our board and volunteered as a reader. In time my Wits engineering friend Steve Tsakiris would join us, setting up operations in Soweto. It was significant for me that we were sowing seeds of inspiration in Soweto where the 1976 uprising had begun and set in motion events that would contribute to the toppling of apartheid. Later even my mother got involved, along with cousins, friends and a vast network of volunteers who covered books and visited schools with us.

I now had a chance to go back to the community of Mitchells Plain where I grew up to invest in the young children there. Crime and gangsterism was an even greater problem than when I grew up so the need for light in the darkness was even greater.

We started in Mitchells Plain and Soweto but soon we'd be operating across the country and Oaky books would be distributed across Africa. On visits to the US and UK I delivered the Read to Rise programme there too and distributed Oaky books.

For me books are not static, inert objects; they are means of delivering inspiration. I had first-hand knowledge of their inspirational power.

In 2013, I was recognised by the City of Cape Town for my community development work with the erection of a concrete bollard in my name – the bollard stands outside the municipal offices in Mitchells Plain along Heroes Walk and bears my photograph and a short biography. A great honour.

While still at Harvard I was advised that if I wanted to read a PhD in political philosophy I would need to complete a theoretically rigorous master's degree first. All of my discussions and research pointed to the prestigious London School of Economics and Political Science (LSE) as the best place to do this. LSE was ranked number 1 in the world in the social sciences and in the top three worldwide for political philosophy. I checked with Oxford and got the same advice. So even though I already had three master's degrees I would need to complete yet another. This was certainly the long, hard route!

I applied to LSE and got some heavyweight reference letters from my Harvard professors. I was admitted and I accepted the offer soon after receiving it. In September 2013, just two months after returning from Boston, Taryn and I headed over to London for me to study towards my *fourth* master's degree.

Exactly as I was warned, the degree was super intense, with massive volumes of readings to do each week. It was an invigorating experience with my seminars filled with astoundingly bright students, many of whom had undergraduate degrees in political philosophy. I had lots of catching up to do relative to my peers, so just as in high school, I got as much additional input as I could. I attended every extra class and seminar that I could attend including undergraduate lectures, student conferences, PhD seminars and faculty seminars. I immersed myself completely in the field and in the end had a successful year being awarded a distinction for my dissertation and receiving the award for the best master's dissertation in political theory.

Taryn carried the load of running Read to Rise during this time with occasional input from me.

While at LSE the sad news broke that the great Nelson Mandela had died. It was the end of an era. I sat at my desk in Northumberland House where I was living in London, had a moment of silence and immediately wrote a dedication to him. The LSE newspaper, *The Beaver* published my personal dedication to Mandela in which I expressed 'deep gratitude and sadness that I say goodbye to this great man, a man who fought for my freedom, a man who inspired me to dream the impossible for my society and for my era'.

Many talked about the time that they met him or pulled out photos with him or items that he had autographed. I hadn't met him and that didn't bother me. What was important for me was that I played a role in continuing his work. His impact on my life could not be captured in a photo, it was in the work that I would do. I concluded the piece: 'What was the magic that he had? What was the "Mandela Magic?" I think if we look closely at his life we will find that his magic is something that we are all fully capable of, and that is the ability to love – to love another person simply because they are a fellow human being. This is his most enduring lesson for us.'

By September 2014, I submitted my LSE master's thesis and was back home in Cape Town, preparing to apply to PhD programmes. I decided not to apply to Harvard and chose to instead focus on Oxford. While at LSE I had rolled the dice and submitted an application to Oxford with the idea that if I got admitted I would defer my entry. Again, my application was rejected. The boulder of my Oxford dream had come crashing down the hill twice already but I would not give up, I would go back down the hill, get behind that boulder and start pushing it up the hill again. I would apply a third time.

After three months of anxious waiting, on 23 March 2015 I received a letter from Oxford that read: 'I am delighted to inform you that your application for admission to the University of Oxford as a graduate student has been successful.' Additionally, I was admitted to Hertford College, one of the oldest university colleges at Oxford.

I was in! 'I am in,' I shouted to Taryn as I rushed to her, 'I got into Oxford.' We embraced, tears pouring down our cheeks. After all the years of dreaming and agonising, I had done it. I was going to Oxford!

Yet another of my dreams had been fulfilled.

At 45 I would be older than many of my professors and be two decades older than my classmates. 'There goes that old man in his old Oxford jacket,' they'd say. But I didn't care. I would be living my dream and everyone I'd meet would be part of the fulfilment of that dream.

The following day I did something that I had run through in my mind hundreds of times. I put on the Oxford jacket that Nick had bought for me 17 years earlier. We had talked about this jacket so many times over the years with me always repeating the vow that I made standing in the street in Oxford, that I would only wear it when (not *if*) I had fulfilled my dream of being an Oxford student.

Salty streams of sweat ran down my face and what felt like a waterfall poured down my back as I stood in the blistering heat outside Nick's house wearing the thick jacket. My heart was pounding as I rang the bell at the gate. I wanted to jump and scream with excitement but I remained calm as he walked out towards the gate where I waited. His walk took forever – *he* wasn't the one about to faint in the heat, he was wearing a cool T-shirt. He pressed the gate's remote control button and waved me in. The gate took an eternity to slide open. I walked into his driveway without saying a word. We were about 2m apart when Nick stopped, looked at the jacket that I was wearing and burst into tears. We raced towards each other and embraced tightly, both in tears.

We were smiling, laughing, holding each other, with tears streaming down our faces (mine mixed with odious sweat). I hadn't said a word to him but I knew he would understand the significance of me wearing that jacket. For a few minutes we stood in his driveway, with the sun beaming down on us, embracing with intense brotherly love, patting each other on the back, shoulder and chest with affection, him congratulating me and me thanking him.

When he gave me the jacket back in 1998 he said: 'This is to motivate you to pursue your dream.' It was a great motivation and I was now going to fulfil that dream. For 17 years I held onto that dream, that vow and that jacket. I would hold the jacket in my hands, caressing the rough woollen texture with my fingertips. I would hang the navy blue and grey jacket where I could see it and just stare at it in hope. I'd run my fingers over the golden embroidery of the badge, three crowns and an open book, which shone boldly in contrast to the navy blue. *Dominus illuminatio mea* the badge read: The Lord is my light.

'You are amazing bro, you can do whatever you dream,' Nick whispered into my ear. There was no one in the world who believed in me more than Nick, through all the years of my victories he had been there celebrating with me and through all the times when I fell, he was there dusting me off, encouraging me to get up and to keep going. If I looked closely at the boulders of my life that I had pushed aside, I'm sure I would see Nick's fingerprints there for he surely helped me push many of them.

I had dreamt of studying at MIT *or* Harvard *or* Oxford. It was always *one* of these. Never did I imagine that I would end up studying at all three. I already held degrees from Wits, MIT, London Business School, Harvard and LSE and now I would add Oxford. As ambitious as I was I had never expected to achieve this, I don't think there are many boys who grow up in poor, gang-infested townships who do. There probably aren't many people growing up in affluent suburbs who expect this. I would be one of the few people in history to have earned postgraduate degrees from five of the world's top universities.

I was reminded that even though my life had been dominated by pushing boulders, life is not about the boulders. Life is about the dream that lay on the other side of the boulders. Life is about the freedom we come to know of pushing our boulders over the hill. I had come to know that within each of us is a deep impulse to flourish, to expand into greatness. I had come to know that life is about discovery – discovering this deep impulse, discovering our true selves, discovering our great purpose and discovering how best we will live out this purpose. Pursuing these discoveries leads us along many paths, some dead ends, some through valleys but many to mountaintops. I had come to know that walking these paths of discovery, these paths of opportunity, invites miracles into our lives that can lead to outcomes beyond even our most ambitious and outrageous dreams.

On 30 September 2015 I departed for Oxford to go fulfil one of my most outrageous dreams. That feeling of me fulfilling my destiny again visited me. A feeling that gave me comfort that I was walking my path. I left with a strong feeling that this walk had a purpose that extended beyond me. What that purpose was I still needed to discover. Perhaps it was to complete the one remaining item on my 1994 dream list of serving my country as president. Perhaps it was to work towards justice and socioeconomic freedom. Or perhaps it was simply to keep telling my story to inspire others. Whatever my purpose I knew that I would continue to push boulders – boulders that today seem impossible to move and boulders that I did not yet know existed but stood in the way of human prosperity. What lay ahead of me was a life of public service in which I would continue to believe in the greatness of humanity and believe that despite our numerous challenges, what lay ahead is better than our past.

Just before leaving home I wrote a note that I left on the living room table, not for anyone in particular, just to capture the feeling that welled inside. It read: 'To be alive is to walk a path, to take a journey; it matters less where the path leads than that we have the courage to walk ...'

I grabbed my suitcase, threw on my Oxford jacket, and was on my way.

Thank you for reading my book and walking this journey with me. I'd love to hear from you. Please connect with me on Facebook and Twitter, or send me an email at atholwilliams@hotmail.com. Please also write a brief review on amazon.com or amazon.co.uk.

I wish you great success in pushing aside the boulders that stand between you and your dreams. You can do it. You owe it to yourself to do it. Visit the Pushing Boulders website for more information on the book and tips on developing the abilities to push aside the boulders in your life.

www.pushingboulders.org